EVANGELISM

AND MISSIONS

SWINDOLL
LEADERSHIP
LIBRARY

EVANGELISM

AND MISSIONS

Strategies for Outreach
in the 21st Century

RON BLUE

CHARLES R. SWINDOLL, *General Editor*

ROY B. ZUCK, *Managing Editor*

WORD PUBLISHING

NASHVILLE

A Thomas Nelson Company

Published in association with Dallas Theological Seminary (DTS):

General Editor: Charles R. Swindoll
Managing Editor: Roy B. Zuck

The theological opinions expressed by the author are not necessarily the official position of Dallas Theological Seminary.

Library of Congress Cataloging-in-Publication Data

J. Ronald Blue
Evangelism and Missions: strategies for outreach in the 21st century / by J. Ronald Blue
p. cm.—(Swindoll leadership library)
Includes bibliographical references.

ISBN 0-8499-1443-4

1. Evangelistic work. 2. Missions. I. Title.   II. Series

BV370.B565   2001   00-068545
266—DC21   CIP

Printed in the United States of America

01 02 03 04 05 06 BVG 9 8 7 6 5 4 3 2 1

DEDICATION

To Victoria Grace Averitt

You have brought great joy and blessing to your grandpa.
I pray that you will grow in God's grace and knowledge
and serve Him with all your heart.

CONTENTS

FOREWORD

A NEW BUZZWORD is circulating in the business community. The word being tossed around by consultants and commentators is *mission*. One manager may say to another, "Well, that's a good strategy, Johnson, but that activity does not fit in with our company's mission." When an organization begins to run afield of its stated purpose, its reason for existence, that company is said to be experiencing "mission drift."

Mission. It's a powerful word, isn't it? When I see a seminary student walking briskly toward a classroom, I think, "There's a person on a mission." At the end of a long day of writing, when I put the finishing touches on a manuscript, I exclaim, "Ahh, mission accomplished!" Then there are those familiar words that opened the old television crime-stopping series, *Mission Impossible:* "Your mission, Jim, should you choose to accept it. . . ." Who among us doesn't lean forward a bit on hearing such a phrase?

Allow me a few candid questions. Do you know what your own mission in life is? If you are working with a team of individuals, do you know where the team is headed? Could you clearly state that team's objective? If you've spent years working for a church or a company, how would you rate the organization's success at reaching its stated objectives? Is your organization "on mission"?

Our Lord never hesitated when the time came for Him to spell out the intent of the movement He was leading. Near the end of His life on earth

Jesus boldly stepped up to that Galilean mountaintop and proclaimed, "All authority in heaven and on earth has been given to me" (Matt. 28:18).

Those are not the unsure mumblings of an insecure leader. The Son of Man knew who He was and what He had been sent to accomplish. In the next breath He laid out once and for all the mission of the church.

"Therefore go and make disciples of all the nations, baptizing them in the name of the Father and the Son and the Holy Spirit, and teaching them to obey everything I have commanded you. And surely I will be with you always, to the very end of the age" (28:19–20).

You will agree, there is no "mission drift" in this clear proclamation. That type of leadership statement is a certain trumpet, sounding right in the midst of eleven fearful, perhaps even confused, disciples.

The book, *Evangelism and Missions,* is a similar certain trumpet in our age of attendance goals, short-term projections, and vision initiatives. I knew I could count on my long-time friend Dr. J. Ronald Blue to "deliver the goods" on this compelling subject, and he hasn't failed. Not by a long shot.

Dr. Blue eats, sleeps, breathes, and lives evangelism and missions. He's truly become a modern-day missionary statesman. He has taught, led, and written extensively on the subject. And he models a passion for seeing lost individuals, wherever they are, receive the best opportunity to hear the wonderful story of God's redemptive plan. In this book he presents numerous ways to introduce people to the Savior. And he discusses every aspect of missions in what is a veritable handbook on missions procedures.

I also knew Ron would base his findings securely on the Scriptures. After reading through the manuscript I noted he began in Genesis and didn't conclude until recounting from the Book of Revelation how men from "every tribe and language" will one day gather around the throne to worship our great God. You don't have to be a cross-cultural missionary to love those words. Think of it. Representatives from across the globe will gather in the presence of the King of kings. No other ruler lays claim to that all-encompassing authority. None other than Jesus Christ is worthy of receiving such worldwide adulation.

As you dive into this study, I hope you'll ask yourself (as I found myself reviewing once again), "What is my life mission? What is my role in God's plan for the nations? Am I fulfilling the role God created for me? How do I fit into His mission for the ages? Whether your role is giver, sender, homemaker, corporate head, prayer warrior, or frequent-flyer, you have a strategic role to fulfill in God's calling people everywhere to turn to His Son for salvation from sin. I'm confident Ron Blue's greatest desire revolves around seeing more and more people seriously consider their mission in the world. I urge you to allow this volume to alter your worldview forever.

Remember, since Jesus Christ promised He would be with you always, He's not asking you to take on a mission impossible. Our Lord is looking for those who desire His mission to become their own. My great hope is that this will transpire in your life, if it hasn't already, as you come to terms with the message of this outstanding book.

—CHARLES R. SWINDOLL
General Editor

ACKNOWLEDGMENTS

I WOULD LIKE TO THANK all those who have influenced my life in evangelism and world missions. I am grateful to my wife, Libby, who prayed me into missions, to my Dallas Seminary professors who molded me with God's Word, and to my colleagues in CAM International who have beem exemplary models and have taught me so many important lessons. My deep thanks to Dr. Roy Zuck for his tireless editorial work; to Carolyn Owens, JoAnn Greenoe, and Judy Bowyer for their invaluable assistance in preparing the manuscript; to Dick Cotton and Larry Moyer for their bibliographic suggestions; and to my family for their constant support in prayer and encouragement. Above all, I thank the Lord for the wonderful privilege it is to serve Him.

EVANGELISM

AND MISSIONS

PART ONE

The Opening Line—Leadership for Evangelism

CHAPTER ONE

Keeping the Main Thing the Main Thing

L EE IACCOCA invested his entire career in the automobile industry. After many years with Ford Motor Company, Iaccoca was tapped to become the new chief executive officer of Chrysler Corporation.

To be CEO of Chrysler was no picnic. The company was virtually bankrupt when Iaccoca accepted the challenge. Somehow this aggressive, no-nonsense leader got a loan from the only "bank" that had enough money to bail them out. Iaccoca secured a loan from the United States government, turned the company around, and paid the loan back ahead of schedule!

It was from Lee Iaccoca's lips that I first heard a phrase that has made an indelible mark on my life. He said, "The main thing is to keep the main thing the main thing."

What a statement! It is simple. It is brilliant. It is practical.

Companies can get sidetracked. The task of Chrysler Corporation is not to keep the enterprise solvent, to make employees happy, to make money for stockholders, or to increase efficiency and production. The "main thing" is not simply to sell more cars. The company exists to produce vehicles that satisfy the customer.

Iaccoca was smart enough to know that ultimately he did not run the company. The consumer ran the company. Iaccoca made sure that the "main thing was the main thing."

WHY ARE WE HERE?

When I served as a professor at Dallas Theological Seminary, one of my goals was to make sure that each student was aware of the "main thing" in the work of God.

I enjoyed the interaction of the students in classes. I loved to launch a challenging question and watch the class come alive in discussion. Early each semester I presented the question, "Why are we here?" I was not asking, "Why are we here for this class period?" or "Why are we here at Dallas Seminary?" My question was, "Why do we exist as Christians in this world?" I knew that this simple question could lead us to the "main thing" in the Christian life.

To prime the pump I suggested a "neighbor nudging" session. Each student paired up with the person next to him or her. Together they compiled a list of every reason they could think of for a Christian's existence.

It was fun to watch the class buzz with animated conversation. At the end of the five minutes I had allotted for the exercise, I asked the class to share some of the items they had listed together.

"Glorify God," one student offered.

Another student said, "Grow in Christ."

Others suggested, "Fellowship with other believers," "Evangelism," and "Reach the world."

The list continued to grow. I finally intervened. "We could probably go on, but let's stop right here and analyze this list for a moment. Look over the list," I suggested. "Of the things we have listed, what will we do better when we get to heaven?"

It didn't take them long to respond.

As we discussed each item on the list, they began to see that we will be able to do every one of those things better in heaven than on the earth, with *one* exception, namely, to evangelize and engage in missionary outreach. "That," I said, "is why we are here."

THE MISSION

This exercise with the students at Dallas Seminary never failed to impress on all of us the importance of evangelism and world missions. Although

I knew where we were headed in the discussion, I was always moved by the incredible assignment God has given to His children.

The priority of our responsibility has been captured in song. Every time I hear Steve Green sing it, I am challenged.

> To love the Lord our God
> Is the heartbeat of our mission
> The spring from which our service overflows
> Across the street
> Or around the world
> The mission's still the same
> Proclaim and live the truth in Jesus' name.[1]

Steve Green grew up in Latin America as a "missionary kid." He knows what he sings. He saw his missionary parents pour out their lives in outreach to people who needed to know the Lord.

Steve is both bilingual and bicultural. He is one of those "TCKs," "Third Cultural Kids," people without a country or, better yet, people who can identify with many countries. Steve was destined to be a global Christian with a heart for the world.

Of all the songs he has recorded, this is still one of the favorites. No wonder so many people have purchased a tape or CD of this amazing selection. They play it over and over again.

The lyrics of this bestseller are potent. Seven brief lines pretty much give the whole story. The mission is to love the Lord our God. This is God's central purpose for us. It is the main thing. The lyrics also reveal that love is not a slushy feeling. This love is seen in action.

If we truly love the Lord our God, we will obey Him. Our love is evidenced in our action. We proclaim and live the truth in Jesus' name. We witness because we worship and we worship by our witness.

One author has suggested that missions exists because worship does not.[2] Actually missions exists *because* true worship does. Because we love the Lord we reach out in world missions. Worship is the driving force. True worship yields world missions. Missions is simply the evidence of worship in action.

WORLD WORSHIP

Worship is both the initiating force for missions and the inevitable fruit of missions. As people respond to the gospel, they then join the chorus adding their voices in praise to God. World missions brings world worship.

Every Sunday I envision the wonderful wave of adoration that starts at the international dateline where Christians arise on remote islands in the Pacific and head to church. They sing in languages most of us don't understand. As the globe turns, other believers awaken and join the chorus.

The rising sun begins to shine on Japan and believers there add their praise with an oriental flair. More believers trudge the frozen tundra of Siberia to their little church while small groups huddle in homes across China.

The sun reaches the masses of Asia. It then peaks across the vast continent of Africa and lights up the rolling fields and historic cities of Europe. The massive pipe organs in Austria mix with rhythmic drums of Angola as the strains of the chorus reach heaven. A thousand counterpoint melodies enrich the celestial composition.

The praise chorus reaches a crescendo as sunlight shimmers on the coast of Brazil and sweeps across Latin America. Guitars and tambourines add vitality to the praise. The volume rises as people in South America, Central America, and North America praise the Lord in worship and in song. Indigenous peoples add a special touch to the joyous anthem. They chant in Mam, Otomi, Cakchiquel, Quechua, and a thousand other tongues.

As the praise rises from morning worship services in the Americas, those back in Asia are already lifting new songs in their evening gatherings. There is ceaseless praise in a myriad of tongues that spans the globe and all time zones.

This is the force that drives the work of missions. This is the fruit of missions. Worship is the alpha and omega of our evangelistic endeavors around the world. Worship is the beginning and the end of our witness.

WORLD WITNESS

Paul said it well: "Christ's love compels us" (2 Cor. 5:14). The Greek verb "compels" (*synechō*) is forceful in Greek. The preposition *syn* attached to the verb *echō* gives it an extra push. This verb might be translated, "pushes me out." I like to call it a "wet watermelon seed" verb. As a boy, I became very adept at "shooting" seeds. I could really make a wet watermelon seed fly. I'd squeeze the seed between the thumb and forefinger and the seed would zoom at the desired target like a bullet. Zing! There it goes.

The love of Christ sends His servant flying to the designated target. My worship to the Lord and love to Him is what thrusts me out to tell others about my Savior. If I worship, I will want to witness.

Worship launches mission outreach, and worship is the outcome of this outreach as new believers join in honoring our Lord. Active witness connects the starting line with the goal.

Every leader in the body of Christ must recognize the overriding importance of evangelism and world missions. Without world witness Christian leadership becomes shortsighted and self-centered and eventually brings stagnation to the church. Church growth is dependent on this key element.

There is no choice. Leadership includes the responsibility of active witness to a lost world. The main thing is to keep the main thing the main thing. As Paul wrote, "Woe is me if I do not preach the gospel" (1 Cor. 9:16).

Each believer is an ambassador of the King of kings, a living witness to the lost, salt of the earth, and light to the world. What a privilege! What an opportunity! What a responsibility!

TELLING THE GOOD NEWS—EVANGELISM

Every believer shares the responsibility of telling others about the Lord Jesus Christ. In the flow of life it is imperative that conversation with lost people turn to the essential relationship each person can have with the Lord. The testimony of each believer should demonstrate to others the vibrant difference that life in Christ makes. Christians should be gracious, kind, polite, considerate, loving, and of such high character that others will want to know what makes the difference.

Every Christian should be deeply concerned about the spiritual welfare of every colleague, every friend, every neighbor. Driven by love for others and a full recognition of the desperate need for each person to experience new birth or be condemned to eternal separation from God, believers should naturally want to share the good news of salvation.

Sharing the gospel need not be forced. It should take place in a normal, natural way. Evangelism should be a part of regular conversation at work, at school, at home, and in the street. While special evangelistic endeavors can be helpful, the ultimate goal is to make evangelism as common as breathing. Telling the good news needs to become normative. Evangelism can become a way of life.

CROSSING THE BARRIERS—WORLD MISSIONS

In contrast to the constant flow of evangelistic outreach through every believer, world missions demands an organized and systematic endeavor in which specific, carefully chosen, and duly screened individuals are commissioned by the church to cross cultural and linguistic barriers to reach people who would otherwise be untouched with the gospel.

World missions is a sending process in which trained individuals penetrate those places that are otherwise unreached in the normal flow of evangelism. Distinct people groups in other parts of the world must be identified and specially trained individuals sent to reach them.

Every church must be engaged in both endeavors. In the normal flow of life every believer must share the good news of Christ in evangelism. In special efforts selected missionaries must be sent to touch the world with the gospel and to establish viable, multiplying churches in those unreached areas of the globe. The effort must be directed both "across the street and around the world."

CHAPTER TWO
~~~~~~

Setting the Pace for Evangelism

I N ANY FIELD OF ENDEAVOR the leader provides the spark for everything that happens. Evangelism does not happen without some encouragement and guidance. Church leaders need to set the pace and point the way.

SOUND THE CALL—SENIOR PASTOR

The character of any church is derived in large measure from the senior pastor. The one who is called to feed and lead the flock is rightly named "senior pastor." However, seniority does not focus on the age of the one who has this assignment. Instead, seniority refers to his position. As the shepherd of his flock, he must lead the way in evangelism.

A good senior pastor must demonstrate by personal example a lifestyle of evangelistic outreach. His teaching must be filled with examples of conversations with unsaved people in which there was a natural opportunity to share the gospel. Especially encouraging are those instances in which people have come to saving faith in Christ. These illustrations taken from his ongoing experience are some of the most effective means for motivating and training others for evangelism. A church known for evangelism is usually pastored by one who is engaged in evangelism.

SET THE PACE—PASTOR OF EVANGELISM

If a church is sufficiently large, a pastor of evangelism can be assigned to give greater attention to this fundamental purpose. He can nurture this work and insure that continuous training and effective means are in place for every member to be engaged in ongoing evangelism.

The key qualification for a pastor of evangelism is his successful and persistent evangelistic activity. Formal training is helpful, but practical experience is far more essential. The pastor of evangelism must be an evangelist with a track record that sets the pace for everyone else.

STIR THE FIRE—EVANGELISM COMMITTEE

Whatever the size of a church, it is wise to involve those who are effective in personal evangelism to give direction to the outreach ministries of the church. New believers who demonstrate a passion for their unsaved friends are often ideal candidates to bring new life to evangelistic outreach.

It is especially helpful to include men and women of all ages, including youth, on this committee. Such a committee can work with the pastor and/or the pastor of evangelism to plan ways to evangelize and to encourage and train church members in evangelism. And as these committed members engage in evangelism themselves, they set the example and they can help stir up a fire that can spread throughout the congregation.

PART TWO

~~~~~~~~~~

The Bottom Line—Biblical Foundations

E VERY CHIEF EXECUTIVE OFFICER is trained to glance through a financial report to find the key dollar figure. The CEO tends to fixate on the "bottom line."

Administrators focus on the bottom line because that is the line the board of directors wants to see. The board is interested in the bottom line because that is the line the stockholders look for. Most stockholders believe that the business of business is to make money.

If the "bottom line" is not in the black, stockholders see red. Investments are made to produce growth, provide dividends, and cause stock values to rise. No investor is looking for a business that has plans to decline, go broke, and bring stock prices down.

Unfortunately some people spell "evangeli$m" and "mi$$ion$" with dollar signs. But evangelism and world missions were never intended to be money-making endeavors. The focus is on people, not profits. Nonetheless there is a "bottom line."

The ledger for God's worldwide enterprise is not a book of fine-line columns filled with cold ciphers. The "bottom line" is found in God's letter of love. He has given us His Word in His Book, the Bible.

All we need is contained in this library of sixty-six books. It reveals lessons from past ages, provides counsel for present existence, and opens windows to future glories.

God's inclusive Handbook provides a "bottom line" that is immovable and unshakable. It is an anchor for every storm. It is the launch for every worthwhile endeavor. It is light to every dark path.

God spoke through human servants who recorded divine truth. Those writers whom the Lord used were common people just like us. But what they wrote was far from common. They penned the infallible words of the heavenly Father, the Creator of the universe.

"All Scripture is God-breathed and is profitable for teaching, rebuking, correcting, and training in righteousness" (2 Tim. 3:16). Just as God breathed into dust and brought forth life, so He breathed and provided written instructions for life. The Word of God is profitable. Follow the instructions. When we give heed to the "bottom-line" truth, "top-line" blessings are assured.

The "bottom line" for evangelism and world missions must be in line with God's Word. We can profit from God's prophets. To be an effective leader in the essential ministries of evangelism and world missions, you will need to establish a foundation in God's Word, to heed the "bottom line."

A few key studies from selected portions of Scripture can help us see that evangelism and missions are at the very heart of God's Word—and an essential part of His plans.

CHAPTER THREE
~~~~~~

To Be a Blessing—Genesis 1–12

FILL THE EARTH

ACH DAY OF CREATION, as recorded in Genesis 1:2–27, added another miracle of God's handiwork. What He made is absolutely amazing. For thousands of years we have explored and marveled at this vast world and all that it contains. Not only is this planet something to admire; the vast universe in which the world turns is even more awesome. It is no wonder God was pleased with His achievements.

Six times in the first chapter of Genesis we read, "God saw that it was good" (1:3, 9, 12, 18, 21, 25).

The satisfaction of the Creator is summarized in a seventh statement, "God saw all that he had made and it was *very* good" (1:31, italics added). In contrast to the seven seals of destruction in the closing book of the Bible, here are seven seals of approval in the first book of the Bible.

God put everything in place and then designed a creature who was given the assignment of taking care of this vast enterprise. God said, "Let us make man in our image, in our likeness, and let them rule" (1:26).

Don't miss the details. "Let us [plural] make man [singular] in our [plural] likeness, and let them [plural] rule." It may be confusing, but the Bible clearly teaches a triune God, three in One and One in three. Father, Son, and Holy Spirit appear in the first page of God's book.

Humankind reflects the image of God. There is a spiritual dimension in the human race that is found nowhere else in creation. Human beings are eternal. The created couple had a personal relationship with God.

No wonder God took such special interest in His culminating act of creation. "God blessed them and said to them, 'Be fruitful and increase in number; fill the earth and subdue it'" (1:28). He blessed humanity with a very specific goal in view—to be fruitful, to fill the earth, and to subdue it.

This is the first commandment of the Bible. *From the outset a world-wide plan was set in motion and a fascinating formula was introduced. God blessed His servants so that they in turn might be a blessing in all the earth.*

God's simple plan of "blessing to be a blessing" is the foundation of missions. This "great commission" is found in the very first chapter of the Bible. The communion God has with His children must be shared with those who do not know the Lord. Blessed to be a blessing was God's plan with Adam and Eve. It is the heartbeat of our mission to this day.

OUT OF THE GARDEN INTO THE WORLD

God could have created humans as robots. Men and women could have been connected to God's pushbutton controls to respond automatically to His programming.

Instead God made Adam and Eve with a will. Freedom of choice had some restrictions but people were designed with the ability to accept or reject. They were created by God with a limited but very real will. People were not made to respond involuntarily to a divine control board.

It is reasonable to assume that God knew that His creatures would fail. It was no surprise to God that Eve believed Satan's lie, or that Adam listened to Eve's persuasion to eat of the forbidden fruit. Sin was an anticipated outcome. God didn't create sin but it was no surprise to Him.

The grace of God is evident in His response to the failure of His creatures. He reached out to these fallen beings who cowered in a dark corner of the Garden, vainly attempting to cover their bodies. But fig leaves did no good in the light of God's holiness.

God called out to the distraught couple, "Where are you?" (3:9). Mercifully God always continues to call out to those who are trying to hide from

His righteousness. He is not willing that any should perish (2 Pet. 3:9). It is not His purpose to destroy. He wants to bless.

The first couple tried to shift the blame for their disobedience. Eve blamed the serpent, and Adam blamed Eve. But God was not fooled. Adam, Eve, and the serpent suffered due consequences for their rebellion. But there was more than mere punishment.

God provided a covering, clothing them with garments of skin. Flimsy fig leaves didn't work. Instead, an animal was sacrificed by God's gracious hand to give the naked couple a covering that allowed renewed communion with the Father.

Then in His grace God banished the couple from the Garden lest they eat of the tree of life and forever be subject to an imperfect life in this small corner of the globe. Angelic beings took their place "to guard the way to the tree of life" (Gen. 3:24).

A battle began at the gates of the Garden, and this war wages throughout the ages. The conflict goes on between the forces of evil under Satan's direction and the forces of righteousness governed by God. However, victory is certain. God will prevail. But just as Adam and Eve were granted a will, so everyone is faced with an eternal choice. Each human may yield to Satan's deception and try to sew together a few wilting leaves. Or each person can listen to God's voice, accept His covering, and walk in His light. It is a matter of life and death.

Every Christian leader must recognize his place in this battle. God's leaders can't tiptoe through the tulips in the global garden and hope that people will somehow choose the right path. *We must declare God's clear message of redemption and restoration in a world that is more a zoo than a garden.* We have to persuade those clinging to fig leaves to turn to the One who has provided a perfect covering. We must point the lost to God's way, for they will not find it without due warning and divine direction.

RAISING CAIN AND REAPING JUDGMENT

The sons of Adam were thrust into the battle. Life outside the garden was not easy. Abel kept flocks and Cain worked the soil. Both labored in a world of thorns and thistles. They endured "painful toil" with a fair share of "sweat" (3:17, 19).

Each son brought an offering to the Lord. Cain brought "some of the fruits of the soil," and Abel brought "fat portions from some of the first-born of his flock" (4:3–4). God's response to their efforts was decisive. "The LORD looked with favor on Abel and his offering, but on Cain and his offering he did not look with favor" (4:4–5).

It seems that God looked more closely at the heart of the giver than at the offering he brought. Evidence that Cain had a heart that was unresponsive to God can be seen in his reaction to the divine verdict. The Lord challenged Cain's anger and downcast countenance.

God asked Cain, "If you do what is right, will you not be accepted?" (4:7). Cain failed to do what was right. God's question did not specify what was right and what was wrong. God may have given orders for blood sacrifice. It is clear, however, that the Lord desired a spirit of sacrifice and generosity in the giver.

Cain's halfhearted offering from the field was no match for what his brother brought to God. Abel gave the best portions from the firstborn of his flock. Cain gave fruit, but Abel gave the firstfruits. Leftover offerings are not pleasing to God. He merits the first and the best. Abel's generous blood-sacrifice gift was accepted with favor, whereas Cain's offering failed the test.

Cain did not do what was right. Sin crouched at the door (4:7). This voracious lion attacked and added to the havoc in Cain's heart. Bitterness and anger soon turned into murder. What a tragedy! Cain was brought under the curse of God.

The human race continues under the burden of sin. People are "raising Cain" and suffering the consequences.

Should we be surprised that modern families are having problems? The first family was dysfunctional. Satan lured the first parents from God's best, and sin brought division and death to their offspring. This lurid scene from the Bible is reflected in the problems that continue to plague the human race.

LONGEVITY PLUS

With all the problems in the first family, it's amazing to see God's gracious provision for every need, including life itself. Even with all the advances in health care, longevity today is radically limited compared to the hundreds of years of the first generations. Something was lost. Sin removed Adam and Eve from the Garden, but it also took its toll on life.

The budding flower of human life was cut when Adam and Eve yielded to Satan's lure and disobeyed God. The flower looked alive but the connection to life-giving nutrients was severed. For succeeding generations death became an increasingly costly influence.

God's story in Genesis moves on through succeeding generations. The battle continues; the war goes on. Satan is pitted against the Lord, and people are caught in the middle. The conflict grows as time marches forward. Things are not getting better; it is readily apparent that the world is in decline.

From the inception of God's divine account He gave evidence of the stark contrast between light and darkness, between obedience and rebellion, between life and death. The battle line between God and Satan is real, and leaders in God's army must acknowledge this line. We fight to win on the side that has already won.

Evangelism and world missions are not extracurricular activities. God has outlined His plan. *He desires fellowship with human beings. And He wants that fellowship to span the globe.*

God blesses us so that we in turn can be a blessing to others. We willingly offer our best as an offering of praise to His goodness and His grace. This is what God desires—and what He demands.

SEE THE FACES

Billions of people dwell in isolated places around the globe, and few take notice of them. Population estimates are presented as cold statistics, mere numbers. The numbers are numbing. The billions lack faces.

But God sees things differently. He sees the faces. He senses the needs. He knows each person intimately and He cares. From God's perspective there are no "hidden peoples."

To make sure we understand His interest in both important and insignificant people, God moved scribes to record names—lots of names. Behind each name is a life, a "someone" whom God loves, someone through whom He has chosen to fulfill His perfect plan. The sons of the sons of the sons of Noah are important, and so are all those who follow in the family tree.

CAREFUL ORDER

Genesis 5 records another genealogical list, extending all the way from Adam to Noah. This timeline points up the long life and certain death of each person. It is especially curious to note the amazing life span of these hearty souls. Adam lived to the ripe old age of 930 years (5:5). Poor Mahalalel lived only 895 years (5:17), and Lamech died at the "early age" of 777 (5:31).

Obviously God did quality work when He created human beings. However, the longevity of humankind suddenly started declining and has stabilized at the present "threescore and ten" years (Ps. 90:10). All the medical advances in the world have not given much hope for more than eighty or ninety years, with only a select few topping the one-hundred-year mark.

Sin has taken its toll on people's physical well-being. Some say that sin does not pay. But sin does pay! "The wages of sin is death" (Rom. 6:23). When Adam sinned, death entered the scene. Spiritual separation was accompanied by physical deterioration and sin continues to take its toll on the human race.

The genealogical record of Genesis 5 is a backdrop for the amazing story of the Flood (Gen. 6:14–8:14), which was a "payback" for the mounting sins of the people of the world (6:1–13). God was ready to wipe out the rebellious masses of humanity. But He saved Noah and his family so that death would not wipe out the entire human race. God provided a way of escape.

STRANGE LANGUAGES

Just as God provided salvation for Noah and his immediate family, He made certain that those He saved would scatter on the earth.

Many people read the story of the Tower of Babel and see languages as a curse of the Lord on His disobedient children. Actually the diverse languages of the world are a great blessing. The story of the Tower of Babel of Genesis 11 must be studied in light of the Table of Nations in chapter 10.

The ongoing genealogy of Noah's family is grouped under the names of each of his three sons. At the conclusion of each list is an intriguing statement recognizing the uniqueness of each son's offspring. For example, of Shem's descendents the Bible says, "These are the sons of Shem by their clans and languages, in their territories and nations" (10:31). Each group had "its own language" (10:5).

Why did God trace the branches of Adam's tree out to the twigs and follow beyond Noah's brittle twig to the fluttering leaves of his hopeless offspring? Is this list really necessary? Why did God include so many names of seemingly insignificant people in His inspired Word? Because God cares about *each* individual!

The eleventh chapter of Genesis suddenly breaks on the scene and seems to contradict what was reported in chapter 10. Chapter 11 begins, "Now the whole world had one language and a common speech."

Repeatedly Genesis 10 makes it clear that there were multiple languages, and 11:1 says that there was but one language in the world. How can this seeming contradiction be resolved?

CLARIFYING FLASHBACK

The migration of humanity came to a standstill at the plain in Shinar many miles southeast of Mount Ararat, a place that eventually became known as Babylonia. They decided to settle down there and forget about God's command to "scatter and fill the earth."

As they settled in, someone got the bright idea of building a "high–rise." The ingenious engineers amongst God's early pioneers decided to build a city with a skyscraper that would reach right up to the heavens. What a wonderful idea! New York's Empire State Building and Chicago's Sears Towers are not so revolutionary after all. Can you help but admire Adam's descendants for their ingenuity?

But there was a problem in this big plan. Someone forgot to check

God's instructions. The Lord said "Scatter," and these people said "Settle." Instead of doing what God said—which seemed to them mere roaming around as busy nobodies hurrying nowhere—they decided to "make a name for themselves" right there in Shinar.

Who wants to be "scattered over the face of the whole earth" when you can congregate in one place and consolidate your efforts?

GOD CAME DOWN

God was not pleased with the city planners who defied His orders. He was not impressed with the architectural prowess of the tower builders. The Bible says, "But the LORD came down to see the city and the tower that the men were building" (11:5). The little word "but" is the first clue that something is wrong. When God came down to take a look, He was not an admiring sidewalk engineer. He was very displeased with the people's disobedience.

After a brief consultation between the members of the Trinity, God said, "Come, let us go down and confuse their language so they will not understand each other" (11:7). This was a clever way to put a halt to the big building project.

A confusion of languages was the tool God used to get His creatures back to His plan. "So the LORD scattered them from there over all the earth, and they stopped building the city. That is why it was called Babel— because there the LORD confused the language of the whole world. From there the LORD scattered them over the face of the whole earth" (11:8–9).

Interestingly the Hebrew word "Babel" sounds like the Hebrew word that means "confusion." God brought confusion through diverse languages and thus brought conformity to His plan to scatter humanity around the globe.

There is more in these verses. "Babel" can be pronounced in two ways. The English word "Babel" has the accent on the first syllable and depicts exactly what the word means in Hebrew. It is confusion.

If the accent is shifted to the second syllable, the Hebrew word has a different meaning. "Bab-El" is a composite word that means "Gateway to God." The tower the early architects designed was more than a showpiece of human skill. This was no simple Sears Tower. This was a plan to reach beyond the heavens and dethrone the Creator.

Just as Adam and Eve thought they could assume godlike qualities by eating of the tree of the knowledge of good and evil, so Noah's descendants thought they could do the impossible and achieve deity status.

The tower that was intended to be a high point in man's achievement became a low point in history. The prosperous plain in Shinar lost its luster. The sands of Babylonia speak of the blatant disobedience and disastrous pride of a people who lost their way. The careful plan of "Bab-El" was no gateway to Elohim (God). Once-clear communication between these industrious people became senseless "babel," a hopeless confusion.

And through it all God spared humankind from another dead-end on the divine timeline toward the goals of heaven.

GOD'S BLESSING

The diverse languages of the earth can best be seen as a blessing from God. Through the mosaic of strange sounds God achieved His plan. The table of the nations in Genesis 10 is the glorious result of the birth of the nations found in Genesis 11.

Rejoice in God's mosaic. Give praise to the Father when you see people from another clan. Smile at the strange sounds that come from shoppers across the aisle at Wal-Mart. This is God's wonderful handiwork.

Cross-cultural missions is a reality that started on the scaffolds of the Tower of Babel. God said, "Scatter and fill the earth." Today He says, "Go and reach the world."

God wants you to lead in this worldwide effort. You are either one whom God thrusts out of the plains of Shinar or you are one who supports those who go. Every Christian leader must respond to God's plan.

Missionaries who move out take the challenge. They learn the language and adjust to a different way of life so that people who are trying to reach up to God may know that God has reached down to them.

God's ambassadors correct the message peddled by religious hucksters. These false teachers say, "Try hard and you might climb up to heaven." The Lord's servants proclaim a revolutionary message of life, "Trust in the One who came down from heaven." People around the world who are focused on what they must *do* to become acceptable to God must hear what God has already *done* so they might be redeemed.

Towers of false religion are abandoned when people around the world, of any culture or language, come to see the reality of a relationship with God the Father through the Lord Jesus Christ. "I am the way, the truth, and the life. No man comes to the Father except through me" (John 14:6). *This message must sweep the globe and reach people scattered around the earth.*

TRAVEL WITHOUT A DESTINATION

One of the great delights of a vacation is planning. My wife and I set our sights on Hawaii more than a year before our twenty-fifth wedding anniversary. I had accumulated enough airline miles for two free tickets to the tropical paradise that attracts thousands of travelers every year.

We collected travel brochures. We talked with friends who had been there. I dropped by our local public library and checked out as many books as I could find on this land of enchantment.

We contacted a Dallas Seminary graduate who had been in one of my classes, and he graciously offered a condominium that had been given to him as an inheritance. During our five-day stay, we paid only a minimal fee for housekeeping. We could hardly believe his generosity.

When we landed in Honolulu we were greeted by an Aloha welcome with flower leis, courtesy of our Dallas travel agent. We felt like royalty. Our dream holiday exceeded all our expectations. It was wonderful. We have fond memories of our long anticipated anniversary trip to one of the world's most popular island destinations.

Can you imagine going on a trip with no anticipated destination? Picture poor Abram puttering around the house one day when a voice out of heaven declares, "Leave your country, your people, and your father's household and go to the land I will show you."

You would expect Abram to engage in a little dialogue at this point. He might ask, "Where is this land? What is it like there? When will You show it to me? And exactly what would You like me to do when I get there?"

In my former role as president of CAM International, I was often included in discussions with prospective appointees about their field assignment. This decision is of great importance. We must be certain that the person being considered for membership in our mission family is adequately prepared. He or she must relate well to other missionaries in the place where they will minister and be able to adjust to the living conditions and culture of the proposed destination.

FAITH TO STEP OUT

The faith of Abram is impressive. Even though he had no idea where he was going, he knew that God would direct him to the place of His choosing in accord with His perfect plan.

It was all so simple. Abram needed only to obey God and watch Him lead. To this day God's plan is simple. Several times Christ said, "Follow Me" (Matt. 4:19; 8:22; 9:9; 16:24; 19:21). It doesn't get much easier than this. No need to ask where Christ will take you. The focus must be on the One leading, not on the destination.

To be an effective Christian leader, you must have the courage and faith to board God's plane even when you are not certain where it will land. In total trust you can settle down into your assigned seat, fasten your seatbelt, and take off for the destination of God's choosing.

SURE PROMISES

Although God did not reveal the destination of Abram's journey, He lavished on His obedient servant some incredible promises. "I will make you into a great nation and I will bless you; I will make your name great, and you will be a blessing. I will bless those who bless you, and whoever curses you I will curse" (Gen. 12:2–3).

For an aging couple with no children, this was quite a promise. How does a great nation emerge from a childless family? And if a nation does not emerge, Abram will undoubtedly experience more ridicule than fame. His name will not be great; it will be mud! And if Abram is held in contempt, he will hardly be a blessing to anyone.

No need for conjecture. God fulfilled His promise. His covenant is always sure. The little saying, "God said it; I believe it; and that settles it," holds true. In fact, it is enough simply to say, "God said it and that settles it." Whether I believe it or not, God's Word is certain.

In the unfolding story of Abram it is evident that this old patriarch had a hard time believing God's promise. At his wife's seemingly sensible suggestion, Abram turned to the Egyptian maid Hagar in pursuit of the needed child. From this humanly devised union Ishmael was born. This only added confusion and interracial strife (Gen. 16), which continues to this day.

In spite of man's futile attempts to intervene, God keeps His promises. Just before Abram reached one hundred years of age, the Lord appeared to him and said, "I am God Almighty; walk before me and be blameless. I will confirm my covenant between me and you and will greatly increase your numbers" (17:1–2).

It is reassuring to know that even when we try to take matters into our own hands, God does not abandon us. We may live with the consequences, but the Lord is gracious. He picks up the broken pieces and brings order in the midst of chaos.

God continued in His conversation with Abram. "As for me, this is my covenant with you: You will be the father of many nations. No longer will you be called Abram; your name will be Abraham, for I have made you a father of many nations" (17:3–4).

The promise is radical enough, but the name change adds to the mystery. How is this elderly man going to be a father, let alone be a father of many nations?

There is more. God said, "The whole land of Canaan, where you are now an alien, I will give as an everlasting possession to you and your descendants after you; and I will be their God" (17:8).

God promised to bring offspring to a man who was nearly one hundred years of age with a wife who was ninety. Furthermore He promised to provide a vast territory of land to this foreigner who hardly had a foothold in hostile, alien territory.

LAUGHTER

Granted, he was wrong in doing so, but it is not at all surprising that Abraham doubled over in laughter. He thought about the sheer magnitude of what appeared as impossible promises.

God in His grace demonstrated patience to His doubtful child and assured Abraham, "Sarah will bear you a son, and you will call him Isaac" (17:19). The Hebrew name "Isaac" means "He laughs." When heavenly visitors returned shortly thereafter to bring further assurance of the Lord's promise, Sarah overheard the promise of a son and she too laughed. She tried to deny it, but the Lord said, "Yes, you did laugh." Nothing is hidden from God.

In spite of the persistent doubts on the part of both Abraham and Sarah, God fulfilled His promise. "Now the Lord was gracious to Sarah as he had said, and the Lord did for Sarah what he had promised. Sarah became pregnant and bore a son to Abraham in his old age, at the very time God had promised him." (21:1).

The laughter of doubt was turned to the laughter of delight. Sarah recognized the Lord's gracious intervention. "God has brought me laughter, and everyone who hears about this will laugh with me" (21:6).

FULFILLED BLESSINGS

All God's promises to Abraham were fulfilled and continue to be fulfilled. God blessed Abraham with a child, and from that child came a great nation, and from that nation Abraham is honored.

In spite of ongoing conflicts that surround the little sliver of real estate called Israel, Abraham's descendants still control the essential center of their promised land, and a day is coming when the entire territory will be theirs. History proves blessing comes to those who show respect to God's chosen people and curses befall those who show violence toward the descendants of Abraham and Isaac.

God in patriarchal times also blessed Melchizedek and Job and maybe others with the knowledge of Himself—but the promise of a land and a nation was unique to Abram.

Does God really love the world? How does His choice of one man

Abram and one nation Israel fit into the broader frame of world evangelization and missions outreach?

BOTTOM-LINE BLESSINGS

The blessings to Abraham, to his offspring, and to a nation of chosen people were not without purpose. God made this clear when He first conveyed His promise to Abram.

"All peoples on earth will be blessed through you" (12:3). God's covenant with Abraham was far from exclusive. Through him and his family blessings would come to every group on the globe.

Similarly God has blessed each believer with new birth and untold benefits as His child so that He might work through you, just as He did through Abraham, to be a blessing to all the peoples of the earth.

WE DARE NOT HOARD HIS BLESSINGS

Christians must not gather in little huddles to enjoy fuzzy fellowship and count their many blessings with no intent of breaking from the huddle to share those blessings with a lost world. God blesses so that His blessings may overflow to those who are outside the huddle.

Every leader must realize the unmerited favor of God and not only share with others the rich blessings received from the Lord but also encourage all those born-again believers under his or her influence to do the same. The world needs to hear of God's blessings so that they might better understand who He is and thus come to know Him.

World evangelism and global outreach to "all the people on earth" should be the natural outcome of the rich blessings God gives to His children. The overflow of blessing brings more and more people into God's family. Then as the larger family swells the choir, multiplied voices bring praise to God. Blessing begets blessing. Praise prompts praise.

Chapter Four

Songs of the Universe—Selected Psalms

GOD'S HYMNBOOK

ONE OF THE MAJOR PROJECTS that CAM International completed months before I became president of the mission was a wonderful new Spanish-language hymnal, *Celebremos Su Gloria*. Thousands of God's children in Latin America and Spain "celebrate His glory" using this attractive hymnal.

One of the most popular versions of *Celebremos Su Gloria* is the word-only version. Musical notes are not needed for many people who use the hymnbook. They have never learned to read music, but they love to sing. They need only the words.

Interestingly God's hymnbook—the Book of Psalms—contains words only. It is likely that the people of Israel sang the psalms, but the notes were never kept for posterity. They are not part of God's inspired revelation. God provided poetic messages so that praise might be lifted to Him.

Hebrew yields itself to a unique revelation of dignified and yet very realistic praise. Contrary to the rhythmic patterns that provide lyrics for contemporary tunes, Hebrew poetry is based on repetition, parallel thoughts, and rich flowing concepts that often crescendo to a defined climax.

This scriptural hymnbook specializes in cascading linguistic patterns that emerge with poetic meaning. God's hymns are usually more than a quiet melodic stream. They are more like Niagara Falls rushing over the brink of life with crashing sounds and deep meaning.

Most of all, God's hymns relate to worldwide needs. They stretch across the universe. They are as big as His world plan. They are as wide as global missions. A few samples from the one hundred and fifty songs recorded in God's hymnal illustrate His heart for world missions.

JOYFUL PRAISE—PSALM 33

God's plans have no room for sad-sack Christians. Repeatedly the Bible calls for joy.

Psalm 33 seems to reverberate with a happy spirit. The opening lines of this hymn turn a frown into a smile. Sorrow is washed away with song. "Sing joyfully to the LORD, you righteous; it is fitting for the upright to praise him. Praise the LORD with the harp; make music to him on the ten-stringed lyre. Sing to him a new song; play skillfully, and shout for joy" (33:1–3).

God's children are identified as "righteous" and "upright," people who want to praise the Lord. A threefold command tells the believer how to praise the Lord: sing, play, shout. "Sing joyfully," God says. Use your vocal chords to give joyous melody to the Lord. "Play skillfully." If you can handle a musical instrument, all the better. "Make music." Let your fingers glide over the strings of a harp or ten-stringed lyre. Something about the stringed instruments lift the soul to heaven, especially the harp.

Don't get worried if you don't happen to play the harp. Few do. God gives His approval of other musical instruments. In the final hymn in God's psalm collection, other instruments are added to the harp and lyre. He accepts other "strings" and lists the "flute." He even provides for the "tambourine" and, of all things, a "resounding cymbal."

With all the controversy over musical style in churches today it is difficult to sustain an argument against the use of any legitimate musical instrument to lift praise to the Lord. God is pleased with both vocal and instrumental music offered in praise to His name. He simply commands that the musicians play with skill.

The third command is, "Shout for joy." If you can't sing well or play with skill, you can shout. The shouter can join the singer in a spirit of joy.

Some may rightfully ask, "Where is the reverence in this kind of bedlam?"

Somehow I do not sense that God is opening a door here for scandalous, irreverent bedlam. God is not the author of confusion. In fact the Bible makes it clear that worship is to "be done in a fitting and orderly way" (1 Cor. 14:40).

God wants us to "sing joyfully," "play skillfully," and "shout for joy" in a way that is honoring to Him. God desires worshipers who express great joy in the midst of order. He desires a happy spirit expressed in fitting ways. Nonetheless an occasional "Amen!" in a church service is, I feel, well-pleasing to God. We dare not sit there like a bunch of dead oysters.

Praise God's Goodness to the Earth

Biblical joy is not the result of some high-powered pep rally spirit. This joy springs from truth. The psalmist wrote, "For the word of the LORD is right and true; he is faithful in all he does. The Lord loves righteousness and justice; the earth is full of his unfailing love" (33:4–5).

The Lord is right and true in all He says. He is faithful in all He does. The Lord embodies righteousness and justice. The whole earth is full of His unfailing love.

Every believer can praise the Lord for His goodness, a goodness that spreads across the globe and reaches into every corner of the world. He is God. He is good. He merits glory.

Ponder God's Greatness over the Earth

Joyful praise springs from the heart. The heart is made glad as the mind meditates on the One who can make every heart glad.

We praise God's goodness as we ponder God's greatness. The psalmist reviews the works of the Creator: "By the word of the LORD were the heavens made, their starry host by the breath of his mouth. He gathers the waters of the sea into jars; he puts the deep into storehouses. Let all the earth fear the LORD; let all the people of the world revere him. For he spoke, and it came to be; he commanded, and it stood firm" (33:6–9).

The Creator is the Commander. He made us so that we might fear Him. He gave us life so that we might revere Him.

The extent of God's handiwork is as broad as the expanse from which

He anticipates rightful praise. "Let all the earth fear the Lord." "Let all the people of the world revere him."

The significance of the opening chapters of Genesis is repeated by the psalmist. World missions is rooted in the creative purpose of God. God spoke and "there it was." As people around the world recognize His greatness, they will surely respond to His goodness.

The only real hope for the world is found in the Lord. "The LORD foils the plans of the nations; he thwarts the purposes of the peoples. But the plans of the LORD stand firm forever, the purposes of his heart through all generations" (33:10–11).

The nations and peoples of the world must yield to their Commander. His plans are sure. They apply to the entire universe, and they also stand firm "through all generations." God's domain is both universal and eternal. He covers both space and time. Little wonder the psalmist concluded, "Blessed is the nation whose God is the LORD, the people he chose for his inheritance" (33:12).

Pursue God's Guidance for the Earth

It is not enough simply to praise God's goodness. All praise must be grounded in the bedrock of faith. Nor is it sufficient to ponder only God's greatness. Meditation on the power and majesty of the Creator elicits praise, but it must do more.

Every believer must pursue God's guidance. We must look to Him, wait on Him, and hope in Him. Obedience to His plan and compliance with His purpose is the ultimate response.

The psalmist wrote of God's close scrutiny over the earth: "From heaven the LORD looks down and sees all mankind; from his dwelling place he watches all who live on earth—he who forms the hearts of all, who considers everything they do" (33:13–15).

God is transcendent but He is not distant. He is nearby. He focuses on every single person scattered across the face of this earth. He considers every single act each person does. So it behooves every one of God's creatures to bow before the Lord and recognize His majesty and His authority.

Rather than put any confidence in the vast armies of this world, people need to rely on the Lord. He is the only One who can "deliver them from death" and "keep them alive in famine" (33:19).

The psalmist concluded the hymn with a reassuring thought and a moving prayer. "We wait in hope for the LORD; he is our help and our shield. In him our hearts rejoice, for we trust in his holy name. May your unfailing love rest upon us, O LORD, even as we put our hope in you" (33:20–22).

Praise springs from the heart of one who recognizes the majesty and power of the Lord. And the one who recognizes the majesty and power of the Lord is the one who has put all his confidence in the Lord. He who pursues God's guidance and ponders His greatness will most certainly praise His goodness.

Psalm 33 shows that *God desires universal praise. World missions springs from the very heart of God.*

Little wonder then that the psalmist prayed that the unfailing love of the Lord might rest on His people. God's love brings hope, hope strengthens faith, and faith bubbles over in joy.

JUSTIFIABLE PRAYER—PSALM 67

Psalm 67 seems to reflect in poetry what Abraham wrote in prose. This unique song opens with a prayer that might well have come from the patriarch's lips: "May God be gracious to us and bless us and make his face shine upon us" (67:1).

God's covenant with Abraham gave fulfillment to the requests of this prayer. God promised His grace; He promised His blessing and goodness; He promised the glory of His presence. And Abraham received what the psalmist asked from God.

The opening phrase of the psalm does not end with a period. Nonetheless it is right to pause at the end of this brief prayer. The word "Selah," which appears in the text at this point, is recorded but not translated. Hebrew scholars are not certain of its meaning. It appears to be a musical term but is sufficiently ambiguous that the term is left in the original language. It is not a total mystery, however. The word comes from the verb "*sālal,*" which means "to lift up."

The confusion comes in the exact application of this term. This could be a signal for a crescendo in the music, a signal to "lift up" the volume. Or it might indicate a hold on the note: "lift up" the note. Perhaps this is the sign for a rest, to stop and "lift up" the name of the Lord or to pause to "lift up" meditation about the Lord. It may be all the above: the choir as well as the readers were called on to increase the volume, to hold the note, and then to pause and praise the Lord.

In a church service I like to give a brief explanation of the term "Selah" and then call on the congregation to respond to the familiar leader's prompt, "And all God's people said. . . ." By habit most people respond, "Amen." No, the response I desire in this case is the word in the text. After a friendly correction I try again, "And all of God's people said. . . ." This time there is a resounding "Selah!"

Prayer with a Purpose

Just as God's covenant to Abraham promised blessings to the patriarch and his descendants so that they in turn might be a blessing to all the families of the earth, so the prayer for God's blessing found in Psalm 67 has a world mission purpose: "that your ways may be known on earth, your salvation among all nations" (67:2).

God's grace, goodness, and glory are bestowed on His children so that the world might see what He has done and come to know Him. The purpose of this prayer is clear. Blessing is given to God's children so that salvation might come to those who are not yet His children.

God wants His message of redemption to extend to all nations. And this redemption results in people around the world rejoicing in Him. "May the peoples praise you, O God; may all the peoples praise you. May the nations be glad and sing for joy, for you rule the peoples justly and guide the nations of the earth" (67:3–4).

After the psalmist prayed for God's blessing, he acknowledged a world-wide purpose. God's grace, goodness, and glory are for world redemption, reverence, and rejoicing, which in turn yield praise around the world. "May the peoples praise you, O God; may all the peoples praise you. Then the land will yield its harvest, and God, our God, will bless us. God will bless us, and all the ends of the earth will fear him" (67:5–7).

The psalm opens with prayer, "May God be gracious to us and bless us." It ends with prayer, "May the peoples praise you, O God." A self-centered prayer becomes a God-honoring prayer. The turning point in the hymn is a look at the world. The sequence is clear: Attention shifts from self to others to the Lord.

Focus on the lost brings praise to the Lord and the assurance of His provision. The "land will yield its harvest, and God, our God, will bless us." God will bless and His blessing will bring praise to His name so that "all the ends of the earth will fear him." God's preeminence is evident. He is Lord over all the ends of the earth. *World missions and global evangelism are an integral part of His divine plan.*

JUDICIOUS PROCLAMATION—PSALM 96

God could have created the world in monotone. Can you imagine an existence in which none of us could distinguish notes, a world in which no one could sing, a world without music?

Thank the Lord for the variety of sounds and the vast range of notes He has provided. No wonder so many psalms start with the melodious little word "Sing." Psalm 96 begins with this scintillating command: "Sing to the LORD a new song; sing to the LORD, all the earth."

The psalmist called for a new song destined to reach heaven sung by an international choir that spans the globe. No small thinking here. This is as big as world missions. This is as immense as global evangelism.

Our Worship

In the opening stanza, five key questions are answered: Who? What? When? Where? and Why? Try to answer these questions as you read verses 1–4: "Sing to the LORD a new song; sing to the LORD, all the earth. Sing to the LORD, praise his name; proclaim his salvation day after day. Declare his glory among the nations, his marvelous deeds among all peoples. For great is the LORD and most worthy of praise; he is to be feared above all gods."

Who? "All the earth."

What? "Praise his name."

When? "Day after day."

Where? "Among the nations . . . among all peoples."

Why? "Great is the LORD and most worthy of praise."

This new song is filled with meaning. It is not some simple little praise song with a few mindless phrases that are repeated until everyone is singing with their brains shifted into neutral. Here is a hymn of profound meaning and ultimate significance. The whole earth is called to praise the name of God in endless worship among all nations and all peoples in response to the greatness of the Lord who is most worthy of praise.

In contrast to the senseless homage given to idols around the world, the Lord is lifted up in praise and adoration. The focus is on the sovereign Creator of the universe who "made the heavens" (96:5). "Splendor and majesty are before him; strength and glory are in his sanctuary" (96:6).

Our Witness

Our worship is a vibrant witness. As we ascribe to the Lord the glory, strength, splendor, and glory due Him, as we bring our offerings to Him, we give witness to the world.

The psalmist burst forth, "Worship the LORD in the splendor of his holiness; tremble before him, all the earth. Say among the nations, 'The LORD reigns.' The world is firmly established, it cannot be moved; he will judge the peoples with equity" (96:9–10).

This refrain of God's inspired song sounds like a page out of some missions text. The psalmist focuses on "all the earth . . . the world . . . the peoples." *God cares about the whole world.* His message must reach the extremities of this globe so that people everywhere might know Him and honor Him. *Missions and evangelism are not some remote attachment to God's plan; they are central to all He desires to accomplish.*

Our Wonder

If for any reason God's children fail to accomplish the intended purpose of witness to the world through worship, nature is forever tuned to God's purposes. "Let the heavens rejoice, let the earth be glad; let the sea resound, and all that is in it; Let the fields be jubilant, and everything in them. Then all the trees of the forest will sing for joy; they will sing before the LORD" (96:11–13a).

This chorus never sings off key. Clouds roll by in their splendor. The sun shines in brilliance. The moon glows, and stars twinkle in perfect harmony. Even in the midst of a storm, the dissonance of thunder and the jagged flash of lightning give glory to God.

Waves roar ceaselessly on every coast, wild flowers burst forth in brilliant colors, beasts and birds alike lift their voices to heaven, and even the trees wave their praise to God as the wind sings in their branches.

If these choir members could talk our language, they would shout their disdain for the pseudoscientists who refer to them as "Mother Nature," as though they were the source of creation. They would laugh at the evolutionists who blindly believe that they all came into existence from some formless lump or floating gas. "Mother Nature" is as absurd as "Mother Goose."

Earth's elements and her creatures all give glory to their Creator. Praise rises in a worldwide anthem to the Lord. This too is a witness to those who need to know the Father.

We stand in wonder before the Creator. We hear the chorus of nature and join in praise. Most of all, we are made aware that He is the One who is in charge. He is not distant. He reaches out to us. "For he comes, he comes to judge the earth. He will judge the world in righteousness and the peoples in his truth" (96:13).

What a God we have! He who created the universe shows special interest in frail children of dust. In fact, He reaches right into the dust bin, picks us up, brushes us off, and pushes us out to spread His message of hope and assurance.

We are not called to judge the world, but we *are* called to reach the world. He rules—and we respond. He calls—and we communicate. The target is clear in the closing verse of this heavenly hymn, "the earth . . . the world . . . the peoples."

Our assignment is big. *We are called to join in the chorus of nature to proclaim the glory of God in all the earth, to point the peoples of the world to their Creator* and to acknowledge their righteous Judge and sovereign Lord.

CONCLUSION

God's hymnbook is a missions handbook. Repeatedly the psalms give glory to God who cares about the whole world. We who know Him want to praise Him, and in praising Him we witness for Him.

Even the short song in Psalm 117 focuses on the nations and the peoples of this world. This shortest psalm in the Bible is a hymn for missions: "Praise the LORD, all you nations; extol him, all you peoples. For great is his love toward us, and the faithfulness of the LORD endures forever. Praise the LORD" (117:1–2).

CHAPTER FIVE

This Troubled World—Isaiah 1–6

I CAN HARDLY THINK of a more thankless job than being a prophet. Can you imagine being the one who must confront a whole generation of sinful people with God's message of condemnation?

Sinners don't like people telling them they are wrong, especially when things seem to be going well. Peace and prosperity do not seem to be the environment in which commitment to God and spiritual vitality prosper.

God's blessings on Israel seemed to breed apathy toward the very One who provided those blessings. In fact, the apathy turned to rebellion. Sin grew like a weed in the souls of people who had been brought out of bondage in Egypt and given the bounty of the Promised Land.

A LITTLE BIBLE

The Book of Isaiah is like a little Bible. The Bible has sixty-six books, and Isaiah has sixty-six chapters. Also like the whole Bible, Isaiah can be divided into two parts. Isaiah 1–39 speak of God's condemnation. We might call these chapters the "Old Testament" of Isaiah. And Isaiah 40–66 (twenty–seven chapters) convey God's consolation, a kind of "New Testament." The first word in this section of hope penned by the prophet is "comfort." "Comfort, comfort my people, says your God" (40:1).

There is hope for people held under the dominion of sin. The prophet was given God's message, "Speak tenderly to Jerusalem . . . her sin has been paid for" (40:2).

This is the message each Christian leader proclaims to a lost world. God has provided a way. The way, the truth, and the life is the theme. People today need to come to the Savior; they need to know the Lord.

In Isaiah's day the only sure hope was in the promise of God. The prophet pointed to the ruling Sovereign and a caring Shepherd (40:10–11). But, Isaiah wrote, "the nations are like a drop in a bucket; they are regarded as dust on the scales; he [God] weighs the islands as though they were fine dust" (40:15).

Before this prophetic message of hope, the Book of Isaiah is filled with pathetic gloom. The picture is dark. The prospects are dim.

A VILE VISION

As Isaiah began his lengthy book, he immediately addressed the apathy, indifference, and outright rebellion of God's people. Quoting the Lord's own words, Isaiah wrote, "I reared children and brought them up, but they have rebelled against me. The ox knows his master, the donkey his owner's manger, but Israel does not know, my people do not understand" (1:2–3).

Dumb animals show more innate intelligence than did these children of the Lord. The conclusion is bleak: "Ah, sinful nation, a people loaded with guilt, a brood of evildoers, children given to corruption!" (1:4).

This doesn't mean the people were irreligious. Instead, they were heavily engaged in ritual and sacrifice. They followed the rites indicated on their calendars, but the holy days had become hollow days. Their hands were dirty, and their hearts were stone cold. God said, "I have no pleasure in the blood of bulls and lambs and goats. . . . Stop bringing meaningless offerings!" (1:11, 13).

Even their prayers had become empty chatter. So the Lord did not hide His stern displeasure. "Even if you offer many prayers, I will not listen" (1:15).

This is serious business. What Christian is not guilty of going through the motions at a church service, of singing a hymn with absolutely no thought of its meaning, of tossing some money into the offering plate as part of the routine? We need to heed the words of the prophet. God despises this kind of mindless activity. He will not tolerate ritualistic activity that does not come from sincere hearts. He does not want gifts offered by dirty hands.

The trend away from God may start with incremental steps, but it always grows into open rebellion. Apathy turns to animosity. A cool heart becomes frozen as unchecked sin takes control.

People who once walked with the Lord were lured away by pagans. God's assessment is astonishing: "They are full of superstitions from the East; they practice divination like the Philistines and clasp hands with pagans" (2:6).

In the midst of seeming prosperity, God's people had fallen into the pit of imminent destruction. "Their land is full of silver and gold; there is no end to their treasures" (2:7). "The women of Zion are haughty, walking along with outstretched necks, flirting with their eyes, tripping along with mincing steps, with ornaments jingling on their ankles" (3:16). Everything *seemed* so good. But actually it wasn't.

God was about to remove His blessings. The coming judgment was severe. "Instead of fragrance there will be a stench; instead of a sash, a rope; instead of well-dressed hair, baldness; instead of fine clothing, sackcloth; instead of beauty, branding" (3:24). God is not impressed with the fashion parade of prosperous and proud people. He has determined that prosperity will be turned to poverty. He will humble those who strut around in high style.

A WOEFUL TUNE

The Lord does not inflict judgment without just cause. There is a legitimate reason for the prophet's warning to the people of Judah.

The alarm sounded on specific faults in the fabric of society. Six times the buzzer echoed across the plains of a land filled with self-centered people. God's prophet relayed six woes, each one directed to a nation that had lost its way in seemingly acceptable activities. But God pronounced His anathema on each one of those trends of society. What the people considered satisfactory God called sin.

Materialism—The Sin of Possessions

Prosperity seems so good. The abundance of goods and money appears to some as evidence of God's blessings. Isn't this what the Lord promised to Abraham, a land "flowing with milk and honey"?

But what happens when people clamor after more things? Can greed for goods and mania for money really be part of God's plan? The prophet recorded the answer: "Woe to you who add house to house and join field to field till no space is left and you live alone in the land" (5:8).

Big mansions will become hollow shells and the skyrocketing return on investments will crash. "Surely the great houses will become desolate, the fine mansions left without occupants. A ten-acre vineyard will produce only a bath of wine, a homer of seed only a ephah of grain" (5:9–10). This is not to say that it is wrong to have money or possessions. But God does condemn the *love* of possessions.

The world today seems to be racing down the track of materialism. Consumers are consumed with making more money. Shopping malls are filled with frantic customers buying more goods. Houses look more like castles than homes. People are inundated with piles of goods that do not satisfy. Materialism is rampant.

God looks down and says, "Woe to you." You have lost your way in the maze of money and all the junk it can buy. Judgment is coming.

Hedonism—The Sin of Pleasure

The entertainment industry prospers. Amusement parks, rock concerts, prime-time shows, sports events, and a thousand other attractions lure masses of people to fill hours of leisure time. Wine brings a ruddy complexion and a light heart. Music drowns out the monotony of life. The theme song is "Eat, drink, and be merry!" What does God say to the lilting theme of the world?

"Woe to those who rise early in the morning to run after their drinks, who stay up late at night till they are inflamed with wine. They have harps and lyres at their banquets, tambourines and flutes and wine, but they have no regard for the deeds of the Lord, no respect for the work of his hands" (5:11–12).

The Lord is not some kind of killjoy. It is not that He wants His children moping around in little pity parties. He is not a God of gloom and doom. In fact, God has provided everything we need to be truly content. The only satisfying joy is to be found in an intimate and fulfilling relationship with the Lord.

The world's ways of entertainment never satisfy. They are a poor substitute for God's way. Disregard for the Maker and disrespect of His handiwork only bring disaster.

Unregenerate people chase after counterfeit systems of glitter and glitz, booze and bangles, foodstuffs and fancies. These only provide a temporary surge of delight and leave the reveler with a splitting headache and a bad hangover. This is not happiness; it's a nightmare.

God says "woe" to these momentary pleasures. He promises exile and starvation to the world's brawlers and revelers. The arrogant will be humbled, and the Lord will be exalted.

The world is ablaze with "hedonism," a term that comes from the Greek word *hēdonē*, which simply means "pleasure." It is not that God opposes pleasure, but He does condemn godless pleasure. Or perhaps more accurately, He brings judgment on those who make pleasure their god.

Hedonism is a philosophy in which pleasure is considered the chief end of man. But people were not created to exert all their energy in self-gratification. On the contrary each person is to bring pleasure to God and to provide blessing to others, not simply to satisfy his or her own desires.

Like so many in the world today, Judah's citizens were chasing after fleeting delights and running from the only One who can bring lasting satisfaction. For this, God pronounced His judgmental "woe."

Narcissism—The Sin of Presumption

Woe to the person who sees a world spinning in a tight orbit around him or her, who feels that God should be his or her personal servant, who elevates self. "Woe to those who draw sin along with cords of deceit, and wickedness as with cart ropes, to those who say, 'Let God hurry, let him hasten his work so we may see it. Let it approach, let the plan of the Holy One of Israel come, so that we may know it'" (5:18–19).

For those who know the Lord it is difficult to imagine someone taunting God. I am reminded of the fisherman on Lake Ray Hubbard near Dallas who raised his fist to heaven from his boat. He looked into the storm clouds above and shouted, "If there is a God in heaven, let Him strike me." Lightning flashed out of the clouds and connected to the man's upraised fist. His self-designed lightning rod worked perfectly. He was instantly electrocuted. His fishing buddy who tells the story has a new appreciation for the power of God!

Narcissism is defined as admiration of oneself. The term comes from the Greek legend of Narcissus, a handsome youth who fell in love with his own image in water. As he pined away over his own beauty, he was changed into a flowering plant known today as the narcissus.

God condemns self-centered individuals who give little regard for Him and His work.

Relativism—The Sin of Perversion

Rising tolerance of opposing views seems admirable. Ready acceptance of those who believe differently sounds like an ideal. Actually this apparently democratic viewpoint presents a major obstacle to strict adherence to the Word of God.

Contrary to prevailing attitudes on earth, unwavering absolutes have been issued from heaven. God did not provide a tablet of "Ten Suggestions." He has given us Ten Commandments. The Lord decreed what is right and what is wrong. Woe to those who try to gloss over these biblical distinctions and turn God's clear mandates into mere choices. As Isaiah wrote, "Woe to those who call evil good and good evil, who put darkness for light and light for darkness, who put bitter for sweet and sweet for bitter"(5:20). Just as certainly as light can be distinguished from darkness, righteousness contrasts sharply with sin.

Excessive tolerance is rampant. It is difficult to believe that some denominational church groups are debating in their national assemblies whether to ordain practicing homosexuals. The so-called alternate lifestyle is defined in the Bible as sin. God calls homosexuality "detestable" (Lev. 20:13). The apostle Paul reiterated God's judgment on this evil practice, which he labeled as "indecent," contending that those involved will receive the "due penalty for their perversion" (Rom. 1:27).

Numerous examples may be cited of similar distortions of God's clear edicts. It may not be "politically correct" to stand firm on biblical truth, but Christians were never called to wave with the winds of politics. They are called to hold forth the Word of life.

Intellectualism—The Sin of Pride

The word *pride* is spelled in such a way that the heart of the issue stands at the center of the word. The letter "I" stands in the middle of the word. The same letter stands in the middle of the word *sin*.

God is not impressed with haughty people. "Woe to those who are wise in their own eyes and clever in their own sight" (5:21).

Repeatedly the Word of God warns those who think highly of themselves that they will be brought low. The prophet Isaiah warned God's people that they dare not continue with self-admiration, neglecting to give rightful tribute and homage to their Master and Maker.

A multimillionaire with whom I spoke in Dallas exclaimed to me, "Who needs God? I'm doing very well without Him." I warned him of his haughty spirit, and assured him that he will sense his need for the Lord. I often wonder what calamity might befall this man. The self-sufficient of this world experience a radical change when cancer strikes, or the stock market collapses, or a family member is killed.

For the nation of Judah, Isaiah's unheeded warning resulted in a hostile armed invasion and years of bondage in enemy territory. God is not playing games. What He says, He will do. "Pride goes before destruction" (Prov. 16:18).

Imperialism—The Sin of Persecution

The Cold War was never very cool. A rampant escalation of destructive armament spiraled out of control. Atomic warheads sat poised at enemy missiles pointed in the opposite direction. The standoff was enough to cause multitudes to build bomb shelters in their own backyards.

The threat of nuclear warfare is only a symptom of the deeper hatred and animosity that rules in the heart of humankind. Injustice reigns. Those in power live in luxury and revel in parties as they manipulate those under their authority. "Woe to those who are heroes at drinking wine and champions at mixing drinks, who acquit the guilty for a bribe, but deny justice to the innocent" (5:22–23).

It is almost beyond belief that human beings could feast at a banquet and consume costly wine while they watched over thousands of desperate Jewish captives who were treated as contemptible slaves and expendable flesh.

In the midst of the rampant revelry guilty officials were set free with unethical bribes, and the innocent masses were brought under the sway of death. This was an obvious perversion of justice. Little wonder God blew the whistle on the sins of Judah. God is a righteous judge, and in contrast to those who exercise unfair control He has good reason for His judgments.

A WONDROUS VIEW

God's woes are devastating. But when the outlook is grim, the "uplook" is grand. After beating a drum of judgment on serious rebellion in the ranks of God's people, the prophet Isaiah turned his look upward to God's righteous throne. The sins of this world are brought under the sovereignty of God. "In the year that King Uzziah died, I saw the Lord seated on a throne, high and exalted, and the train of his robe filled the temple" (6:1).

The death of the king was probably the low point of the prophet's experience. Sin was rampant, but now the only hope of authority that might bring reform was removed. The king was dead; the picture was bleak.

In the darkness of the hour God's light broke through. Isaiah looked up and saw the Lord's preeminence; He was "high and exalted." He ruled from His heavenly throne, and the glory of His presence filled the scene.

In addition to His preeminence there is evidence of God's purity. Angelic beings hovered above the Lord. Seraphs are angels who attend to the altar. Their name comes from the Hebrew root that means "to burn." Each seraph had six wings. With two they covered their faces, probably to keep from looking on the holiness of God. Two wings covered their feet, to hide their unworthiness. And with two they flew, perhaps in serving God.

Most significant is their message: "Holy, holy, holy is the Lord Almighty; the whole earth is full of his glory" (6:2–3). In Hebrew the way to highlight a characteristic is to repeat it. Contrary to what some contend, the three-fold "holy" is not a reference to the Trinity. The repetition is for emphasis.

The Lord Almighty is holy and His glory extends throughout the earth. No corner of this planet can escape the preeminence and purity of God.

Isaiah then painted an awesome scene. "At the sound of their voices the doorposts and thresholds shook and the temple was filled with smoke" (6:4). At the angelic announcement the heavenly dwelling place was shaken as though some catastrophic earthquake took place. A modern Richter scale could not measure the effect of this heavenly tremor.

I remember my first experience with a major earthquake when I was a fairly new missionary in El Salvador. We were meeting together for prayer on the third floor of a downtown office building. When the walls began to tremble, I opened my eyes to see what was going on. I was the novice in the group. Arturo, who was leading in prayer at the moment, did not even raise his head. He only increased the volume and the urgency of his prayer, *"Estamos en las manos de Dios,"* he exclaimed. "We are in the hands of God!" How right he was.

God has power. He could shake this earth down to a pile of dust in a moment. By His grace He does not consume us. The Almighty is longsuffering and gracious.

A PERSONAL TOUCH

Almost as an echo to six thundering "woes" of God's condemnation found in Isaiah 5 is a lone "woe" in chapter six. "'Woe to me!' I cried. 'I am ruined! For I am a man of unclean lips, and I live among a people of unclean lips, and my eyes have seen the King, the LORD Almighty'" (6:5).

It only takes a glimpse of the preeminence, the purity, and the power of God to sense the awesome conviction of personal sin. We deserve to be consumed in God's wrath. We are ruined. We are unclean, and the generation in which we live merits destruction.

The prophet's conviction of sin is moving. Perhaps many Christians are not more sensitive to the horror of sin because they do not fully appreciate the holiness of God. Perhaps the greatest cure for apathy to the needs of the world and to our own personal limitations is to come to know the Lord more intimately, to bask in His holy presence.

Isaiah's cry to God is the only proper response. "Woe to me!" We need to confess our sin to the only One who can take away the rightful condemnation of our sin.

The dark picture is again bathed in light. Confession brings cleansing. The problem in the world is not so much unchecked evil as it is unwillingness to admit wickedness and bow before their King in humility, to plead for His forgiveness with a broken spirit. "Then one of the seraphs flew to me with a live coal in his hand, which he had taken with tongs from the altar. With it he touched my mouth and said, 'See, this has touched your lips; your guilt is taken away and your sin atoned for'" (6:6–7).

God is in the business of cleansing. He atones for sin. He redeems those who seem to have no hope. He restores the brokenhearted. He gives new birth to those who are considered dead.

What a wonderful example of God's amazing grace. Isaiah experienced the touch of God. Cleansing in his own life brought the prophet to deeper consecration. He was ready to submit to the Lord who brought him out of the dark pit of condemnation to new purpose and privilege.

Conviction brought confession, and confession resulted in cleansing. Then cleansing was followed by God's call, and His call led to a response of commitment. "Then I heard the voice of the Lord saying, 'Whom shall I send? And who will go for us?' And I said, 'Here am I. Send me!'" (6:8).

Who calls the missionary? It is not some supremely righteous or pious response to say, "God calls the missionary." This is as it should be. The "missionary" or "sent one" is a mere messenger saved by His grace, who is commissioned to take the message of salvation so that others might look up and see the Lord and experience His cleansing from sin.

The Trinity is evidenced here. "Who will go for us?" God the Father, Son, and Holy Spirit appoint the sent one. God calls, the Son cleanses, the Spirit controls the servant who responds.

This passage in Isaiah is a favorite for mission leaders who seek to motivate and mobilize God's people to become engaged in worldwide outreach. However, one detail is often overlooked. The message God told the prophet to convey was not all sweetness and light. God's judgments are far from consoling. Condemnation is the theme that occupies much of the Book of Isaiah.

Nonetheless the message of condemnation is followed by an assuring note of consolation. The Book of Isaiah contains a clear message of judgment for sin, but it also provides a message of hope and salvation. God sends His messenger with a complete message. Isaiah was an obedient and faithful voice of what God wants to tell His people. He warned of sin and God's condemnation, and he pointed to salvation and God's consolation.

Every Christian leader can learn from Isaiah. Leadership is not derived from innate strength and admirable talent. Leaders are obedient servants who convey God's full revelation, His righteous judgment, and His gracious forgiveness.

True leaders are aware of needs in the world around them. They don't gloss over sin. Instead they acknowledge and clearly identify iniquity and injustice, which are so evident in society.

True leaders have a clear vision of God's glory. They come into God's presence and sense His preeminence, His purity, and His power.

True leaders recognize their unworthiness. They humble themselves in God's presence and rejoice in His cleansing. They acknowledge His call and yield to His purpose.

True leaders care about the world. True leaders love the Lord. *True leaders walk in obedience and fulfill the work of the Father to reach the world. True leaders are linked to missions and evangelism, God's sending and cleansing work.*

CHAPTER SIX
~~~~~~~

Who Cares?—Jonah

TRUE BASEBALL FANS always have their eyes on the minor leagues. This is the player pool from which the great stars of America's favorite pastime come. The great strikeout king of the Texas Rangers, Nolan Ryan, began his career in a little-noticed minor league club.

The Bible has its own major and minor leagues: five "major" prophets and twelve "minor" prophets. In God's Word, however, the major prophets are not more adept in their task nor are their pronouncements of greater significance than those of the minor prophets. Their writings are simply of greater length.

The minor prophets are more concise. Their writings comprise only a few pages in God's divine library. Of these twelve books the little Book of Jonah is somewhat unique, for it is more a personal testimony than a prophetic utterance.

Just who was this man named Jonah? A quick trace yields one little sound bite from God's Word about the man. Jonah was one of God's spokesmen during the reign of one of Israel's many wicked kings.

I call Jeroboam II "wicked" because the Bible says, "He did evil in the eyes of the Lord." This is no fairy tale. He was a genuine historical bad man (2 Kings 14:23–24). In spite of his rotten record, Jeroboam II was able to extend Israel's borders. The Bible does not give the credit for this advance to the king, however. This happened "in accordance with the word of the Lord, the God of Israel, spoken through His servant Jonah the son of Amittai, the prophet from Gath Hepher" (14:25).

But Jonah's story is not the greatest leadership manual. He was not very cooperative. In fact he was downright disobedient. He went in the wrong direction. At least he started that way. God had given him clear orders: "Go to the great city of Nineveh and preach against it" (Jon. 1:2). This "fax" from heaven is about as specific as you can get. God told His prophet exactly where he was to go and what he was to do there.

JONAH RAN

Great leaders follow orders. But not Jonah. He "ran away from the LORD and headed for Tarshish" (1:3). This is most revealing. Jonah was not simply running; he was running away from his Commander. He was running from God.

A quick check on details adds to the significance of Jonah's rebellion. Go back to the brief statement about Jonah in the story of King Jeroboam II. There we read that his hometown is Gath Hepher (2 Kings 14:25). This town was so small that it appears as a little dot on the map. The town may be insignificant, but its location was important in the story. God said for Jonah to get up and head to Nineveh—northeast. But Jonah got up and started toward the port town of Joppa—southwest. He was 180 degrees off course. He went in the exact opposite direction!

At Joppa he found a ship heading to Tarshish. Although not totally certain, most cartographers place Tarshish on the Iberian peninsula that today is called Spain. In the days of Jonah, Tarshish was considered the end of the world.

This Jonah was impressive. He looked like a star missionary. Willing to go to the very ends of the earth, he even paid his own fare. But Jonah was running from God, and he knew it.

GOD CHASTENED

Graciously, God the Father intervened when His child needed correction. "Then the LORD sent a great wind on the sea, and such a violent storm arose that the ship threatened to break up" (Jon. 1:4). When God moves in, big things happen. To capture Jonah, bring him back to his senses, and put him on track again, God churned up the wind and the waves. The storm was so bad that even the crusty sailors were terrified.

Seasick? Exhausted? For some reason, Jonah was not on deck. He was down in the lower part of the ship fast asleep.

The ship's captain roused the negligent passenger. "How can you sleep?" This was incredible. His crew was working frantically, but his passenger was in the sack. "Get up and call on your god! Maybe he will take note of us, and we will not perish" (1:6). The preacher may not be able to help the crew, but he should at least be able to say a prayer or two in this crisis.

The Jonah scene is repeated around the world to this day. The world is in a violent storm with eternal consequences. People are perishing and God's people are fast asleep. It seems that they do not care and there is little prayer.

Jonah was finally singled out as the lone culprit of the chaos. Surrounding him, the sailors pumped him with a multitude of questions: "What do you do? Where do you come from? What is your country? From what people are you?" (1:8). Jonah's response was impressive. "I am a Hebrew and I worship the LORD, the God of heaven, who made the sea and the land" (1:9). The words were right, but Jonah's actions denied his noble declaration.

"What have you done?" The sailors were terrified. They demonstrated more respect and awe for the Lord than the preacher did! The crew knew Jonah was running away from the Lord, because he had already told them. (1:10). In desperation they finally asked Jonah, "What should we do to you to make the sea calm down for us?" (1:11).

Jonah had a simple solution. "'Pick me up and throw me into the sea' he replied, 'and it will become calm. I know that it is my fault that this great storm has come upon you'" (1:12). The pagan sailors found this solution difficult. They worked frantically to avoid what they considered an unacceptable loss of life. Finally there seemed to be no alternative.

Amazingly, the sailors prayed to the true God, not to their gods. They asked for His forgiveness for what they were about to do, and they acknowledged God's sovereign control. They concluded their prayer, "For you, O LORD, have done as you pleased" (1:14).

Through Jonah's poor testimony and God's great sovereignty, these pagan sailors came to faith in the Lord. They tossed Jonah overboard and, sure enough, "the raging sea grew calm" (1:15). God had worked, and the ship's crew recognized it. "At this the men greatly feared the LORD, and they offered a sacrifice to the Lord and made vows to him" (1:16).

Leaders in God's work may take heed. It is God who does spiritual work. Even if we fail to follow Him, even in our moments of disobedience and failure, God can work to accomplish His purpose in ways that we can't fully comprehend.

Give the right answers to the questions lost people ask, and God can use them to touch the heart. Human leaders are dispensable, but not God. He is all-powerful, sovereign, and eternal.

God in His sovereignty spared Jonah and rescued him. But the story had just begun. Suddenly Jonah was inside the belly of a great fish. We don't know if this was a whale. This might not be a tale of a whale, but it is certainly a whale of a tale!

JONAH PRAYED

It is amazing how an impossible crisis can drive us to prayer. Could it be that God allows us to be in a tight spot so that we turn anew to Him?

From inside the fish Jonah prayed. Jonah's three days and three nights in the whale provide an amazing parallel to the Lord's three days and three nights in the tomb. Jonah's prayer ended with a promise, "What I have vowed I will make good. Salvation comes from the LORD" (2:9).

GOD CLEANSED

As soon as Jonah expressed his vow of obedience, God set his servant free to get back to the work of the ministry to which he had been ordered in the first place. God gave Jonah a new opportunity.

God is in the business of giving new opportunities to those who bow before Him. I am so grateful that He has included the promise, "If we confess our sins, He is faithful and just to forgive our sins and cleanse us from all unrighteousness" (1 John 1:9).

JONAH PREACHED

In round two, Jonah did better. God reissued the order, and Jonah obeyed. He marched right into the wicked city of Nineveh and started proclaiming his assigned message, "Forty more days and Nineveh will be overturned" (3:4).

The message was not one of salvation. It was one of doom, a message in which Jonah predicted total destruction. This was hardly the way to win friends and influence people.

Amazingly, God's message of coming chaos prompted a time of intense confession that swept through the city. From the king to the lowest servant, the citizens repented. In sackcloth and ashes they humbled themselves before the almighty God.

The world today needs to hear the message of condemnation, the consequences of judgment, and the reality of hell. Why? Because most people don't realize that they are lost. Little wonder that talk of salvation seems meaningless to the average person.

One night in Segovia, Spain, I received a phone call from one of our new converts. She said, "Mariano is here in our apartment. You know, the one with marital problems."

"Oh, yes," I acknowledged.

"Well, he is here. Could you come and talk with him?"

"Sure," I replied.

I jumped into the car and dropped by the home of another of our recent converts. After the typical Spanish pleasantries and a brief explanation of Mariano's situation, I said, "Raimundo, it looks like we have some work to do, can you come along?"

"*Sí*," he said, and we headed to Juana's apartment.

There was Mariano pacing back and forth. He was a nervous wreck. As soon as we entered the room, Mariano exclaimed, "My wife is going to leave me tomorrow!" He continued his story, "I cannot prove it for sure, but I am quite certain she has been out with other men."

Mariano kept talking about his plight when Raimundo finally interrupted, "Wait a minute, I used to do that, to excuse myself and blame everyone else. No. You're a sinner!"

I was standing there thinking, "Raimundo, don't be so direct." I had learned to start with a nice little phrase, "God loves you and has a wonderful plan for your life." Here was my friend giving this poor guy the direct statement, "You're a sinner!"

However, that was exactly what Mariano needed to hear. We sat down, talked through his marital problems, and discovered a major mess. *He* had been out with other women. It was bleak.

I finally said to Mariano, "Look, there are no easy solutions to complex problems like this, but we know where you need to start. You need a new life in Christ." We explained the gospel as fully as we could. Finally, I asked Mariano, "What about it? Would you like to put your trust in Christ?"

He responded, *"Sí."*

"We need to talk to God," I explained. "I don't know how you pray. I sometimes pray standing, sometimes seated, sometimes kneeling."

"We usually kneel," he replied.

We knelt at the couch. "Do you know how to pray?" I asked Mariano.

He said, *"Orar, no; rezar, sí."* (Pray, no; say prayers, yes.) Typical of many Spaniards, Mariano had only read and said prayers; he had never prayed.

"Mariano," I suggested, "let me say a sentence and if you can say it to God, just repeat what I say. Otherwise remain silent and I will know you can't honestly say this to God."

"Good," Mariano agreed.

"O Dios," I started. He repeated what I had said, "Oh, God."

"I realize that I am a sinner." Mariano again repeated what I had said.

Mariano continued on his own in prayer. He cried out, "Oh God, forgive me! Forgive me!" He wept like a baby. Mariano confessed his sin and cried out to put his trust in Christ. His life was transformed.

It all started with the declaration of my friend Raimundo, "You're a sinner." This was not a judgmental attack. It was reality and it was expressed in love. Raimundo cared enough to declare God's message and to reveal a spiritual need.

Jonah's message simply made the need of Nineveh clear. In forty days the city would be destroyed. This was God's call to repentance and it worked. The entire city bowed before an almighty God.

GOD CONVERTED

The people of Nineveh repented and God withheld His judgment. "The wages of sin is death, but the gift of God is eternal life" (Rom. 6:23). When people repent, God withholds the destruction they rightfully deserve. He is not willing that any should perish.

We who serve the divine Master need to convey His message. It is a message that includes a warning of dire circumstances for those who reject Him as well as wonderful promises to those who humbly turn to Him. We dare not present a distorted good-news message without an equally clear presentation of the bad news.

The bad news of the consequences of sin is what brings conviction. The bad news makes people want to hear the good news of life in Christ. You can't get people saved until they realize they are lost.

JONAH POUTED

You would think that Jonah would be overjoyed to see the incredible citywide response to his evangelistic campaign. It would seem natural to read of Jonah's follow-up efforts to organize Bible-study groups and discipleship training in light of the marvelous response.

On the contrary Jonah headed out to a hillside and started the countdown to see if what God had told him to preach would really come true. Destruction was coming in forty days.

While he waited, Jonah prayed. At first glance the prayer looks like a model of praise. "I knew that you are a gracious and compassionate God, slow to anger and abounding in love, a God who relents from sending calamity" (Jon. 4:2).

No. Jonah was furious. He knew God's character. He knew that if people repented God would spare judgment. This was so infuriating to Jonah he wanted to die. Jonah was burning with anger and self-pity, and he was suffering under the scorching heat of the desert sun.

God in His grace provided a vine and caused it to grow. Jonah was blessed with refreshing shade. Then God provided a little worm that devoured the vine, and Jonah found himself under a heat alert all over again.

For the second time Jonah cried out in frustration, "It would be better for me to die than to live" (4:8). The suicidal thoughts clouded his mind all over again.

GOD CARES

The point of the Book of Jonah is found in the closing verses. God used this amazing experience to teach Jonah, the nation of Israel, and each one of us a great lesson about His character.

The Lord challenged His prophet, "You have been concerned about this vine, though you did not tend it or make it grow" (4:10). In other words God was telling Jonah that he was concerned about his own little head. This self-centered leader wanted things to go well for him. He sought the comforts of life. He was angry when those who were of a lesser race, the scum of society, were not duly judged for their evil.

This biblical account is convicting, especially to those of us who bask in the comforts of the United States while the majority of the people on this globe are caught in the grip of Satan. Their only destiny is eternal destruction.

Who cares? God cares! Jonah focused on his personal welfare and comfort. God focused on the masses of lost people in Nineveh. The point of the Book of Jonah is found in the final sentence. God declared, "Should I not be concerned about that great city?" (4:11).

The compassion of the Lord for the lost people of the world is beyond our full comprehension. He is a God of mercy, grace, and incredible love. He hates sin. Judgment is certain. But at the same time He loves His creatures and longs for them to turn to Him and worship Him.

In His grace God has called His children to go to the distant Ninevehs of the world to proclaim His message of judgment and His message of love. He cares. Do we?

I remember the day I pulled the mail from our box one morning in San Salvador. We had just returned from an exhausting trip in a distant rural area of the country where there was neither running water nor electricity. The trip by mule back in and out of the isolated communities in this area was no adventure. It was backbreaking work.

I looked forward to the uplift of mail from home. As I pulled the treasure of letters from the box on our front door, a folder dropped to the floor. I picked it up. Big bold letters splashed across the brochure, "Who Cares?" It was announcing the missions conference program of Camelback Bible Church in Phoenix where I had been ordained.

How appropriate this question seemed. "Who cares?" I thought about it. "Do the people back home care about those humble people in the mountains of El Salvador?" I had to be honest. Most did not care. Even those who had attended the missions conference with this penetrating question as the theme probably cared little about what is happening in some small banana republic in Central America.

But I was encouraged as I began to consider those who cared enough to send us, pray for us, and sustain us. Yes, they cared.

Suddenly I was convicted of my own indifference at times to the people to whom I had been sent. Our home in San Salvador had running water and electricity. What about those we had just visited who had so little?

And then I thought of the many expressions of love from Salvadoran friends and believers in the remote corners of the country who had become like members of our family. In fact, these vibrant Christians *were* members of the family. They cared for me and I cared very much for them. What a wonderful blessing to be part of the family of God that spans geography, time zones, cultures, and languages.

Suddenly I was overwhelmed by the thought of the One who cared so much He died for me. I was reminded again of the apostle's moving declaration, "Christ's love compels me" (2 Cor. 5:14). God cares. Oh, that we might capture more of His compassion and let it govern our lives!

Missions and evangelism is ultimately driven by a passion from within. Programs and plans can never match the burning reality of God's love manifest within us. God cares! This message to Jonah must burn in our hearts.

CHAPTER SEVEN

Here Is Your Assignment—The Gospels

MARK AND BECKY were seminary students. They met while ministering to people in inner-city Dallas. In the course of time they fell in love with each other and were married. Their commitment to ministry only increased after they were married. Mark prepared further, earning a second degree at Dallas Seminary while serving as a youth pastor.

I was thrilled when Mark and Becky sensed God's direction to missions. They applied to CAM International and were appointed to serve in Mexico in evangelism and church planting, an assignment for which they were uniquely qualified.

They moved to Becky's home area in York, Pennsylvania, to further enlist friends on their support team so that they might soon be on their way to Latin America. Things progressed well until suddenly Mark developed a congestion that the doctors could not seem to identify. I was made aware of Mark's persistent cough when we spent a day together in Washington, D.C. I was speaking in a church in the area. Mark and I arranged to meet in the nation's capital for some time together. Becky had her hands full with the children, so she stayed in York.

"I have another doctor's appointment next week," Mark reassured me when I questioned him about the cough. Then I received the alarming e-mail message. They discovered that Mark had a rare form of cancer. It was considered terminal. I could hardly believe it.

Mark went through chemotherapy. He lost his hair but never lost his spirit. In fact he joked with me about how much we looked alike. It was good that we could laugh together.

The cancer continued to grow, but Mark regained some strength. Mark's doctor gave his counsel: "Now is the time to do what you have always dreamed of doing. If you want to take a cruise, now is the time. If you have ever longed to go to Disneyworld, by all means do it."

Mark and Becky looked at the doctor in amazement. "We don't want to take a cruise. We aren't interested in Disneyworld. We want to get to the mission field!" They set their sights on Mexico. Soon they had their full support and their paperwork in order. They were ready to leave.

Suddenly Mark faced a reversal. He spent a few days in the hospital, and although he was released, he never recovered. On a cold day in February, I received a call from Becky. Mark was with the Lord. Mark slipped from a weakened body into heaven's glory while Becky held him close to her.

I have never felt as close to the Lord as I did at Mark Kramm's graveside service. We trudged through the falling snow and then huddled together around the coffin under a canvas covering. We sang hymns Mark had chosen. The words took on new meaning.

After a meditation from God's Word on the wonderful hope and assurance we have in Christ, two young men took the Christian flag from the coffin, folded it with military precision, and presented it to Becky with the reassuring words from the Lord, "Well done, good and faithful servant" (Matt. 25:21).

At the memorial service that evening the church was packed. The vibrancy of youth was evident. So many who attended were young. Mark was not quite thirty-three when the Lord took him. The memorial service bulletin contained two priceless pages. One was a poem Becky had written before Mark was diagnosed with cancer. The first stanza of Becky's "An Open Hand" captures the intensity of this trial.

> The hardest earthly task
> That God has given me
> Is holding with an open hand
> My earthly family.

Becky concluded her poem with reassuring words.

> When trials come across my path
> I'll hold on to His Word,
> "My child, I will carry you!
> Remember, I'm still Lord!"

This was but an echo of the facing page that was reproduced exactly as Mark had written it the day before he died. Mark had scratched out a farewell to all of us.

"I have strong feelings that it may not be long now," he wrote. "As I have always said, I would love to hang out but since I am not totally in charge of that I do trust in our God's loving care. God has been . . . is . . . and will always be good. Serve Him with all you have. It is worth it! Looking forward to being together again. Mark Kramm."

LAST WORDS

The final words of a person ring with importance. The comments my friend Mark jotted before he died have greatly impacted my life. I can almost hear him saying to me, "Serve Him with all you have. It is worth it!"

At the end of each Gospel account, the final instructions of the Lord Jesus Christ bear special significance. Commonly called the "Great Commission," these instructions are of utmost importance. This task is given not only to the apostles but also to all those who bear the name of the Savior. This commission is included in each of the four Gospels.

MAKE DISCIPLES

In the brief forty days between Christ's resurrection and ascension, He ministered to His confused followers and gave ample proof that He was alive. Most of all He gave them an assignment and promised to empower them and us to fulfill this assignment.

Matthew presented Jesus' final words in the best-known Great Commission text, a commission based on His authority that encompasses both heaven and earth. "Therefore, go and make disciples of all nations, baptizing them in the name of the Father, and of the Son, and of the Holy Spirit, and teaching them to obey everything I have commanded you" (Matt. 28:19–20).

I can well remember when I made the personal discovery that the central command of this Great Commission text is not "go." It is "make disciples." The assignment is to reproduce productive followers of the Lord Jesus Christ, not to buy a plane ticket and travel to some distant place.

The process to accomplish this discipleship goal is given in the instructions. Of course, going is necessary if all nations are to be included. As His ambassadors we need to reach out with the message of the gospel.

Those who respond to the gospel must then be rooted in their newfound faith and associated with the body of Christ through baptism. Baptism is a testimony of identification with Christ in His death and resurrection. Baptism visualizes the fact that the believer has died to the dominion of sin and is raised to newness of life. It is a testimony of an everlasting identification with the living church, the worldwide body of Christ.

The one who has been *reached* for Christ and *rooted* in Him and His church must then be *readied* for further outreach. True disciplers are teachers. So the next step in the discipling process is clearly outlined, "teaching them to obey everything I have commanded you." For many years I erroneously focused on the "everything" and stressed teaching the full counsel of God's Word. While this is important, this verse focuses less on teaching content than it does on the disciples' response to the content. The stress needs to be on "obey." The discipler must encourage believers to cultivate an attitude of obedience to everything Christ has commanded, including this Great Commission text.

Picture a growing spiral. We reach people for Christ, root them in the Lord, and ready them as obedient servants of the Lord so that they too can reach, root, and ready others in a never-ending multiplication process.

This commission is as big as the world, for we are to make disciples "of all nations." Following Christ's authority and assignment are His words of assurance: "And surely I am with you always, to the very end of the age" (28:20).

There could be no greater commitment. Christ assures each ambassador to whom He has given His assignment of His abiding presence and His encompassing power. His disciples are not left alone to fulfill the task by themselves, for believers are assured of divine assistance that will endure to the very end of time.

Why would a person want to get wrapped up in petty matters of earthly existence when he or she could become a part of a worldwide enterprise that brings eternal rewards? The Great Commission recorded in Matthew gives purpose to life. It challenges every child of God. It provides something worth living for—and something worth dying for.

PREACH THE GOSPEL

I was sitting under the mighty redwood trees near the Mount Hermon Conference Center in California, having some time alone with the Lord. I had taken just enough Greek in my first year at Dallas Seminary to be able to use my Greek New Testament.

It was then that I made a personal discovery. As I mentioned, the "go" commands in the Great Commission passages of Matthew and Mark are not imperatives in Greek. In both Gospels the word expressed in English as "go" is really a participle, an "-ing" verb, in Greek. The translators have not been negligent, however, for the Greek participle assumes the force of the main verb.

Without getting entrenched in the details, I would simply emphasize that "go" is not central to God's Great Commission. The main verb in Matthew is "make disciples." And the main verb in Mark is "preach." Going is important in both passages, but it is not at the heart of Christ's orders.

Christ said, "Go into all the world and preach the gospel to every creature" (Mark 16:15, NKJV). The Lord instructed his disciples to preach, to herald, to proclaim the good news. We are God's spokespersons. We are to communicate the gospel in "all the world" and "to every creature."

This is a big assignment. To fulfill the global scope of this mandate, somebody needs to go "into all the world." Missions is not an option, it is essential. God is not satisfied with a community of believers who stay in the huddle. He wants a team that breaks out of the huddle, takes the play to the scrimmage line, and gains yardage toward the goal of world evangelization.

Tom Landry, the first and undoubtedly the finest coach of the Dallas Cowboys football team, was a member of the Dallas Theological Seminary Board. One day I asked him, "Coach, how did you win so many games?" His answer was revealing. "I demanded one thing from my players," Landry said, "I insisted that they execute the play." He went on to explain, "I didn't want the team to be distracted by the score or by the crowd. I trained each player to focus on one thought, 'Execute the play!'"

Coach Landry sent every play into the huddle. As soon as the quarterback called the play, those men broke from the huddle, lined up, and did their assignment to "execute the play."

God has called the play, and Christ has passed it on to us. "Go into all the world and preach the good news to every creature." We need to step up to our assigned position, face our opponent, and execute the play! We must move the gospel "down the field" and around the world.

The text in Mark provides an intriguing focus. The inclusive "all the world" is followed by a very individual "every creature." Although some have translated the second phrase "all creation," the construction is such that I feel the preferred translation is "every creature."

Billions of people encompass the earth. But those billions are individual beings who need the message of Christ's love and salvation. Rather than be overwhelmed by the masses, we need to focus on a few. We must see crowds by focusing on faces.

In successfully executed plays each player has an assignment. The defensive players have specific opponents they must bump, cover, or tackle. If every player in the defensive lineup does his task, the other team makes little or no gain. They might even be thrown for a loss.

Offensive players likewise have their specific tasks in each play. Each one knows whom he must block. If all goes as planned, the running back cuts through the opening. He gains yardage. He might break free for a touchdown. Or the quarterback finds a receiver who has timed his pattern to be open at the perfect moment to connect with a pass. It is carefully designed. Each player does his part.

Do you hear our heavenly Coach? "Into all the world." "Preach the gospel." "Every creature." Execute the play!

What must we do to stop the advance of evil in this world? Whom has God assigned us to touch with the message of salvation in Christ to help advance toward God's eternal goal line? Are we faithful in carrying out our assignment? Have we done our part in obeying His divine call? Do we faithfully execute the play?

YOU ARE WITNESSES

The days following Christ's death were not easy. The disciples were understandably confused and discouraged. The One they thought would be the Messiah had been executed as though He were some common criminal.

Early on Resurrection Sunday some of those who had been closest to the Lord discovered the empty tomb. Mary Magdalene, Joanna, Mary the mother of James, and others reported the news to the apostles (Luke 24:10), and then Peter verified their astounding report (24:12).

Two men trudged their way home that same Sunday. On the seven–mile journey they had ample time to discuss the sad events that had occurred during their time in Jerusalem. It seemed unbelievable that Jesus could have been crucified. These men were not the only ones who were convinced that He was the One who would redeem Israel. Three days had passed. Hope seemed dim.

Even more confusing news had come to the two travelers. The body placed securely in the tomb was reported missing. These reports were verified by trusted colleagues. Visions of angels might be disputed, but without doubt the body was gone.

While they engaged in conversation, an apparent stranger came alongside and interrupted. This inquisitive unknown traveler asked, "What are you discussing together as you walk along?" (24:17). Some less tolerant and gracious individuals might have rightly responded, "It's none of your business!"

The two travelers were kinder, gentler types. They stopped. Dismay and concern were evident in their faces. "Are you only a visitor to Jerusalem and do not know the things that have happened there in these days?" (24:18). You can sense the frustration and surprise in Cleopas's voice. How could anyone have missed this news?

However, the stranger was no stranger at all. He was the resurrected Lord Jesus Christ. The men, however, were kept from recognizing Him.

The Lord's response to Cleopas's question is amusing. "Don't you know the things that have happened there in these days?" Christ responded, "What things?" (24:19).

Cleopas blurted out, "About Jesus of Nazareth." The men outlined all the amazing things that had occurred—the trial, the crucifixion, the dashed hopes, the three-day wait, the women's discovery, the empty tomb, the vision of angels, the verification by trusted companions (24:20–24).

The extensive recap of the disturbing news centered on the very One with whom they were talking. Jesus might have chuckled within at their impassioned explanation.

"How foolish you are, and how slow of heart to believe all that the prophets have spoken! Did not the Christ have to suffer these things and then enter his glory?" (24:25–26). The Lord then began to review the prophetic Scriptures. The Bible study continued as they walked together toward the village of Emmaus.

When the two men urged their stranger friend to stay with them for the evening and they sat down to continue their Bible study, Jesus finally revealed Himself. He took bread, gave thanks, broke it, and began to give it to them. Suddenly Cleopas and his companion recognized Him. This stranger was no stranger at all. This was Jesus!

Then, in the very instant in which Christ was revealed to them, He mysteriously disappeared.

The men rushed back to Jerusalem. They huffed and puffed the seven miles right back to the city from which they had come. They hustled to the place where the apostles and other guests had assembled that night and exclaimed to them, "It is true! The Lord has risen."

While they were relating all that had happened during their brief encounter on the road and in their home in Emmaus, Jesus suddenly appeared in the room. "Shalom," Christ said to them. "Peace be with you" (24:36). As might be expected, those in the room were frightened. They thought the figure before them was a ghost, some wild apparition. But the Lord quickly calmed their fears. He identified Himself as the risen Savior and then voiced an unusual request. "Do you have anything here to eat?"

Nothing could match the fellowship with the Lord around the Word. Instead of talking about His experience of death and resurrection, Jesus turned to God's revelation. He outlined the prophecies that were written about Him in the Law of Moses, the Prophets, and the Psalms. He led a study that moved right through the Bible (24:44), opening their minds so they could understand the Scriptures (24:45).

In an age when many people focus on unusual experiences, personal testimonies, and scintillating stories, people all too often yawn when we convey the truth of the Word of God. The stories may tickle the ears, but they will not satisfy the soul. The power of God is found in the Word of God.

The Lord set the standard. Effective leaders in God's work must communicate God's message. The title Theodore Epp chose when he launched his radio broadcasts from Lincoln, Nebraska, was perfect. "Back to the Bible" might well be the theme for every Christian leader.

Christ started with God's Word. God prophesied salvation. The whole plan was carefully designed in eternity past and clearly revealed in the Bible.

Christ then turned to His work of salvation. "The Christ will suffer and rise from the dead on the third day, and repentance and forgiveness of sins will be preached in his name to all nations, beginning at Jerusalem," the Lord explained to His disciples (24:46–47). In accord with the eternal plan, Jesus suffered, died, and arose on the third day. God's Word and Christ's work are at the heart of our witness.

Repentance and forgiveness of sins are to be preached to all nations. This, too, is part of His plan. Matthew and Mark recorded the worldwide scope of our assignment. Make disciples of all nations, and go into all the world and preach the gospel to every creature. Luke, too, identified the extent of the assignment. Repentance and forgiveness of sins will be preached "to all nations." And how is this vast target to be reached? Amazingly, God's plan includes each one of His children. Christ concluded His Bible study with a simple application, "You are witnesses of these things" (24:48). There is no command here. This is a simple statement of fact. We are His witnesses. Good or bad, we are it.

This is an awesome responsibility. It is through our witness that repentance and forgiveness of sins will be preached to all nations. Through our actions and words the message will spread around the globe and people will be convicted of their need, turn from the way of destruction, and turn to the Lord Jesus Christ for His cleansing, His forgiveness, His redemption.

This is lifestyle evangelism. This is world missions. No other option is offered. God's plan is set. *Through believers God spreads the news of new life in Christ to all nations, beginning in Jerusalem.*

SO SEND I YOU

To be an ambassador is no small task. The one who is assigned to this responsibility becomes the official representative of the country he represents.

Could there be any greater assignment than serving as God's ambassador? Christ came to this dusty planet to represent the Father. He was sent by God from heaven to reveal His glory and His grace. Through Him we have come to know the Father, and in Him we have come to be fellow heirs in an eternal family with everlasting hope.

In John's Gospel account, the Great Commission presents the responsibilities of God's children to touch the world with blessings that can come only from heaven itself.

When the resurrected Christ appeared to His disciples that Sunday evening, they were huddled in fear behind locked doors. With good reason they were afraid. The officials had martyred the One they loved and the One in whom they had placed their hope. It seemed only natural that one of them might be the next victim. Death was at the door.

What a shock when Jesus appeared in their midst with the comforting greeting "Peace." The disciples were overjoyed when they saw the Lord (John 20:19–20). Again Jesus said, "Peace." Why did the Lord repeat it? I am convinced that He wanted to make sure the disciples recognized that this was more than a common greeting. He came to offer true peace.

Then Christ said, "As the Father has sent me, I am sending you" (20:21). This is an incredible statement. Just as God the Father sent His Son to bring life to a dying world, so Christ is sending us to bring light to a dark world.

There is no command in His statement. As certain as we are witnesses, we are sent ones. It is not a matter of choice. We have been appointed to the task. We can either be effective or ineffective, but witnesses and sent ones we are.

As His ambassadors, what do we have to offer? The Lord made it clear in His assignment. We are ambassadors of *Christ's peace*. Even in the midst of turmoil, God's peace can calm the heart. His peace is unique. Earlier Christ promised His peace and contrasted it with the vain promise of peace the world offers. "Peace I leave with you; my peace I give you. I do not give to you as the world gives. Do not let your hearts be troubled and do not be afraid" (14:27).

We are also ambassadors of *the Spirit's power*. Christ gave a foretaste of what His disciples were to experience at Pentecost. He breathed on them and said, "Receive the Holy Spirit." The Spirit who came on God's servants for special assignments throughout the Old Testament and in the time of the Gospels came to indwell us who continue to serve as God's ambassadors. Christ made this clear when He said, "The Spirit . . . lives with you and will be in you" (14:17).

We are ambassadors of *God's pardon*. "If you forgive anyone his sins, they are forgiven; if you do not forgive them, they are not forgiven" (20:22). This is an unfortunate translation. Some church authorities wrongly use this text to claim that they are responsible for hearing confessions of their parishioners and providing absolution. But the verse should read, "If you forgive anyone his sins, they have been forgiven; if you do not forgive them, they have not been forgiven." The apostles carried the message of forgiveness of sins to those who were lost in sin. The message was simple: Believe on the Lord Jesus Christ and you will be saved. Peter preached it, "Repent, then, and turn to God, so that your sins may be wiped out" (Acts 3:19).

Just as the early disciples did, we are to communicate to people that they need to acknowledge their sin and turn to Christ. For each person who by God's grace responds in saving faith, sin is washed away. God grants His pardon, and the one who believes is redeemed.

What a privilege it is to be one of the Lord's ambassadors. We are sent into the world to represent Him, to serve as His emissaries, to honor His wishes and His commands.

A BIG ASSIGNMENT

In each Gospel account the assignment is given. Christ has commanded us to *make disciples*. We multiply productive followers of the King (Matt. 28:18–20). Christ has commanded us to *preach the gospel*. We herald the good news of the Servant (Mark 16:15). Christ has commissioned us as *His witnesses*. We demonstrate the work of the Son of Man (Luke 24:48). Christ has commissioned us as *His ambassadors*. We represent the wishes and the will of God (John 20:21).

In every assignment the scope is presented. The fulfillment requires a view of the whole world, all nations, every creature, the entire globe. *Evangelism and missions are at the core of all God wishes to accomplish.*

CHAPTER EIGHT

To the End of the Earth—Acts

No BOOK IN THE BIBLE more clearly outlines the growth and expansion of the church than the Book of Acts. Acts is a book of action, a book of advance.

The outline of the Book of Acts is divinely inspired. "But you will receive power when the Holy Spirit comes on you and you will be my witnesses in Jerusalem, and in all Judea and Samaria, and to the ends of the earth" (Acts 1:8). The church *started* in Jerusalem, as recorded in Acts 1–7. The church *scattered* throughout all Judea and Samaria, as recorded in Acts 8–12. And the church was *sent* to the end of the earth, Acts 13–28. (While the New International Version has "ends of the earth," the Greek word for "ends" is singular and should be rendered "end." This might signify the outer extremity or "edge" of the world. Or it could mean the "last people group" or "final person" who might be saved).

THE CHURCH STARTS

The church had a rather inauspicious beginning: eleven men hiding in an isolated upstairs room in Jerusalem (Acts 1:13).

This small handful of men who had been touched by the Lord in their personal walk with Him took action to find a replacement for their colleague who had surfaced as a traitor. Treasurer Judas committed suicide when he finally realized the horrible outcome of his betrayal. Two candidates to fill the apostolic vacancy were proposed. Matthias was selected (1:15–16). Their action may have been a wise move, but it was hardly the step that advanced church outreach. Recruitment endeavors are no substitute for divine intervention.

A band of 120 believers joined the apostles to celebrate the Feast of Pentecost. They could hardly have anticipated what transpired. Suddenly God intervened.

An unprecedented audiovisual display drew thousands of curious onlookers—the sound of a rushing wind and the sight of flames of fire that seemed to hover over them. An even more amazing phenomenon followed. When the twelve men from Galilee spoke, the people who rushed to the scene heard languages being spoken by the Twelve.

People from every continent of the then-known world were there. Asia, Africa, and Europe were represented (2:9–11). No one knows how many languages were represented, but the Scriptures list the nations from which these people had come. From its inception the church had a focus as big as the world.

In the middle of conflicting analyses by those who witnessed the scene, Peter stood tall and spoke up. The results from Peter's powerful preaching were amazing. Like some city-wide evangelistic crusade, thousands responded. In this campaign, however, those who responded did not simply sign decision cards. Instead, they were baptized, all three thousand new converts.

Not long after that, Peter preached again to a crowd that gathered when a well-known beggar was healed. The response was even more spectacular. The number "grew to about five thousand" (4:4). Since the Greek word *androi* means "men," not "people," it is likely that many women and children responded too. So undoubtedly many more than five thousand were converted to Christ.

The growth of the church continued at an amazing rate. "More and more men and women believed in the Lord and were added to their number" (5:14). However, these growing multitudes of believers engendered great jealousy among the religious leaders. But acts of persecution only fanned the flame that resulted in even greater expansion of the church (5:17–18).

With growth comes conflict. The apostles were unable to keep up with the pressing needs of the masses. Wisely, these divinely appointed leaders did not give up their priority tasks. "It would not be right for us to neglect the ministry of the word of God in order to wait on tables" (6:2). They were willing to assist in distributing food to needy widows, but they did not dare neglect their time in the Word.

The example of the apostles provides a red alert to leaders today. Wise leaders recognize priorities and are quick to enlist others to assist in appropriate assignments when time requirements for the most important responsibilities are in danger.

By engaging carefully selected "deacons," the apostles were able to "give attention to prayer and ministry of the word" (6:4). Could it be that so many of today's churches are limited in their evangelistic and world missions outreach because their spiritual leaders have neglected prayer and Bible study?

The process of delegating some of the tasks to others not only took care of pressing needs. Also the "word of God spread" and the "number of disciples in Jerusalem increased rapidly." In fact "a large number of priests became obedient to the faith" (6:7).

Conflict was correctly addressed, priorities were maintained, key people were selected to assist, and the church continued to grow.

Church growth can bring internal conflict. But it can also produce external opposition. Stephen, one of the deacons, "a man full of faith and of the Holy Spirit" and "full of God's grace and power," became a threat to the religious establishment (6:3, 8).

When the religious zealots could not "stand up against his wisdom or the Spirit by whom he spoke" (6:10), they started a smear campaign and finally brought Stephen to trial. This "deacon" knew the Word of God. He reviewed the Scriptures from Genesis through the Prophets, but when he sensed that the court was less than interested and clearly antagonistic to his message, Stephen spoke forthrightly, "You stiff-necked people, with uncircumcised hearts and ears! You are just like your fathers: You always resist the Holy Spirit!" (7:51). This was not exactly the way to win friends and influence people!

Stephen's opponents rushed at him, dragged him out of the city, and stoned him. His heavenly vision and final prayer seem to parallel Christ's death. His final words were, "Lord, do not hold this sin against them." And then he died. True leaders have a drive and a compassion that no death threat can challenge.

Opposition can be a wonderful blessing. It is a clear sign that something is happening. Yet opposition is not the real foe; apathy is. If church members are comfortable and there are no signs of conflict or opposition, the prognosis might not be God's blessing. It might mean the church is dying. A leader should never be content with inactivity and ineffectiveness. Playing church is the worst of modern games.

Stephen's death was the beginning of expanded outreach. Persecution intensified. The church came under attack, and so God's people started to move out. Furthermore Stephen's martyrdom undoubtedly made an indelible impression on a young man who eventually became one of the most effective missionaries in human history. "Saul was there, giving approval to his death" (7:60).

THE CHURCH SCATTERS

The divinely ordained outline of the Book of Acts is unmistakable. The church started in Jerusalem and then scattered throughout Judea and Samaria. The plan outlined in Acts 1:8 is exactly the progression recorded in the remainder of the book.

The scattered believers carried with them the message of hope in Christ. They "preached the word wherever they went" (8:4).

In particular, Philip, a "deacon" colleague of Stephen, made a great impact in Samaria (8:5–8). Peter and John traveled from Jerusalem up to Samaria to verify the reports of Philip's amazing ministry. Conflict was evident even in this visit. Simon the Saint, better known as Peter, confronted Simon the Sorcerer, who thought he could buy God's power (8:9–24).

Peter and John returned to Jerusalem, and Philip was obedient to God's leading. He left the flourishing ministry in Samaria with multitudes of converts to encounter one lone man, an Ethiopian, on a deserted road connecting barren Gaza with the capital city of Jerusalem (8:26–40).

Philip's move does not make sense to most leaders. Many people are looking for a position of greater influence, more responsibility, and larger numbers. To leave the crowd and focus on an individual is seen as a step backward.

However, obedience to God is always a step forward. The fixation on numbers, influence, and position can be a subtle temptation leading to spiritual failure. Leaders need to focus on obedience, not "success." Actually true success can be found only in obedience.

The Ethiopian official would have been left in spiritual darkness if God's servant had not been obedient. With careful biblical exposition Philip led this influential leader to the Lord and baptized him. It is likely that through this one official an entire nation received the gospel. The famed Coptic church of Ethiopia continues to this day.

Leadership is best measured by effective reproduction. All our preaching and teaching is futile if individuals do not apply the truth and pass it on.

In the years I spent in Guatemala as a missionary with the Central American Mission, now know as CAM International, the most productive time was the limited months I spent with two promising young men.

Reflecting on my time alone with the Lord in the Gospels at dawn, I remarked to my wife, "Honey, why don't we do what the Lord did. Let's invite twelve guys to come and live with us. We could study together, pray together, minister together."

My wife interrupted. She blinked a bit and sputtered, "Could we start with two?"

We agreed on the plan and began the search for two. God led us first to César Montenegro, a young man who had never been to school a day in his life. He had taught himself to read so that he could study the Bible. The other candidate to whom God led us was Edwin Martínez, who was just then making his plans to attend university to be an engineer.

My plan was to "disciple" these young men. But *I* was the one who was discipled.

There really is only one Disciple-Maker, the Lord Jesus. God worked through each of us to make of us His disciples.

After just a few months studying, praying, and serving together, God developed César and Edwin into amazing leaders. César became a prolific church planter in eastern Guatemala. The gospel continues to flourish in communities that might still be in spiritual darkness had it not been for this wonderful servant leader.

Edwin was touched by the Lord to give up his plans for engineering. He enrolled in the Seminario Teológico Centroamericano, CAM International's seminary in Guatemala City, and he became a noted evangelist and international leader in missions. I recently received a copy of Edwin's prayer letter in which he pointed back to the months he spent in our home as a turning point in his life. Edwin and his wife, Evie, now mentor others. They open their home to young people interested in the ministry.

Which is more important, crowds or disciples? Leadership must not be measured by large masses meeting together. Leadership is reflected in the number of productive followers of Christ who are multiplying God's work.

Sometimes God uses drastic measures to get the attention of one He wants to use as a leader. It is doubtful that anyone would have considered Saul a candidate to spread the gospel. He was a murderous opponent to the Lord's disciples.

Surprise! The Lord had plans to use Saul for His glory. The Lord literally knocked Saul down, flashed a spotlight on him, and spoke to him right out of heaven. Saul got the picture but could not see. Blinded, this tough guy suddenly turned passive. In a holding pattern for three days, he didn't eat or drink.

Then God sent a messenger to outline His plan for Saul. The newly baptized Saul began a frenzy of activity first in Damascus and then in Jerusalem. It seems that he spent more time winning arguments than souls. He stirred up opposition but brought little growth to the church.

So the believers took Saul down to the coast and shipped him off to his hometown, Tarsus. "Then the church throughout Judea, Galilee, and Samaria enjoyed a time of peace" (9:31). The link between Saul's departure and the church's peace is not contrived. The translation "Then" is more emphatic in Greek and could be translated "So then therefore."

Saul does not appear again in the Book of Acts until the end of chapter 11 when Barnabas searched for him in Tarsus. When Paul wrote his testimony in Galatians, he gave a detail that is often unnoticed: "Fourteen years later I went up again to Jerusalem, this time with Barnabas" (Gal. 2:1). Fourteen years is no small amount of time. Apparently Saul was not ready at the time of his conversion for the leadership role to which God would later assign him. Perhaps he was too enamored with his intellectual abilities and his talent for debate to be effective in ministry.

Sometimes leaders must first be humbled. Self-effort must yield to Spirit control. Saul was obviously tempered during his time back home. Finally ready to serve under Barnabas's guidance, he emerged as the leader in missions God meant Him to be.

While Paul was being groomed for his place of leadership, Peter appeared as the recognized spokesman for the church. In ways that only God could devise, the gospel spread to a Roman commander who was searching for spiritual answers. God always provides a messenger to bring the gospel to every lost person on this globe who responds to the limited revelation available. Peter was God's servant to explain saving truth to Cornelius and his extended family (Acts 10).

The leadership in Jerusalem was not pleased with Peter's visit to a Gentile home. The pattern is consistent. Every advance brings conflict. Church growth is not always smooth sailing.

Fortunately, the conflict between Peter and his colleagues was resolved. Their conclusion was revolutionary: "So then, God has granted even the Gentiles repentance unto life" (11:18). This is no idle verse in the Bible. Here the door was opened to worldwide missions. As God had promised Abraham, "All peoples on earth will be blessed" (Gen. 12:3).

The church continued to be scattered. "Now those who had been scattered by the persecution in connection with Stephen traveled as far as Phoenicia, Cyprus, and Antioch" (Acts 11:19). Antioch was especially blessed. Both Jews and Greeks turned to the Lord. Barnabas was sent to investigate, and in this visit he found Saul in Tarsus and brought him to Antioch, and in the following year Barnabas and Saul headed for Jerusalem with an offering taken in the mission church to help the mother church.

In keeping with the pattern, the advance of the gospel brought both conflict and opposition. James was martyred and Peter was incarcerated. King Herod determined that he would have Peter executed at the end of the festive week when masses of visitors would be in Jerusalem to witness the spectacle (12:1–4).

In difficult moments God's power is most evident. Peter wasn't worried, for he knew God was in control. In fact Peter was sleeping between two tough soldiers to whom he was chained. While Peter slept, the believers prayed (12:5). And God worked in answer to their prayers. Chains were broken and prison doors opened. Although it seemed like a wild dream, it was real. Peter was freed.

Peter rushed to the home where the prayer meeting was being held and pounded on the door and called out to those inside. A servant girl heard the commotion and responded. She was so shocked to hear Peter's voice that she failed to open the door. She rushed to the group to tell them the exciting news, but they refused to believe her. Finally when they went to the door and opened it, there was Peter! He had to raise his hand and calm the group to explain what had happened (12:6–17).

Did the people in the prayer meeting have much faith? Apparently not. The answer was literally at the door and they couldn't believe it. Did God answer their prayers? Yes!

Church leaders must guard time alone with the Lord to be nourished by the Word and engaged in prayer. This is not enough, however. Leaders must also engage other believers in corporate prayer. Prayer is central to God's plan. Power is unleashed as we depend on Him.

THE CHURCH SENDS

The prayer meeting recorded in Acts 12 is the launching pad for the amazing missionary outreach that followed. Peter was freed, but what about the rest of the story?

King Herod was furious. He had assigned sixteen soldiers to guard Peter. He ordered all sixteen executed. Then he left to attend a political rally on the coast. When the crowds shouted their praise to Herod, "This is the voice of a god," God struck the vain king dead, eaten of worms (12:22–23). Peter was free. Herod was dead. And the Word of God spread (12:24).

During all this excitement Barnabas and Saul were in Jerusalem. They then returned to Antioch to report back to the mission church that had sent the offering to assist the believers in Jerusalem (12:25).

The first thing Barnabas and Saul did in Antioch was to call a prayer meeting. Barnabas and Saul may well have been among those in Jerusalem who had prayed for Peter's release. The prayer meeting had been held in the home of Mary, mother of John Mark (12:12). Interestingly, John Mark joined Barnabas and Saul in the trip to Antioch. The link is hardly coincidental. Having seen the power of prayer in Jerusalem, Barnabas and Saul were wise to focus on prayer in Antioch.

Those who prayed in Antioch were moved to launch one of the most historic movements in history. Somehow it was apparent to the five leaders who were participants in the prayer meeting that two of the five were to be "set apart" for the work to which God had called them. Barnabas and Saul were sent out (13:1–3).

World missions was born in the Antioch prayer meeting. The scattered church became a sending church.

Interestingly, of the five men named in this historic prayer meeting, not one of them was from Antioch. Barnabas was from the island of Cyprus. Simeon was called Niger, meaning "black." Lucius of Cyrene, the northern coast of Africa, was probably also a man of color. Manaen, the Greek form of the name Manahem, had been brought up with Herod the tetrarch. Saul was from Tarsus (13:1–2).

An international, interracial prayer meeting was the perfect setting for the birth of missions. Three men commissioned two men and sent them out. And all that transpired was governed by the Holy Spirit. Although the Antioch leaders commissioned the two missionaries (13:3), they were "sent on their way by the Holy Spirit" (13:4).

By the Holy Spirit's leading, God sends His ambassadors into the world through the local church. *God initiates missions, the Spirit empowers missions, the church fulfills missions.* Believers in the local church send those of the Lord's choosing to take the good news to the very ends of the earth.

The rest of the Book of Acts records the conflicts, difficulties, opposition, and persecutions that accompanied the expansion of the gospel to the then-known world. Yet in the midst of all the problems there were amazing breakthroughs.

On the third of Paul's missionary journeys, the apostle called for the elders in the church in Ephesus to meet him at the port city of Miletus for a farewell gathering. Paul's address to them outlines the inclusive responsibility of a leader.

Paul said, "You know how I lived the whole time I was with you" (20:18). Paul lived with the people. He spent time with them. He was an example. Leadership begins with what we are. *We must be what God wants us to be.*

Paul continued, "I served the Lord with great humility and with tears" (20:19). Paul diligently worked for the people. He served them. He was a laborer. What we do is also basic to leadership. *We must do what God wants us to do.*

Paul told the Ephesians, "You know that I have not hesitated to preach anything that would be helpful to you but have taught you publicly and from house to house" (20:20). Paul faithfully taught the people. He instructed them. He was a spokesman. What we say is important to leadership. *We must say what God wants us to say.*

Paul spoke at length of the coming trial he was facing. "And now, compelled by the Spirit, I am going to Jerusalem, not knowing what will happen to me there" (20:22). He revealed the likely hardships and imprisonment, even pending death, of which he had been warned. "I consider my life worth nothing to me, if only I may finish the race and complete the task the Lord Jesus has given me—the task of testifying to the gospel of God's grace" (20:24). Paul was fully dedicated to the people. He loved them. He was a friend. What we feel is also part of leadership. *We must feel what God wants us to feel.*

What we are, what we do, what we say, what we feel—all are part of effective spiritual leadership. The capstone of the leadership role is found in the bond of love. Love for the Lord and for the people is the driving force for this demanding task.

Every successful missionary has experienced the emotional farewell recorded in Acts. "When he had said this, he knelt down with all of them and prayed. They all wept as they embraced him and kissed him" (20:36–37).

The whirlwind of trials that followed for Paul were humanly frightening, but all were divinely planned. Paul had the unique opportunity to testify for the Lord to the most influential authorities of the day, including two successive governors (Felix and Festus) and a king (Agrippa).

Mission outreach extended all the way to Rome, the nerve center of the empire. Interestingly, the government paid for Paul's fourth missionary journey! Although he was a prisoner, Paul emerged as the recognized leader on the ship that carried him to Rome. He was the one who took charge when the ship ran aground and was wrecked, and because of his courageous leadership everyone on the ship survived (27:42–44).

The Book of Acts ends on a somewhat positive note. After the Jewish leaders in Jerusalem had seemed less than open to the good news he brought them, Paul explained to the Jewish leaders in Rome the expanding missionary challenge. "Therefore I want you to know that God's salvation has been sent to the Gentiles, and they will listen!" (28:28).

Although the apostle was under house arrest, he was able to continue an effective ministry both to the Roman guards who were chained to one of the most vibrant evangelist missionaries in the history of the church and to those who came to visit him. "Boldly and without hindrance he preached the kingdom of God and taught about the Lord Jesus Christ" (28:31).

Paul was not only an active missionary. He penned numerous letters that provide God's instruction to the church. Each of his thirteen letters is filled with sound doctrine and practical advice. Together they probably form the best guide for leadership available.

God chose one who was constantly on the move to record His divine instruction. On occasion God put His servant in prison to give him extra time to write, but most of the letters were written on the field in the heat of battle. No wonder they ring true.

Paul's epistles are not pious fairy tales. They were forged in the reality of life. All the problems, conflicts, opposition, and disappointments are there. Best of all, God's instruction for resolution, advance, encouragement, and hope are recorded. Good leaders are saturated with God's Word.

The seed planted among eleven common men sprouted and then spread around the world. *The task continues. It is the responsibility of every Christian to be involved in evangelism and global missions.* The final chapter has not yet been written. The Book of Acts is but the beginning.

CHAPTER NINE

Are They Really Lost?—Romans

YOU MEAN TO TELL ME that God sends people to hell because they have failed to respond to a message they have never heard? It doesn't sound fair." Many people, including many Christians, ask this question.

In a survey of students who attended the Urbana conference only 37 percent believed that "a person who doesn't hear the gospel is eternally lost."[1] This was not a poll of disinterested or ignorant Christians. This response came from college students who took part of their Christmas vacation to attend the massive triennial missionary conference held in Urbana, Illinois.

Of more than five thousand who responded to the questionnaire, over a third of these dedicated Christian students concluded that the un-evangelized are not lost.

The question, "Are the heathen lost?" may seem like a peripheral issue designed for debate among theologians. This seems like a great question for late-night discussions in college dorms, far removed from issues important to life. On the contrary, this simple question strikes at the very foundation of basic biblical truth. It affects every area of theology:

The character of God (theology proper) is questioned: "Is God just?"

The sufficiency of Christ (Christology) is questioned: "Is Christ the only way?"

The necessity of the cross (soteriology) is questioned: "Did Christ have to die?"

The depravity of man (anthropology) is questioned: "Is man inherently sinful?"

The judgment of sin (hamartiology) is questioned: "Is not evil relative?"

The role of the church (ecclesiology) is questioned: "Is the church God's witness?"

The finale of history (eschatology) is questioned: "Is there a future reckoning?"

A question of this magnitude demands an answer.

A RELIGIOUS SUPERMARKET

Some react strongly to the mere suggestion that those who have never heard about Christ might be eternally lost. They contend that all religions are basically the same, and so we shouldn't concern ourselves with those outside of Christianity.

Theologian E. O. James argued, "To discover the reality of Christ in all the religions of the world is the essence of the ecumenical approach."[2] "God does not condemn anybody," R. Pannikan wrote. "God is at work in the 'pagan' religions."[3]

While diverse religions of the world may reflect man's thoughts about God, they do not thereby present God's message to humankind. Human reason is a poor substitute for God's revelation. To consider Christianity as just another brand in the world market of religions is to reject the unique authority of God's Word, the Bible.

"Pagan" religions are just that—pagan. They blind people from the truth. They turn people from the supernatural God to hopeless superstition.

A GENEROUS GESTURE

Some scholars attempt to find a mediating answer in the Bible. They appeal to Scripture to predict a hopeful future for those who have never heard the saving message of Christ. Clark Pinnock proposes a "second chance" for those who did not hear of Christ in their lifetime. He contends that Christ's "proclamation to the spirits . . . who were once disobedient" (1 Pet. 3:19–20) means that the unevangelized have opportunity after death to make a decision about Jesus Christ."[4]

Contrary to Pinnock's comments, 1 Peter 3 records a historical fact that Christ spoke, by the Holy Spirit, through Noah to the ungodly prior to the Flood.[5] The spirits of these rebellious people are now locked in a prison of eternal separation from God (compare 3:20 with 1:11 and Gen. 6:3). The Bible gives no hint whatsoever of any chance for salvation after death. "It is appointed for men once to die . . . and after this comes the judgment" (Heb. 9:27).

Others find a loophole for the lost in the Book of Romans. Years ago S. D. F. Salmond wrote, "We need nothing beyond Paul's broad statement that those who have the law shall be judged by law, and that those who are without law shall be judged without law."[6]

The verse Salmond quotes, Romans 2:12, teaches that those who have sinned without the Law will perish just as surely as those who have sinned with the Law. The verb *apollymi* does not mean "to be judged." It should be translated "to perish, be destroyed, be lost." The passage does not excuse people; instead it shows that they have no excuse.

Pinnock vainly tries to satisfy his concern for those who have never heard of Christ by concluding, "Of one thing we can be certain: God will not abandon in hell those who have not known and therefore have not declined His offer of grace."[7]

However, these attempts to gloss over the tragic end of those without Christ fail to consider adequately the clear teaching of God's Word.

GOD'S ANSWER

The only valid conclusion to the burning question "Are the heathen lost?"—and to the related question "Is God just?"—is found in the Bible.

Does God send people to hell because they have not accepted a message they have never even heard? This does not seem just. How can this dilemma be reconciled? In his letter to the Romans, the apostle Paul affirmed that God neither sends people to hell nor does He judge them on the basis of their response to One of whom they have not heard.

GOD'S REVELATION

The judgment of God in relation to the unevangelized of this world is based not on their response to unrevealed truth but on their response to revelation they have received.

God's righteousness is revealed to those who believe in the gospel of Jesus Christ (Rom. 1:16–17). We who know the Savior are blessed with this revelation of righteousness. But there is more to God's revelation.

The wrath of God is revealed against "all the godlessness and wickedness of men who suppress the truth" (1:18). Those who are without Christ suffer the wrath and condemnation of God. This wrath is the dark side of God's revelation.

It is important to notice that a person does not face God's wrath because he has failed to accept a gospel he never heard, or because he failed to put his trust in a Savior he has never known. Instead, people experience God's wrath because they have turned from the truth they *have* received.

Some confusion exists because of the faulty translation of Romans 1:18 in the King James Version, where the verb *katechō* has been translated "to hold." Actually it means "to hold down" the truth, or as R. C. H. Lenski puts it, "to suppress the truth, to prevent the truth from exerting its power in the heart and the life."[8]

What is this truth that people have suppressed? The truth of God has been revealed to all humanity in two ways. First, the truth or reality of God is an integral part of every person's *conscience.* Even those who have never heard of Christ know of God. "What may be known about God is plain to them, because God has made it plain to them" (1:19). This knowledge is not as superficial as some would like to make it. Paul used the verb *ginōskō*, "to know by personal experience."

Through their conscience people know of God and instinctively know of His Law. The "requirements of the law are written on their hearts, their consciences also bearing witness" (2:15). Richard DeHaan writes, "Even though the light of conscience has been dimmed because of deliberate wickedness, it still exists everywhere."[9]

Second, the truth of God's power has been clearly seen through *creation.*

"For since the creation of the world God's invisible qualities—his eternal power and divine nature—have been clearly seen, being understood from what has been made, so that men are without excuse" (1:20).

The truth of God is revealed to everyone through both their *conscience* and God's *creation*. But in their unrighteousness people suppress this revealed truth. So they are without excuse. As Gleason Archer explains, "There is sufficient knowledge for each person after the fall to be criminally liable for sin."[10]

The issue therefore is not that the unevangelized have failed to put their trust in a person of whom they have never heard. The issue is that they have suppressed the truth they have both received and understood. So God is totally just in His judgment.

MANKIND'S REBELLION

Just how do people suppress the truth God has revealed? Paul explained why the unsaved are inexcusable before God. "For although they knew God, they neither glorified him as God nor gave thanks to him" (Rom. 1:21). The Greek word rendered "for" is not the general Greek word *gar*. Instead it is *dioti*, a stronger word for "because." In this way Paul was exposing the cause for God's judgment.

Humanity has descended a sin-slick staircase to destruction. The first two steps downward are convicting. They might be labeled "no glory" and "no thanks." To move down these two steps requires little effort. In fact it requires *no* effort. The person who does nothing is not standing still. He is sliding from God. When a person fails to honor God and to thank Him, he or she is sliding away from Him.

Failure to honor or thank God brings futile thoughts and foolish feelings: People's thinking "became futile and their foolish hearts were darkened" (1:21). They became dead in the head and dark in the heart.

"Although they claimed to be wise, they became fools" (1:22). Pride is the precipice from which sinners fall into perdition. Fully confident of their own capabilities, like some puffed-up toad, the unsaved jump to their destruction.

The basement of the sordid seven-step descent is where people perform their most rebellious act. They exchange "the glory of the immortal God for images made to look like mortal man and birds and animals and reptiles" (1:23). The sovereignty of God is depicted as some slimy serpent. This is blatant idolatry.

When I was at a conference in Thailand, I looked with respect but then with deep concern on those who placed sacrifices and burned incense before the massive gold statue of Buddha. My immediate thought was, "Look how these people reach out toward God." But I was wrong. Idolatry is not evidence of a thirst for God. It reveals rebellion against God. As Malcolm Watts states, "The idolatrous systems of the world are actually states of man's departure from God and expression of his desire for other gods rather than the true, living God."[11]

By taking these seven steps down to the cellar of idolatry, the unregenerate have clearly demonstrated their rejection of God. They have suppressed the truth. Their downward path can be pictured this way:

No glory
    No thanks
      Futile thought
        Darkened heart
          Prideful boasting
            Foolishness
              Idolatry

God is totally fair in His judgment of this blatant rejection of His clear revelation, and people are without excuse.

GOD'S RESPONSE

God might be charged with injustice if He sends people to hell because they fail to respond to a message they have never heard. But God's judgment is based on His clear revelation. Robert McQuilkin expresses it well: "They are not condemned for rejecting a Savior of whom they have never heard. They are condemned for sinning against the light they have."[12]

Paul's argument in Romans not only outlines the basis of God's judgment. It also shows that God does not *send* people to hell. He simply *lets them go* to their self-determined destruction.

Like a terrible drumbeat of disaster God's judgment is repeated three times. "God gave them over" sounds forth three times in Romans 1. The verb used here, *paradidōmi*, stresses God's judicial act. Since those who have suppressed the truth are determined to self-destruct, justice decrees that it be so. It is as if God responded, "Let them go!" God gave them over to the lusts of their hearts (1:24–25), to degrading passions (1:26–27), and to a depraved mind (1:28–32).

In direct contrast to the "Great Commandment," "Love the Lord your God with all your *heart* and with all your *soul* and with all your *mind*" (Matt. 22:37; italics added; compare Deut. 6:5), people have pursued a pathway leading to a darkened *heart*, degraded *soul*, and depraved *mind*.

One of the most sordid lists in all of Scripture stands like a lineup of devastating character witnesses against the accused (Rom. 1:29–31). Paul concluded with the disturbing comment, "Although they know God's righteous decree that those who do such things deserve death, they not only continue to do these very things but also approve of those who practice them" (1:32). These are not innocent acts of the misinformed; these actions are willful.

God's judgment is warranted and sure. He does not send people to hell; He let them go. This awesome judgment of eternal damnation, however, is not for us to make. This is God's call. "You, therefore, have no excuse, you who pass judgment on someone else" (2:1). We yield to His justice. "Now we know that God's judgment against those who do such things is based on truth" (2:2).

THEY ARE LOST

Are the heathen lost? Yes! Is God just? Yes! Does God send people to hell because they have not responded to a message they have never even heard? No! God judges people on the basis of His revelation through conscience and creation. He lets those who suppress and spurn His truth go to their own destruction.

These seemingly isolated theological questions strike at the heart of missions outreach. If the people who have not heard of Christ are not lost, it would be far better to leave them alone than to have people running around the world with the gospel message.

Billions on this globe are caught in the downward spiral of eternal destruction. One burning question remains: How will they hear about the Lord Jesus Christ, the only Way?

God in His sovereignty has chosen believers to be His witnesses. He uses common people like us to spread the good news of our Savior. As Herbert Kane pointed out, "There is not a single line in the Book of Acts to suggest that God can save a human being without employing a human agent. On the contrary there are several examples of God's going to great lengths to secure the active cooperation of one or another of His servants."[13]

When an unevangelized "heathen" seems to show a positive response to the revelation he or she has received through conscience and creation, God mobilizes one of His children to bear the message of hope in Christ. When Cornelius started to respond to the revelation he knew, God communicated miraculously to Peter in a trance so that he might accompany the centurion's messengers and take the message of salvation in Christ to Cornelius and his family and friends (Acts 10).

Could God shake you loose to help fulfill this task? People are desperately lost. They are without hope on their way to eternal destruction. *Responsive, responsible agents are needed to serve as Jesus' ambassadors in the exciting enterprise called world missions.*

CHAPTER TEN

Every Tongue and Tribe—Revelation

I WAS IN A STATE OF SHOCK. I had just returned to my room at Camp of the Woods in upstate New York. The night was crisp and cool as I walked across the grounds after the evening meeting. I had wanted to join all those who headed to the campfire service. When I'm a speaker at a conference, I always try to participate in as many activities as possible. I feel that if the conference guests are gracious enough to be present at the Bible hour, I should join them in other events on the program. But for some reason I felt compelled to return to my room rather than go to the campfire. I was glad I did.

Shortly after I entered my room the phone rang. My wife was calling from Dallas. Libby sounded distant and the news disturbing, I asked her to repeat what she had said. Her voice quavered as she told me, "The doctors have discovered that Lew has a very rare form of bone marrow cancer."

I could hardly believe it. This was not the news I expected to hear. Lew Whittle, vice president of field ministries and my close colleague in CAM International, had been under medical investigation for more than two weeks, but I would never have imagined something this serious.

Two weeks earlier, Lew and his wife, Dianne, were on vacation in California when Lew suffered a strange seizure. By God's grace they were staying in a hotel located just a few blocks from the city hospital. The emergency squad arrived at the hotel room in minutes.

After days of testing, the doctors concluded that Lew had meningitis. He was treated for a full week and then released to travel back to Dallas and be transferred to Baylor University Medical Center. Further testing ruled out the diagnosis given in California. I was grateful when the Baylor medical experts declared that Lew did not have meningitis. However, it was disconcerting when further extensive tests left the doctors mystified. They could not determine the cause of Lew's ailments. Lew was finally released from the hospital, but within days further complications arose and he was back in the hospital.

"The cancer is serious," my wife continued. "Many who have been diagnosed with this type of cancer have lived only two to five years."

Much of the night I spent in prayer asking God to intervene. I realized in a new way how helpless and dependent we are. So many factors in life are beyond our control.

Like some hidden enemy, cancer can strike at any moment. Lew's vigorous exercise and healthy diet could not exempt him from an insidious attack by this dreaded disease. A young man who may appear to be in perfect health can be cancer's target.

The word *cancer* is frightening. Even for Christians filled with hope, news of this disease is not a welcome thought. I prayed earnestly for Lew, his wife Dianne, for the Whittle family, and our CAM mission family. Up to this point God has graciously answered our prayers in sustaining Lew's life and in giving all of us strength and hope through this trial.

FUTURE ASSURANCE

If there were no other benefit from knowing Christ, the hope and assurance we have in Him would be worth it all. No matter what happens to us, we know that He is in control and we know where we are headed.

We are not moving blindly down a path with no destination. History is not some cyclical mystery or blind alley. The Bible gives clear forecasts of the future; a bright and everlasting outcome is at the end of the tunnel.

The tunnel leading to our future hope, however, is very dark. Everyone faces trials. However severe our trials may seem, they are small compared to the seven-year Tribulation that will sweep the earth in the coming age.

In graphic and picturesque detail the Book of Revelation outlines incredible horrors that will occur just before Christ returns to reign on the earth. The Bible's closing book gives a vivid account of end-time events and a reliable description of the new heavens and new earth prepared for those who are a part of God's family.

This single book of prophecy in the New Testament builds on the seventeen books of prophecy of the Old Testament and outlines a fitting conclusion to God's stirring revelation through the ages.

THE ONE WHO IS

The apostle John described the One "who is, who was, and who is to come" (Rev. 1:4, 8). This threefold division of time forms an outline of the Book of Revelation.

Chapter 1 vividly describes the One "who is." The word picture is inspiring. John saw "someone 'like a son of man' dressed in a robe reaching down to his feet with a golden sash around his chest. His head and hair were white like wool, as white as snow, and his eyes were like blazing fire. His feet were like bronze glowing in a furnace, and his voice was like the sound of rushing waters. In his right hand he held seven stars, and out of his mouth came a sharp double-edged sword. His face was like the sun shining in all its brilliance" (1:13–16).

No wonder John fell down. But imagine the comfort he felt when the Lord placed His hand on the trembling prophet and said, "Do not be afraid. I am the First and the Last. I am the Living One; I was dead and behold I am alive for ever and ever!" (1:17).

THE ONE WHO WAS

The Lord instructed John to write seven letters. These letters, recorded in Revelation 2 and 3, contain historical significance of the One "who was" with fascinating descriptions of seven churches.

These churches were located in seven cities in what is today western Turkey. I believe the letters were written to actual church fellowships in the time John wrote his prophecy. These bodies of believers needed these pointed messages from the Lord.

It is disturbing to realize that all these churches were eliminated by the sweep of militant Islam. Today Turkey is one of the least evangelized countries in the world. Unfortunately any local church is always but one generation from extinction. Many Christians in Turkey no doubt suffered martyrdom at the hands of Muslim warlords. Others, however, may have turned their back on the Lord. When spiritual fervor dies, evangelism becomes stagnant and mission outreach diminishes. And when evangelism and missions die, the church dies!

THE ONE WHO IS TO COME

Before He revealed the devastation and destruction that was to come on the world, God first opened a door to heaven and gave the prophet a peek at incredible beauty.

"Come up here, and I will show you what must take place after this" (4:1). The One "who is" and "who was" is the One "who is to come," the Almighty One who is about to bring human history to a close.

All future activity is directed from heaven. When I was in the Navy, I stood duty in what is called "C.I.C." The Combat Information Center is filled with electronic equipment and sophisticated communication systems. Navigation is directed on the ship's "bridge." All other activities are directed in the C.I.C., the tactical nerve center of the vessel. From heaven God is manning His C.I.C. We need to recognize God's sovereign plan. Before showing John the terrors of the Tribulation that will befall the earth, God gave him a glimpse of heaven, from which all directives come.

God's throne was the center of attraction. Seated on the throne was One who "had the appearance of jasper and carnelian. A rainbow, resembling an emerald, encircled the throne" (4:3). John tried to describe the beauty of this scene by referring to precious jewels and a majestic full-circle rainbow. I can remember the unforgettable sight of a circular rainbow on a flight high above a thunderstorm over Louisiana. Most rainbows we see are a mere arch stretching from the sky to the earth. High above the Louisiana storm clouds that day, I saw a ring rather than a bow. In a similar scene John witnessed a 360-degree rainbow encircling the throne of God.

"From the throne came flashes of lightning, rumblings and peals of thunder" (4:5). The scene was awesome. Feel the power. Sense the grandeur. Listen to the roar. God is there. He is the sovereign Lord.

Around the throne were four "living creatures" that looked like a lion, an ox, a man, and an eagle (4:7). These seem to depict the four Gospels. Matthew pictured Christ as the Lion. Mark wrote about an ox-like Servant. Luke emphasized the human nature of Christ, the God-Man. John focused on Jesus' divine nature, like a flying eagle.

Day and night the four creatures never stopped saying, "Holy, holy, holy is the Lord God Almighty, who was, and is, and is to come" (4:8).

THE HEAVENLY CHORUS

Surrounding the four creatures are twenty-four "elders" who fell down "before Him who sits on the throne, and worship Him who lives forever" (4:10).

At the right hand of Him who sat on the throne John saw One who was declared worthy to open the "scroll with seven seals" (5:1). To this One who is depicted as both Lion and Lamb, the four living creatures and twenty–four elders sang a new song. "You are worthy to take the scroll and to open its seals, because you were slain, and with your blood you purchased men for God from every tribe and language and people and nation" (5:9).

If there is any question about the eventual success of world mission endeavor, God's Word settles all doubt. As time on earth ticks down to its climactic close, an international chorus in heaven is joined by "thousands upon thousands, and ten thousand times ten thousand" angels in a doxology of praise. Human voices join an angelic host to sing, "Worthy is the Lamb, who was slain, to receive power and wealth and wisdom and strength and honor and glory and praise!" (5:12).

One of my favorite choruses is the classic tune written by Don Wyrtzen with this triumphant text taken from the Book of Revelation, utilizing the wording in the King James Version. The central phrase, "Worthy is the Lamb that was slain," is repeated three times as the music crescendos. Then the song builds again with the words, "to receive power and riches and wisdom and strength, honor and glory and blessing. Worthy is the Lamb, worthy is the Lamb, worthy is the Lamb that was slain." Here the music reaches full volume, giving rightful significance to Christ's sacrificial death. Then the chorus ends with a more subdued and highly worshipful phrase, "Worthy is the Lamb." The melody for these four words of tribute is sung on one sustained note. A hushed underlying harmony provides dignity as the chorus closes and seems to demand a moment of silence for quiet prayer and meditation.

Can you see those redeemed saints who encircle the throne to join the massive choir? They come from every tribe, every language, every people, and every nation.

"Every tribe." Ethnic representation will be complete.

"Every language." Linguistic representation will be complete.

"Every people." Cultural representation will be complete.

"Every nation." Political representation will be complete.

Do you hear the music? In a "loud voice" they sing. Suddenly the whole universe joins the heavenly chorus. "Every creature in heaven and on earth and under the earth and on the sea, and all that is in them [are] singing: To Him who sits on the throne and to the Lamb be praise and honor and glory and power for ever and ever!" (5:13).

GOD'S FUTURE MISSIONARY FORCE

When waves of judgment fall on the sin-sick world in the seven-year Tribulation, God will provide an army of choice missionaries to sweep the globe with a message of hope. From each of the twelve tribes of Israel the Lord will select twelve thousand flaming heralds, a total of 144,000 Jewish evangelists (7:4–8).

At best the number of missionaries scattered around the globe is now approximately eighty thousand. With all the diligent efforts of mission agencies, the active force today is small compared to the force from God's chosen people to be assembled by His direct intervention in the closing days of history.

Then John was again given a glimpse of heaven. "After this I looked and there before me was a great multitude that no one could count, from every nation, tribe, people, and language, standing before the throne in front of the Lamb" (7:9).

In this ingathering of the redeemed, as a result of missions outreach, the number will be of such magnitude that it will be considered innumerable. Every missionary can rejoice in this God-decreed outcome. Success is divinely ordained.

Whatever is lacking in world evangelism through past and present endeavors will be fully completed in the time of the Tribulation by God's missionary force. The international gathering in heaven will be so large that no one will be able to count the number of people.

If you are engaged in some way in evangelistic and mission outreach, you can thank the Lord for the part you have in this wonderful endeavor. If you are only a spectator of evangelism and missions, you should be motivated to get involved. Rather than merely watching what God is doing, each believer needs to be actively engaged in this worldwide enterprise. We can be sure that it will succeed in accord with His perfect plan.

Reaching people for Christ across the street and around the world is not an option in God's program. This is top priority. Every leader must acknowledge the ultimate God-ordained goal and get involved.

GOD'S SELECT WITNESSES

In the course of the final events in history, God will empower two witnesses who will prophesy for forty-two months (11:2–3). In spite of incredible divine power granted them, at the end of three and a half years these two will be martyred. "Now when they have finished their testimony, the beast that comes up from the Abyss will attack them, and overpower and kill them" (11:7). This may seem like a terrible defeat. But the effective witness of the two in life will be superseded by what will happen after their death. Their witness will go on. "For three and a half days men from every people, tribe, language, and nation will gaze on their bodies and refuse them burial. The inhabitants of the earth will gloat over them and will celebrate by sending each other gifts, because these two prophets had tormented those who live on the earth" (11:9–10).

The entire world will gaze on the bodies of God's prophets by means of television or the "web" or some other yet-to-be-devised means. People all over the globe will be touched by the valiant witness of just two of the Lord's servants. This prophetic scene should be a challenge for us to make greater use of global communication networks. Satellite hookups can provide a witness for Christ all around the world.

When these servants of God will be martyred, multitudes of unbelievers from every people, tribe, language, and nation will celebrate. In contrast with the heavenly scenes in which those from every ethnic, social, linguistic, and political segment of the world will praise God, this scene depicts people on earth who rebel against God. Around the globe God's enemies will believe that His witnesses have been defeated. For three and a half days they will have a gigantic gift exchange. But we who love the Lord need not be distraught. These worldly festivities of celebration over the martyrdom of God's two servants will be cut short. After three and a half days the two martyrs will be resurrected and God will take them "to heaven in a cloud, while their enemies look on" (11:11–12).

The festive Christmas-like spirit of God's enemies will suddenly be interrupted by God's Easter-like resurrection of His two witnesses. God is not mocked. His witness is sure, and His witnesses are secure.

GOD'S EVIL ENEMIES

In contrast to God's anointed witnesses described in Revelation 11, two beasts are identified in chapter 13. The New Testament prophet rightfully presents these ungodly world leaders as beasts.

Empowered by Satan himself, the first beast will be worshiped by survivors in the time of this terrible apocalyptic holocaust. The whole world, John wrote, will be astonished and will follow the beast (13:3).

Rebellion against God is evident. "The beast was given a mouth to utter proud words and blasphemies and to exercise his authority for forty-two months. He opened his mouth to blaspheme God, and to slander his name and his dwelling place and those who live in heaven" (13:5–6).

While limited to a rule of a mere three and one half years (forty-two months), this evil political leader will extend his rule to the whole world. He will have "authority over every tribe, people, language, and nation" (13:7).

Again the contrast is significant. While multitudes from every tribe, people, language, and nation will assemble in heaven in praise to the Lord, masses from every tribe, people, language, and nation on the earth will bow in worship to an ungodly leader.

Another beast of this evil empire will perform "great and miraculous signs," thereby deceiving "the inhabitants of the earth." He will force everyone to worship an animated image of the first beast and to receive the "666" mark of the Beast imprinted on their right hand or their forehead (13:11–18).

One more heavenly scene will precede the final destruction on earth. John saw the Lamb "standing on Mount Zion and with him 144,000 who had his name and his Father's name written on their foreheads." In contrast to those on earth who bear the mark of the beast, these "who had been redeemed from the earth" and "who did not defile themselves" will offer a great musical anthem of praise (14:1–5).

One last opportunity will be given those on earth. An angel will be sent to "proclaim to those who live on the earth—to every nation, tribe, language, and people." The angelic message is clear: "Fear God and give him glory, because the hour of this judgment has come. Worship him who made the heavens, the earth, the sea and the springs of water" (14:6–7).

The repeated reference to "every nation, tribe, language, and people" in the Book of Revelation is significant. God's purposes are universal; His goal is global. "God so loved the *world* that He gave His only begotten Son" (John 3:16, italics added). He is not willing that *any* should perish (2 Pet. 3:9).

Nonetheless those who spurn God's message of redemption and refuse His gracious provision will suffer divine punishment. The final judgment will be poured out on the earth from seven bowls of God's wrath. The corrupted religious establishment and false political empire will fall, and then heavenly choirs will again raise their voices in praise to the conquering King of kings and Lord of lords.

"Blessed are those who are invited to the wedding supper of the Lamb" (19:9). The Beast and the False Prophet who will perform "miraculous signs" will be "thrown alive into the fiery lake of burning sulfur" (19:19–20). The "ancient serpent, who is the devil, or Satan," will be bound "for a thousand years" (20:3).

Believers who will refuse to bear the mark of the Beast and will be martyred will reign with Christ during the one thousand years that Satan and his forces are bound. You would think that the world's peoples would be so pleased with the perfect reign of the Lord that they would never turn from Him.

However, when Satan will be given one last moment of freedom, at the end of the thousand years, he "will go out to deceive the nations in the four corners of the earth" and will assemble a force "in number like the sand on the seashore" to fight against God. But fire will come down from heaven and devour them. Satan, the Beast, the False Prophet, and these rebellious masses will suffer immediate defeat and suffer the consequences. "They will be tormented day and night for ever and ever" (20:7–10).

The Great White Throne scene that follows is inspiring. Two books will be opened as the resurrected dead "great and small" stand before the throne. From one book each person will be "judged according to what he had done" (20:13). The point is that no one has done enough to merit eternal life.

This final judgment will be based on what is recorded in the second book, "the book of life." "If anyone's name was not found written in the book of life, he was thrown into the lake of fire" (20:15).

A person is either born twice and dies once or is born once and dies twice. I was born twice in Milwaukee, Wisconsin. My first birth was in Misericordia Hospital. Then I was "born again" at Garfield Avenue Baptist Church when I put my trust in Christ.

Those who are not born again will experience physical death and will also suffer the "second death" (20:14) of eternal separation from God in the lake of fire. This is an awesome truth that should drive every one of us who know the Lord to reach out in evangelistic and world mission endeavors.

THE NEW JERUSALEM

Christ told His disciples that "heaven and earth shall pass away" (Matt. 24:35). No need to get overly attached to the "stuff" of this world, because it will all go up in smoke.

People are eternal. Some pass on to eternal life in God's presence. Others face eternal damnation apart from God. We who have put our trust in Christ are forever grateful for our destiny, new heavens and a new earth where there "will be no more death or mourning or crying or pain" (Rev. 21:4). "The glory and honor of the nations will be brought into it" (21:26).

A "river of the water of life, as clear as crystal, flowing from the throne of God and of the Lamb" will satisfy all thirst, and the "tree of life" will bear fruit sufficient for every appetite. "And the leaves of the tree are for the healing of the nations" (22:1–2).

How intriguing it is to see the continued reference to "the nations" in the Book of Revelation. God's work is universal. It is global in its scope. The closing scenes demonstrate anew the fruit of evangelistic efforts that reach into every tribe, language, people, and nation. World missions is a theme that runs from cover to cover of God's revealed Word, from Genesis to Revelation. The "Alpha and Omega, the First and the Last, the Beginning and the End" has made His purpose clear (22:12).

Christ who is "the Root and the Offspring of David, and the bright Morning Star" gives His gracious invitation, "Whoever is thirsty, let him come; and whoever wishes, let him take the free gift of the water of life" (22:16–17). We are given the privilege of proclaiming this invitation to people of every nation.

But time is limited! Christ said, "Yes, I am coming soon," to which John responded, "Amen. Come, Lord Jesus" (22:20). The closing phrase of the Bible is fitting. "The grace of the Lord Jesus be with God's people," to which we declare, "Amen" (22:21). *We long for His coming, but in the meantime it is urgent that we pass along His message of salvation and hope to a world caught in sin and havoc.*

PART THREE

The Connecting Line—Strategies for Evangelism

CHAPTER ELEVEN

Three Ideas on How to Introduce People to Christ

THE LARGEST CHURCH IN THE WORLD is in Seoul, Korea. The main auditorium seats ten thousand people, and there is an overflow auditorium for an additional two thousand. This massive church was filled for the fourth service the Sunday I visited.

I was there to train missionary candidates from Korea who were planning to serve around the world. Our classes were held in a ten-story facility that occupied a prominent place right next to the huge church auditorium that looked like some state capitol building. Our classes extended from early morning to late afternoon each day with little time for meals or breaks. Not one student ever complained about the schedule, which lasted for two full weeks.

The Sunday in the middle of our two-week class schedule provided an opportunity to be involved in church services. I spoke in a large Presbyterian church for all three services Sunday morning. Over a thousand attended each service.

Sunday afternoon I noted that services were being held at the massive auditorium next to our classroom building. Thousands were arriving in taxis and public transportation for what I discovered was the fifth service of the day. I joined the throngs who crowded into the church auditorium. I was ushered up to the third balcony where instantaneous English translation was provided through convenient earphones at each seat in this section of the auditorium.

One of the announcements of the morning was an impassioned plea for people to attend no more than one of the five identical services offered each Sunday. Another interesting feature was the large number of ushers positioned at each entrance and in the stairwells and hallways to help direct the flow of so many people entering and leaving the church between each service. Crowd control was even more organized than what you would see at football stadiums in the United States.

After the service I chatted for a few moments with the "sub-deacon" who served as an usher in the English translation section in which I was seated. The church is obviously well organized with a large staff and numerous elders, sub-elders, deacons, and sub-deacons.

I asked my new friend, who spoke some English, if we might spend a few minutes together in prayer. He readily agreed and seemed pleased. I asked him, "What are some prayer requests you have for which I might pray?" Without hesitation he replied, "Please pray for two families who have not attended church the past three Sundays."

Here I was in the fifth Sunday service, and each had been attended by ten thousand people. I asked him, "And how do you know they have been absent?"

"Oh," he replied, "they are in my cell group." Everyone in this massive church is accounted for. There is a personal interest in every individual.

After we had prayed together I asked this cell-group leader, "How does this church keep on growing?" "Very simple," he responded. "When anyone joins our church, among other commitments, each person agrees that whenever a friend, relative, or neighbor has a problem, whatever the problem, he or she must act by making a visit.

"We go to the home or apartment of the friend, neighbor, or relative with the problem. We take a gift, usually fruit or flowers. We present our gift and tell the friend, neighbor, or relative we heard about their problem and say, 'Do you mind if I pray for your problem?' We pray aloud with this person asking that God might intervene. We may visit for a few minutes and then leave. Two or three days later we return, always with a little gift, and ask, 'How are things going with the problem?' We pray again and leave."

Then the sub-deacon added, "We have seen many wonderful answers to prayer. We don't usually ask people to come to our church. They ask us, 'Could we go with you to your church some day?'"

I was stunned by the simplicity of this plan, and as I have meditated on their unique system for evangelistic outreach, I have concluded that this is not culturally bound. This will work anywhere in the world.

Friendship evangelism, which involves every member in perpetual outreach, is the key. And the process is triggered with problems in the life of one who is already a known friend, relative, or neighbor. While the gift might vary from place to place in this world, the sacrificial interest in others and in their problems is something that merits a personal visit and dedicated prayer. The prayer need not be fancy.

Through this simple evangelistic process the largest church in the world just keeps multiplying. When the membership reaches five thousand, these Korean believers set their sights on ten thousand. When they jump to a membership of ten thousand, they set a goal of twenty thousand. And so forth. The multiplication factor never seems to end.

The dynamic growth process I discovered in Seoul, Korea has prompted me to seek other methods to advance similar growth in evangelistic out-reach. These ideas can serve to encourage evangelism in a church of any size and bring about much-needed multiplication of new believers.

HOME SWEET HOME—HOME BIBLE STUDIES

When people ask me for a definition of a church planter, I love to reply, "A church planter is one who has the ability to make friends and get them into the Bible."

There is amazing power in the Word of God to solve problems and transform lives. One of the most successful means of evangelism I have found is interactive home Bible studies. People seem to have a natural desire to know what the Bible says. Most people are fully aware that the Bible is a worldwide bestseller. And yet for most unsaved people, the Bible remains a mystery. To be able to dedicate some time with other interested friends in probing for an understanding of the Bible is attractive.

The informal setting of a living room, family room, or dining room in which there is freedom to ask questions and discuss openly what the Bible says is ideal.

In my limited experience in home Bible studies both in the United States and in settings overseas I have discovered some pointers that might help in the success of this unique method of evangelism. First, it is important to build the study on a base of sincere open friendship. From the first invitation it must be apparent that there is no trickery. This dare not be perceived as some kind of trap to get a person into some religious group or church. There must be an honest desire to explore the Bible together with no devious designs.

It is good to suggest the home Bible study with an unsaved friend by saying, "How would it be if a group of us got together to study the Bible? I won't be the teacher. We will let the Bible be the teacher."

If the friend seems to express some interest, then ask, "What would be the best night of the week and the best time for you to try a study like this?" Help them feel that this is not your study but their study. Getting them involved in the planning can help insure a greater sense of ownership on their part.

Second, make sure that the first study is a trial among those friends you have invited. It takes extra effort to keep reminding those invited of the coming trial study, but this is the only way to ensure good attendance. Keep confirming a commitment to attend the initial trial study. Confirm the enjoyable time that you are sure it will be. People must be drawn to something of value with a sense of return worthy of their time investment, even in a trial endeavor.

If those who attend know each other already, this is ideal. However, even if those who attend the first study are not close friends, a good host can make everyone feel right at home with warm introductions.

Third, be sensitive to every detail. In our first home Bible study in Segovia, Spain, we had on hand enough Bibles for everyone who came, including Catholic Bibles and some so-called Protestant Bibles.

Fourth, timing is important. Don't allow an excessive amount of time for casual conversation. A warm, friendly setting is essential, but there must be a sense of purpose that drives the gathering. As the host, I find it best to take charge, and after a mere five or ten minutes of friendly conversation, I call for everyone's attention so that we can start the study.

Fifth, it is often good to launch the study with a discussion question. In the first study in Segovia, I asked the men, "When you think of God, what comes to your mind?"

Discussion questions are unique. To be a question that truly elicits discussion, it must be an opinion question. There must not be a right or wrong answer. A good test for an effective discussion question is found in the phrase, "What do you think?" Any question that can be answered with a mere yes or no is not effective. Nor should there be a simple "fill in the blank" with a predetermined answer. Any question that requires a predetermined right answer will only create tension. Furthermore, if a person answers the question with a wrong answer that requires correction by the leader or the group, he will feel ostracized and never want to return.

The men in Segovia found my question, "When you think of God, what comes to your mind?" to be very stimulating, and the answers were enlightening. One of the first responses came from Jaime Pintor Santamaría. "*Dios es el eje*" (God is the axle), he offered. "Good," I confirmed and jotted the phrase on a portable blackboard. Many excellent suggestions flowed from the group, and I recorded each one until there was no more room on the board.

"Let's see what the Bible says about God," I then suggested. "Please grab one of the Bibles and look for Psalm 139." I had to help them find this passage. Most of these men had never opened a Bible before. I gave them time to find the page, and I watched with satisfaction as they helped each other in the process. Once I was sure everyone had found the psalm, I asked them, "Do you mind if I pray before we start?"

Later the men told me how much they appreciated the fact that I asked if it would be all right to lead in prayer. Then some of them told me how moved they were to hear me pray. Some had never heard anything but "said" prayers and "read" prayers. To hear a person talk with God was revolutionary to them. It is amazing how such a little thing in our minds can have such a great impact on those who have not yet come to know Christ.

Sixth, I have found it important to stick with one passage in an evangelistic Bible study. Unbelievers are embarrassed when they can't find the passages being referred to. Furthermore it's easy to keep on track when you are moving through one verse or one paragraph of verses. Most important, I find it wholesome to study the Bible as it was written. We do not have to piece together a string of different verses from various Bible books to get the Scriptures to say what we want them to say.

Seventh, the study needs to involve ample discussion on the part of those in attendance. The opening discussion question helps prime the group for participation, but further discussion questions are often needed as you move through the passage.

In the first stanza of Psalm 139, for example, the group can consider the question, "Why do you think the writer of this psalm said, 'Such knowledge is too wonderful for me, too lofty for me to attain?'" The phrase "do you think" in the question brings out helpful discussion.

It does not hurt to point out the progression of the passage. Psalm 139 reveals how God knows everything, seems to be everywhere, and has unlimited power. It is wise to consider difficult points as well. For example David wrote, "Do I not hate those who hate you, O Lord. . . . I have nothing but hatred for them; I count them my enemies" (139:21–22). A good question might be, "Why do you think the writer seems to speak of hatred in positive terms here?"

Eighth, in a home Bible study the gospel should be shared in a normal, nonthreatening way. This can best be achieved through personal testimony. Psalm 139, for example, opens the door in the final prayer. "Search me, O God, and know my heart; test me and know my anxious thoughts. See if there is any offensive way in me, and lead me in the way everlasting" (139:23–24).

Ninth, be sure the study concludes within the agreed-on time span. Nothing is more distasteful than to feel trapped when the hour extends beyond what was anticipated and there seemingly is no escape, especially if a person has made plans for things to do after the study.

In Segovia, I remember that on our first night the hour was about to end. Even though we had not gone through the entire psalm, I said, "I'm sorry. The time is up. Do you want to have more of these studies?" The men were very animated in their desire to repeat this intriguing process. If the study had not been successful or the men had been hesitant, I was prepared to drop it and look for some other means to reach them. But in their excitement to continue, I was prepared to offer a plan.

"Let's try five more studies," I suggested. "We have studied what God is like. Now let's see what man is like according to the Bible. Read the first pages of your Bible, Genesis 1–3, for next week. Then let's study the God-Man, Jesus Christ. Then we can study salvation in Christ, security through Christ, and service for Christ."

I didn't try to explain the studies I was proposing, but I wanted them to know that there was a plan and that it wouldn't go on forever. They liked the idea of five more studies.

So we concluded our study and those who had to leave could go. Most stayed, however, for refreshments. My wife, Libby, was a wonderful hostess. The men loved the food and coffee.

As the study progressed, it was often in the informal time of refreshments in private conversation that I was able to answer key questions and to lead men to the Lord. I never gave an invitation in the study itself. The great beauty of a home Bible study is that the setting is perfect to deal with individuals who are being touched by the power of the Word of God. The Holy Spirit will bring people to a place of conviction. God will accomplish His saving work. We simply need to be available for Him to do His work.

It is especially encouraging to see how God uses selected passages to touch hearts. For the topic of salvation, I had selected John 3 for our study. It didn't take long for the men to see in Nicodemus the struggle of a man who was religious but lost. It soon became apparent to me that the barrier of Judaism in the time of Christ and His disciples was a perfect parallel to the barrier of Roman Catholicism in a place like Spain. Through the six weeks of home Bible study in Segovia a number of the men had come to know the Savior. From these men the gospel spread to their wives and children. The wives came to my wife and asked what this Bible study was. Their husbands were now more considerate and loving. They actually spent more time at home rather than in the neighborhood bars. Libby was able to explain the gospel and to lead these ladies to Christ.

At the end of the six weeks, the men wanted to have another series. I proposed five weeks in the Book of James, a chapter each week. This book proved to be revolutionary. It was intriguing to see the men grasp the balance between faith and works from this practical book of the Bible.

This home Bible study resulted in many men coming to Christ. This group became the foundation of the very first evangelical church in the province of Segovia. It was not complicated. We simply sought to make friends and get them into the Bible. What better way to watch God work in evangelistic outreach, even in a tough place like Segovia, Spain.

A FORMULA THAT WORKS— CONVERSATIONS THAT LEAD TO THE GOSPEL

People often ask me, "How do you get started talking about the gospel, especially when you don't even know the person?"

I don't believe in cold-turkey evangelism. I like to "warm up the turkey." I have found a formula that works. This "FORMula" is a simple series of four questions that are easy to remember. To engage in conversation with someone I have not yet met and one with whom I would like to share the gospel, I ask four intriguing questions.

First, I ask about "Family." This opening question always sparks interest. Who doesn't like to talk about his or her family?

The formula works well with travelling companions I meet on commercial flights as I crisscross the country to speak at conferences. I love to talk to people on planes. They are strapped in and can't get away from me. It is an ideal setting.

On a flight from San Francisco to Dallas I started a conversation with a young man seated next to me. I looked for a wedding ring and didn't see one, so for my "family" question I asked, "Are you married?"

"No," he replied, "but I'm living with a gal." I didn't roll my eyes and express my disdain for the evil lifestyle of this young man. I just moved to my next question.

The second question in the FORMula is "Occupation." "What kind of work do you do?" I was very interested in this man's profession. He explained his employment as a zero-based budget consultant. He was working on contract with a municipality in central Texas.

"I'm from Connecticut," he said. "On a two-week job like this, my company lets me fly anywhere I want to on a weekend up to the limits of my home. I had never been to San Francisco so I decided to check it out. The company pays for it."

I thought to myself, "Of course. You flew to San Francisco so we could be on this flight together on your way back to Dallas." But I didn't let him know what I was thinking. Instead I moved to my next question.

It doesn't take long to move through the FORMula. Family, occupation, and now, "Religious background."

There is no need to breathe hard and stumble through a question about religion. I asked with the same tone of voice and friendly composure as the other questions, "Do you have a religious background?" The guy did not hesitate. "I am of Jewish background. The gal I am living with is Roman Catholic." Then he looked me right in the eye and said, "As far as I am concerned, everything I have seen of religion is a rip off."

"You may be right," I agreed, "and who am I to talk to you about religion. But I would like to talk with you about a relationship with God through the Lord Jesus Christ."

We were already sliding into home base on the FORMula. Family, occupation, religious background, and now the "Message."

I took the bag from the seat pocket in front of me and began to draw the bridge illustration to explain the gospel. The guy did not seem very interested. I could see that I had some work to do, so I decided I would be a little more direct.

"Say, do you know what God calls living with a gal like you are?"

"No," he replied.

"He calls it fornication. This is sin."

The guy looked at me in shock. "No one has ever talked to me like that," he complained.

"Don't look at *me*," I said, "I didn't say this. God is the one who says it is sin."

I suddenly got his attention. This guy wanted to talk. For over three hours we talked about the Lord Jesus and how through His death on the cross He paid the price for all of us. I explained how He gives new life to everyone who puts his or her trust in Him.

Somehow the truth began to touch him. As the plane was making its approach to the Dallas/Fort Worth airport, my new friend said to me, "Look. Do you perform wedding ceremonies?"

It is fun to talk to people about the Lord. I have talked with hundreds of people using the simple FORMula, and in only two cases have they stopped the conversation before I was able to share the gospel. By the way, it is important to ask the questions of this FORMula with the right spirit. It should not be seen as some gimmick to set people up for some high–pressure sales talk. When we ask a person about his or her family, occupation, religious background, and then share the message, we need to "Use Love Always." The FORMula is not complete without the "ula."

As redeemed Christians it is only natural that we should care very deeply about people around us. People can sense whether we really love them. We dare not engage in some little evangelistic ritual that does not stem from the heart. We want people to know the Savior. We care about every facet of people's lives, and above all we care about their eternal destiny.

We want people to put their trust in Christ. I have discovered that talking to people on airplanes is a perfect setting to explain saving faith. Faith in Christ for salvation is just like the faith we place in an airplane and crew for travel.

When I share the gospel on a flight I use this simple illustration. "I don't know if the guy up there has a license," I explain. "I hear his voice but I can't be sure he is in the cockpit. It could be a recording.

"Furthermore, if I didn't know better, I would hardly believe that this massive pile of metal loaded with cargo and passengers is going to get off the ground. Yet I board this flight with the confidence that we will get to our destination.

"This is intelligent faith. By contrast it would be rather ridiculous to stand on the tarmac, wave my arms up and down, and say, 'I'm going to Chicago.' That would not make sense. No, we get on this plane, fasten our seatbelts and say, 'Here we go to Chicago.'"

On a flight to Chicago's O'Hare Airport I was talking with a Muslim. I pointed out the crazy idea of flapping my arms to get to our destination. I made it quite direct in his case, "This is what you are doing. You are trying to reach God through your own efforts." The man was visibly shaken. He realized the truth of this pointed illustration.

What an opportunity we have to witness to people whom we have never met. This simple FORMula opens the door in a wholesome and natural way. Start asking questions. Get acquainted with strangers. Enjoy conversations that explore important aspects of life: family, occupation, religious background, and God's transforming message. Use the FORMula and use love always.

ALONG THE WAY—
FINDING THE LOST AMONG THE SHEEP

Although the FORMula can successfully open doors with any stranger, in some settings it does not seem appropriate to engage in conversation about family, occupation, religious background , and the message of the gospel.

For example, in a church setting it may seem a bit forced to engage in a conversation like this. Rightfully so, it is often expected that those you meet in a church are brothers and sisters in Christ. Usually they are.

However, it is of utmost importance that we discover the destiny of every person we meet. Everything else is secondary. We want to be sure that every person we talk with is certain of eternity with the Lord.

In a church setting I love to ask one simple question, "Tell me, how did you come to know the Lord?" If there is any hesitation, if the person does not immediately respond with the story of his or her conversion, we must be prepared to give an alternative question. If "How did you come to know the Lord?" elicits a confused look, we must continue with the words, "Or are you somewhere along the way?"

In a church in Houston I was chatting before Sunday school with a gentleman who seemed to be a visitor in the class. I asked him, "Tell me, how did you come to know the Lord?" He hesitated, so I added, "Or are you somewhere on the way?"

"I guess I am somewhere along the way," he confided.

We talked together about what the Lord has done for us and how we can find new life through faith in Him. I simply explained the gospel. He was obviously prepared by the Holy Spirit to respond. Before the class started he prayed with me to put his trust in Christ.

Can there be any greater joy than that of leading a person to the Lord? All too often we miss these opportunities because we do not focus on the things of greatest value. Instead of talking about the weather or the score of some football game we need to find out the spiritual condition of every person we meet, even in churches.

There is great blessing in hearing the testimony of others. The question, "How did you come to Christ?" prompts conversation of great encouragement from those who know Him. In most cases there will be little hesitation on the part of those we meet in church. They will tell that story of God's grace in bringing them to Himself. We can learn something helpful from each testimony.

And for those who have not yet come to the Lord, who have not yet experienced the miracle of the new birth, the alternative clause, "Or are you somewhere along the way?" provides an acceptable answer that does not seem offensive or abrupt. It is difficult for someone to reply, "I don't know the Lord." Even more difficult would be a response, "I don't want to know the Lord." When the more acceptable alternative is offered, people seem to be relieved to say, "I guess I am somewhere along the way."

If someone is "along the way," it is only natural to do what we can to encourage them to place faith in Christ. This diagnostic question helps us find the lost who are among the sheep and bring them into the fold.

Chapter Twelve

Three More Ideas on How to Introduce People to Christ

DRAW THE BRIDGE—
A PERFECT HOMEMADE TRACT

EXCELLENT, EFFECTIVE GOSPEL TRACTS are readily available. I continue to be impressed with the variety of outstanding full-color, high-quality tracts. Many may be purchased at relatively low cost and are excellent ways by which to share the gospel with those who do not know the Lord. Tracts are especially helpful when there is little or no time to engage in conversation.

I was moved by the testimony of Domingo Treviño, a Spaniard who lived in a remote town in the province of Avila in the heart of Spain. We discovered from one of our colleagues in CAM International that this man had successfully completed a dozen Bible correspondence course lessons. In a letter sent with one of the completed lessons he indicated that he had put his trust in Christ. He wrote that he had experienced new birth in the Savior.

Our CAM colleague, John Miller, sent me Domingo's address and asked that I make an attempt to visit this new believer. In a trip with Raimundo Galán, one of our vibrant new believers from Segovia, we drove into the little town nestled in the barren landscape of old Castille. The village was so small there were no street signs or house numbers.

We asked many people about Domingo Treviño, but no one could identify him. Finally, one person suggested we check at the post office.

"Why didn't we think of this?" I asked Raimundo as we made our way to the little post office tucked in the corner of a small store.

The postmaster knew right away who we were looking for, "Oh, yes, Pepe Treviño!" Domingo Treviño was known only by his nickname.

With clear directions Raimundo and I finally found the home of "Pepe" and knocked on the door. An elderly woman responded. She called and a middle–aged man sporting a dark blue beret appeared. We were welcomed into their humble home. We sat on crude wooden chairs before a massive fireplace. Smoke-blackened cast-iron pots hanging in the open hearth were evidence that we sat in a room that was as much kitchen as it was living room. We were grateful for the warmth of the fireplace and the kindness of our new friends.

In our conversation together it became evident that this dear Spanish man had discovered new life through his diligent study of the Word of God. I asked him how he became aware of the correspondence course. With enthusiasm, Pepe related the story.

One wintry day he encountered several young men and women who had come into this remote town distributing literature. A small contingent of Operation Mobilization workers on a short-term ministry project covered this part of Spain. In a blitz through these little towns, they passed out literature to anyone they could find. The literature contained a coupon for a Bible correspondence course. Pepe Treviño was interested. By mail he requested the course, and then he began working diligently in his study of the Bible.

Pepe expressed his thanks to God for these studies. He was very grateful for the quick return of each lesson and for the helpful comments penned along the margins by the grader. John Miller had encouraged this stranger from the province of Avila to continue his excellent work.

The young men and women with Operation Mobilization who passed through this town could never have imagined the way God would work in this man's life. In spite of repeated efforts to reach out to others in this town, as far as I know, Domingo "Pepe" Treviño was the only one in this town ever to come to saving faith in Christ. Even his elderly mother with whom he lived never responded to the message of the gospel. She attended her son's baptism held in nearby Segovia where we lived and served, but she never made a personal profession of faith in Christ.

God used a simple piece of literature to redeem a lone Spaniard searching for answers. Domingo has never wavered in his newfound faith. Through continued Bible study he has become an amazing Bible scholar in a town were he is an isolated believer in a hostile environment. I am amazed at his ability to discern sound doctrine and provide wise biblical counsel. I would not hesitate to have him match most seminary students in his ability to handle the Word of God.

Literature distribution is a very effective means of evangelism. I thank the Lord for gospel tracts. However, if at all possible, I prefer to engage people in conversation. I like to utilize a makeshift "tract" that I draw on the back of my business card. There is a great advantage in personalizing the gospel presentation. By drawing my own "tract" I am able to explain step by step the meaning of the message of salvation.

I carry a supply of business cards on which I can diagram the gospel from a key Bible verse, "But God demonstrates His own love toward us, in that while we were yet sinners, Christ died for us" (Rom. 5:8, NKJV).

On the back of my business card I draw a cloud and put the word "God" at the top of the card. "Here is God," I explain, "and He is holy. He is perfect." Below the word "God" I pen the word "holy."

"But we live here on this earth," and I draw a circle below the cloud to represent the world. I pen the word "Man" on the globe and explain, "We are not perfect. We have a problem here on earth. It is called 'sin,' everything that falls short of the glory of God." Below the word "Man" I write the word "sinner."

I then start drawing little arrows from the globe up toward God. "All religions tell you that you need to do something to reach up to God. Some do better than others in fulfilling the rules." I draw an arrow that rises above the others. "But no one attains perfection. Everyone falls short."

Religious leaders tell you, "You just need to try harder." I write the word "Try" to the left of the little arrows that fall short of God.

"The Bible does not say we need to reach up to God. The Bible says, 'God demonstrates His own love toward us.' God reaches down to us." I draw a big arrow down from God to the earth. I circle the words "Man" and "sinner" as I continue quoting the verse, "'in that while we were yet sinners, Christ died for us.'" I then draw a cross on the large arrow reaching down from God.

"The Lord Jesus Christ, the God-Man, born of the Virgin, the only One who was ever perfect, died in my place to give me eternal life." I point to the key words in the diagram "God" above and "Man" below.

"The answer is not 'Try,'" I explain, as I cross the word out on the left side of the little arrows. "The answer is 'Trust,'" and I write the word "Trust" at the right side of the large arrow reaching down from God to man that I have turned into a cross. "We must put all of our trust in Christ. He died for us. He died in our place. He paid the penalty of our sin and gives us eternal life if we trust him." I draw a little arrow from the word "Trust" to the cross.

I often like to explain, "You may be aware that Jesus is the Savior of the world. But what you need to realize is that He wants to be *your* Savior. He died in your place to give you eternal life if you put all of your trust in Him."

I am amazed how this simple hand-drawn tract touches people. It moves those who are wrapped up in some religious system. They know in their hearts that their religion is taking them nowhere. They find the message of faith in the Lord Jesus Christ very appealing. I have found most people are tired of trying to fulfill the rules and follow the rituals of a religion. They are deeply moved by the good news from the Bible of a relationship that can change their lives.

"You need to talk with God and let Him know that you want to put all of your trust in Christ. I can't give you eternal life. Only God can do this. Would you be willing to tell God that this is what you want? Will you let Him know that you want to put all of your trust in Christ right now?"

It is always exciting to see the Holy Spirit use this clear, simple message to touch hearts. I have led many people in prayer to put their trust in Christ. By God's grace, they respond to the gospel.

For those who are not yet ready to respond, there is a distinct advantage to drawing the "tract" and explaining it to the person who needs the Lord. I am able to hand my business card to those with whom I have talked and to encourage them to contact me when they make their decision to put their trust in Christ.

The simple bridge, the cross of Christ linking a holy God to sinful man, is one of the most effective illustrations I know to explain the gospel.

Start using your business card. Draw your own tract to provide people with whom you talk the most revolutionary and meaningful message in the world. This little homemade tract is priceless. God can use it to bring many to the saving knowledge of Christ.

"I NEED YOUR OPINION"—THE USE OF SURVEYS

Public opinion surveys have become common and are generally accepted by people of all backgrounds. Politicians are increasingly dependent on polls. They no longer have to ask, "What do my constituents think about this matter?" They hire specially trained pollsters who utilize an intricate system to provide an authoritative answer to this seemingly elusive question. The statistical ranges of possible error in the results of the poll are included with the results.

Surveys can be used effectively in evangelism. A trained believer can approach a total stranger with a carefully prepared religious survey and discover an open door to investigate the spiritual health of a person and have an opportunity to engage in conversation about the gospel.

If this method is used, it is imperative that the survey be genuine and that results be tabulated. To employ a "religious survey" only as a method to talk to people about the Lord with no intention of tabulating results is at best somewhat deceptive and might be considered totally dishonest.

A questionnaire used to survey public opinion must be carefully designed so that a limited number of questions provides easily tabulated returns. In contrast to open–ended questions used in Bible studies to illicit discussion, survey questions need to offer options or invoke a simple yes or no answer.

Here are some sample survey questions:

1. I consider myself to be ___ atheist ___ Buddhist ___ Christian ___Hindu ___ Jewish ___ Muslim ___ other.

2. I feel my religious affiliation is ___ very important ___somewhat important ___ of little importance ___ of no importance.

3. I attend religious services ___ several times each week ___ weekly ___ monthly ___ quarterly ___ for special occasions ___ never.

4. My relationship with God is ___ very strong ___ somewhat strong ___ rather weak ___ very weak ___ nonexistent.

5. On the average I pray ___ several times a day ___ once or twice a day ___ once or twice a week ___monthly ___ infrequently.

6. I believe in eternal life. ___ yes ___ no.

7. At death I think I will go to ___ heaven ___ hell ___ purgatory ___ I am not sure ___ I do not believe in these ideas.

8. My religious experience is ___ very satisfying ___ somewhat satisfying ___ not very satisfying ___ totally unsatisfying.

9. I sense the need to strengthen my spiritual life ___ very much ___ somewhat ___ a little ___ not at all.

10. If someone were to ask me how I can have an intimate relationship with God, I would tell them _____.

The final question in this sample list is open-ended to give the census-taker the opportunity to give a personal testimony of how he or she found an intimate relationship with God through faith in the Lord Jesus Christ.

After recording the answer to the final question the census-taker can simply say, "I am intrigued by your answer on how a person can find an intimate relationship with God. Could I share with you how I found this relationship with the Lord?"

Most people will not object. If they do, the conversation should conclude with an expression of gratitude for the person's help on the survey. But if the person gives permission to share your own answer to the final question, this is a perfect opportunity to tell about coming to Christ and then let the conversation flow in whatever way God might lead.

It is important that the survey be conducted in a professional and courteous way. The printed survey is best used with a clipboard in a public place where the person has the time to answer the questions. Airports, bus depots, and parks are ideal locations.

A good opening comment is, "Hi. We are conducting a brief religious survey this month here in Dallas. Could you please help by answering a few questions? It will take only about five minutes." The person being asked to participate should see the questions to show that the survey is not complicated or lengthy and that it is a legitimate, official survey.

Attitude is important. The census-taker should be cheerful and anticipate cooperation from the one approached. It is amazing how anticipating a positive response usually meets with participation. Those who anticipate rejection often receive exactly what they anticipated. To approach a person with "I don't suppose you would have the time to take a survey, would you?" will almost guarantee rejection.

From personal experience I have discovered most people like to help in any way they can. They are especially pleased when someone shows interest in their opinions. It is generally fairly easy to engage a stranger in the survey process.

If at any point, the person being interviewed indicates that he or she doesn't want to continue with the questions, the survey should be suspended with courtesy and gratitude immediately. Never should there be any sense of pressure. The survey must be strictly voluntary.

It is ideal if the census-taker can sit or stand next to the one answering the questions so he or she can follow each question and indicate the answer. If there is a place to sit down side by side with the printed survey readily visible by the interviewer and the one interviewed, this is preferred. The one conducting the survey, however, should always record the answers. It is not professional to hand the clipboard to the one being interviewed and let them record their own answers.

The census or poll provides wonderful insight into the person being interviewed. The answers reveal a person's spiritual condition, and their demeanor can be very revealing. Through the interview process a friendship can be established that will open the door for sharing the gospel.

Surveys provide a natural means to approach strangers and explore important aspects of the stranger's religious and spiritual condition. They are useful in providing unique opportunities to present God's plan of salvation.

There is a significant added advantage. If enough people are surveyed to provide an adequate sample of the population, the tabulated results are exceedingly helpful to understand better the people of the city or area from which the people have come. It is of interest to everyone who participates in the survey project to see the tabulated responses to each question. A well-conducted survey can provide material for a helpful article for publication in an appropriate local newspaper or magazine.

I have been involved in surveys in several nations utilizing both English and Spanish. I am amazed how open people are to share their opinions and beliefs. I remember a gentleman in the "Parque Central" in San José, Costa Rica, who seemed pleased to participate in a survey. He claimed to be a devout Roman Catholic, but he readily admitted that his relationship with God was tenuous and his religious experience not satisfying. As expected, he was totally uncertain about his future, and he suggested "good works" as the way to establish a good relationship with God.

Any time someone presents the "good works" approach to God, I like to ask the person, "How many good works do I need to complete to be accepted by God?"

In this case the man replied, "Oh, you have to be really good."

"But how good do I have to be?" I persisted.

"You have to be real, real good!"

I was relentless. "How good is that?"

He finally admitted his dilemma, "I don't know."

"I used to think just what you have expressed," I continued. "I thought that if I could do enough good works to offset my bad works, God might accept me. But I was never sure how I was doing in this difficult game.

"Then someone showed me that the Bible does not say that God requires good works for salvation. He knows our limitations. He made us. He knows us. Instead of expecting us to attain the perfection He demands, He sent His Son, the Lord Jesus Christ, born of the Virgin, the only One who ever was perfect, to pay the price of our sin and give us eternal life. The God-Man, the Lord Jesus, has bridged the gap. The Bible says that if we put our trust in Him, we can have a perfect relationship with God.

"No one is capable of doing enough good works to build a bridge to God. Christ is the One who has done every good work. The sinless One died in your place. He died in my place. Through faith in the Lord Jesus Christ as our Savior, our only and sufficient Savior, God gives us eternal life. The relationship comes through 'total faith in Christ' not 'endless good works.'"

I could tell my newfound friend was touched by the truth. "You know, right now you could find this relationship with the Lord you have been looking for. I can't give it to you, but God can. You need to talk with Him. You need to tell Him that you want to put all your trust in His Son, the Lord Jesus Christ. Would you like to do this?"

The man responded, "*Sí, quisiera hacerlo.*" "Yes, I would like to do it." His prayer was obviously sincere and direct. The man who only moments earlier was a total stranger to me had suddenly become an intimate brother in the Lord.

God used a simple survey, a single sheet of paper with a limited number of printed questions, to open the door for this man to come to eternal life in our Savior.

Surveys work. They provide a wonderful opportunity to approach unknown individuals and explore their inner concerns and needs. God can use surveys to share the gospel and lead others to a saving relationship with Christ.

COMMON GROUND—
UTILIZING COMMON INTERESTS

I am always attracted to people who speak Spanish. When I heard two couples chatting *Español* on a street corner in Los Angeles, I drew closer to get acquainted with them.

"*¿De dónde son Vidas?*," I asked, "Where are you from?"

When they seemed to have the confidence that I was not an agent with the United States Immigration Service, they responded politely, "*Somos de Guatemala.*" "We are from Guatemala."

As you can imagine, I was immediately drawn closer to these dear people. Without thinking, I found myself stepping closer as I continued my pursuit, "*¿De cuál parte de Guatemala?*" "From what part of Guatemala?"

"*Del Oriente,*" one of the men offered casually. "From the Eastern part."

"*¿De qué provincia?*" They obviously noted my intense interest and excitement. "From what province?"

"*De Jutiapa.*" "From Jutiapa." The man seemed a little suspicious at my persistent questions and growing enthusiasm.

"*¿De cúal ciudad?*" "From what city?" I needed specifics.

"*No somos de una ciudad. Más bien es un pueblo, una aldea.*" The spokes-man seemed apologetic. "We are not really from a city. It could better be called a town, a village."

"*¿Pero cómo se llama el pueblito?*" My curiosity had to be filled. "But what is the name of the little town?"

"*Somos de un lugar que se llama El Sitio.*" "We are from a place called El Sitio." He seemed embarrassed to admit their origin.

"I have been to El Sitio!" I said with deep satisfaction.

"*No me diga.*" He could not believe my statement.

I quickly explained how we had lived for years in the city of Jalapa and had traveled throughout the province of Jutiapa and on several occasions had gone to El Sitio. I even mentioned some of the people who were part of our little Central American Mission church in this tiny town.

We immediately became like long-lost friends. To meet someone in the heart of Los Angeles who had been to a place as remote as El Sitio seemed like a miracle to these dear Guatemalan couples.

What was it that bound us together so quickly? A common interest. In this case a remote location that was common in our experience was like glue. Even though we had never met before, the unusual encounter on a street corner and the eventual discovery that we had a common site called El Sitio in our backgrounds made us like intimate friends.

As you might expect, they were curious. They wanted to know more about my visits to El Sitio. I explained in detail the Easter conference we held in this small town. My wife, Libby, and two keen young people from the city in which we lived, Jalapa, made the long trek to this little town for a special resurrection emphasis.

It was only natural that I conveyed to them the importance of a risen Christ, how He died for us, and how He conquered death to give us eter-nal life. In other words I presented the wonderful news of the gospel.

Out of deep respect for a person who had been to their town, the two couples listened intently to everything I had to say. I had discovered that they had not been a part of the evangelical church in El Sitio. These were new friends who were wide open to the good news of God's Word.

People that I had not had the opportunity to reach in a distant corner of Guatemala, even though I had actually traveled there with much difficulty, I touched in the heart of Los Angeles. God seems to have a great sense of humor in the way He provides open doors like this for us to share the good news of salvation.

Evangelism can best be accomplished when a believer has something in common with the person who needs Christ. In many cases one who shares God's message of redemption can find a common interest in conversation as I did in Los Angeles. Another effective means is to use common interests as a base for evangelistic outreach.

Hobbies, sports, music, literature, and any number of personal interests can serve as the ground on which to build friendships and from the friendships to share your faith with those who need to know Christ. Instead of forming Christian clubs around a common interest, believers can become a part of an organized group with this interest to enjoy friendship with a wider circle and to touch people in that circle for the Lord.

For example, if you are adept in volleyball and love to play the game, you could be an asset to a team in your community and be a welcomed witness for Christ while engaging in volleyball. Your lifestyle will be noticed and ample opportunities will arise in a natural setting to share your testimony. If a church team seems to be a more feasible course of action, the church team can be part of a league that includes unbelievers.

Isolation from unbelievers is one of the great obstacles to evangelism. Yet there are natural bridges to people who need the Lord. In fact, the more specialized or unusual an interest, the more readily another person with a common interest will welcome a friendship.

The ideal witness is one who is closely involved with unbelievers who share a common interest. Showing interest in another's hobby can build a bridge. Special interests can be an attraction to any number of unbelievers. Every church needs to explore this unique avenue for evangelism. A congregational survey of hobbies and interests will provide the church leaders with a list of people to challenge with new evangelistic opportunities. Obviously the church must not become a hobby or sports center, but church members can use their interests in any hobby or sport to reach others for Christ.

Even common professions or work can provide the glue needed to bind people together for spiritual enrichment. Somehow, I sense the Lord knew how to do this when he challenged first John and Andrew and then Peter and John to follow Him. He took these men with a lifelong common interest and formed the nucleus of His band of disciples. He called professional fishermen to become fishers of men.

Do you have a unique hobby, a special interest, a unique profession, a hidden ability? Use your talents and interests for the Lord. Watch God work as you reach out along the avenues He has already prepared for you.

CHAPTER THIRTEEN

Still More Ideas on How to Introduce People to Christ

DEVELOP THOSE TALENTS—
SPECIALIZED TRAINING CLASSES

I HAVE ALWAYS CONTENDED that if I were to become a high school teacher I would want to be a coach or a music teacher. Students usually desire to excel in these areas. They have built-in motivation.

Sports and music are often called extracurricular activities. In contrast to what often seems like distasteful academic requirements students are anxious to participate in sports and music. They are predisposed to give their utmost to succeed, actively engaged in what they deeply desire to do.

Helping people achieve in areas of personal pursuit is an ideal way to make contact with those who need to know the Lord. Any talent can be used to attract others of similar interest who would like to improve their abilities.

Sports and music are but two broad categories that can provide a bridge to share the gospel. Sewing, crafts, photography, foreign languages, and other special-interest classes are ideal avenues to win friendships and provide a witness for the Lord.

While serving as a missionary in Segovia, Spain, I was asked to give classes in English at a prestigious language institute in that historic city. The director was the only other North American living in the city at that time. She was from Canada and was married to a Spanish businessman.

Expecting her first child, she planned a trip to Canada for the birth of the baby. She desperately needed someone to take charge of the institute in her absence.

Although I was exceedingly busy in numerous evangelistic and discipleship ministries in our emerging church fellowship, I felt that assuming the responsibility for this institute might further advance the work of the Lord. I knew that I would have contact with students from all backgrounds and of all ages who were anxious to learn English.

So I became the interim director and teacher of the English institute. It was an exciting challenge to help businessmen, leading women of Segovia, and motivated young people to become fluent in English. Binding friendships were a natural outcome.

I did everything in my power to help these students be successful. Their goal was my goal. We labored together with high intensity. None of their valuable time was wasted. I felt I owed them my utmost attention and assistance in the difficult task of achieving fluency in one of the most difficult languages in the world, English. I was very pleased with their progress.

At no time did I utilize classroom time to present the gospel to these captive students. I worked diligently to do what they had paid me to do—to teach English. However, each day when the class ended, I took advantage of the friendship we enjoyed to get together for coffee or engage in some other casual activity. In this informal setting ample opportunities arose to share my faith in the Lord Jesus Christ.

It is both unethical and ineffective to use special-interest classes as some "phony front" to trap people for a high-powered gospel presentation. Such deceptive methods are especially distasteful when students are paying for the classes they receive. By teaching English with diligence and excellence, I gained the respect and gratitude of my students. My hard work in helping them advance in language facility did not go unnoticed.

Students felt honored to spend time with their professor outside the class periods. They were very interested in my deep commitment to Christ. They saw how my faith served as an anchor for my life. It was only natural to share the gospel in an informal way with ample time for questions and further exploration.

Every student advanced in language facility and a number of them were introduced to saving faith in Christ. God used this unique outreach for His glory in the lives of a select group of Spaniards. I rejoice in the way He worked to accomplish His purpose.

When my Canadian friend returned, she noted the advance the students had made and was grateful for the new prominence her institute had achieved. Furthermore, she sensed the positive, wholesome spirit in each class, a byproduct of what the Lord had done in the lives of these students. There could be no more effective testimony. Christ's power and love were reflected in a visible way in those students who had placed their faith in Him.

What talents, what experiences, what training could you share with others? People are all around you who would love to engage in classes that would help them improve their talents and develop their interests. You can help them. Consider this unique bridge to unsaved people.

BLOCKBUSTER BAZAAR—
VIDEOS AND BOOKS ON LOAN

We live in a very visual age. The old Chinese proverb, "A picture is worth a thousand words," probably needs to be updated. "A picture in color is worth ten thousand words." Or better yet, "A picture in color and motion is worth a million words."

The well-known *Jesus* film is a prime example. Originally produced by a group known as the Genesis Project, this dynamic presentation of the life of the Lord Jesus Christ as portrayed in the Gospel of Luke has been used mightily by God to bring thousands of people to saving faith in our Savior.

Campus Crusade saw the untapped potential of this very professional production, filmed on site in Israel with amazing attention to detail and benchmark quality. Bill Bright and his colleagues purchased the rights to the *Jesus* film and launched a distribution system that has covered the globe. The biblical narrative taken directly from Luke has made it relatively easy to dub in a voice track for every significant language in the world.

Campus Crusade has worked with mission agencies and other organizations in this gigantic translation task. For example, contact was made with CAM International missionary, John Miller, in northern Spain to provide a copy of the *Jesus* film in the ancient Basque language. "Vanscongada," as the language is officially registered, seems to be related to Sanskrit or Hebrew, even though it is written with Roman characters.

Through the diligent effort of many key individuals the Basque project was completed with excellence. Through persistent prayer and relentless personal contacts, John Miller was eventually able to get the *Jesus* film broadcast on a Basque television station as part of the Easter celebration. This may well be one of the most resistant regions of Spain. To touch Basque people in the privacy of their own homes with a visual presentation of the life and work of Christ was a major breakthrough.

Sometimes television networks are not willing to schedule an evangelical presentation, even if it is of the quality of the now renowned *Jesus* film. There are other ways to spread God's good news. A lending library of videotapes, audiocassette tapes, and quality books provides an opportunity to present the gospel in an appealing way.

Missionaries with CAM International have established excellent lending libraries that are having an increasing influence in the communities in which they live and minister. People who might not normally attend a service are more open to viewing a video tape, listening to a cassette, or reading an engaging book in the privacy of their own homes. A videotape is an especially effective means of bringing a family together.

Furthermore a lending library provides personal contact with people when they check out the materials and return them. In these moments of friendly contact the believer has a unique opportunity to demonstrate the love of the Lord and a sincere concern for each unsaved individual.

THOUSANDS ARE COMING—
CITY-WIDE EVANGELISTIC CRUSADES

I first met Luis Palau in El Salvador. It did not take long for me to realize that here was a man of unique abilities. I could sense immediately Luis's passion for evangelism.

A Luis Palau city-wide evangelistic campaign was scheduled for the soccer stadium in San Salvador. I was a fairly new missionary in the city.

My wife and I were housed in the mission home that served as the base of operations for the campaign.

The San Salvador campaign was sponsored exclusively by the association of CAM-related churches. This may have been one of the last Luis Palau campaigns with a single sponsoring church. Future Luis Palau campaigns required a more representative cooperative sponsorship of the city-wide Christian community in keeping with the well-established policies of Billy Graham.

I knew that many of our church leaders had worked diligently for more than a year on this major event in San Salvador, but I had no idea of the magnitude of this task. In addition to a host of Salvadoran leaders and CAM missionaries, there were numerous Luis Palau team members. It soon became apparent that these were the experts who brought invaluable experience to the task. I soon began to recognize the immense preparation and coordination needed to hold a major evangelistic crusade. A myriad of details demanded attention according to a strict timetable. One failure could put the entire crusade in jeopardy.

Systematic announcements, radio coverage, personal invitations, billboard advertising, and many other means were evident long before the crusade began to provide widespread awareness. Media coverage rose to a well-timed crescendo right before the opening night. Saturation advertising was clearly achieved.

Numerous volunteers were carefully trained and each one fulfilled the duty assigned. Musicians, ushers, counselors, and many others with key assignments accomplished their tasks with a deep sense of responsibility. Many unique requirements called for experts. For example, sound engineers were needed to ensure that everyone in the vast stadium would be able to hear. Also we needed a myriad of counselors who were ready to meet those who would come forward. And appropriate follow-up literature was essential.

I thank the Lord for well-known evangelists and all those who work with them to make an impact in key cities around the world. I was especially grateful that Luis Palau was willing to work with our CAM-related churches in this massive endeavor. The influence extended beyond the thousands who attend the campaign. Heightened awareness of the Lord and increased evangelical influence were helpful byproducts.

Luis Palau has touched thousands of people with the gospel all over the world. His crusade ministry extends far beyond those who attend the city-wide crusade meetings. Unbelievers have been touched through press releases, news coverage, and radio and TV call-in programs. In San Salvador, Luis was used mightily of the Lord in nightly TV broadcasts on which he talked live with those who called in to the studio. I watched God use Luis to lead people to Christ by phone with thousands of TV viewers watching the eternal transaction take place.

City-wide crusades are a wonderful means of reaching thousands with a message of salvation in Christ. Because of the great energy expended and expense involved, it is best to plan no more than one crusade every five to ten years in any given city. Yet it is an extraordinary means of evangelism. If you think this is something that could be effective in your city in the next ten years, now is the time to start planning.

Here are three key points of advice for a city-wide crusade. First, plan ahead. As I have pointed out, the numerous details will require hundreds of workers to give of their time and energy to make the crusade successful. This all takes time. That's why it's necessary to start planning several years ahead.

Second, rely on an evangelist who has a team of experts and the needed networking to launch such a crusade. This is not something a few volunteers can accomplish. Set the dates and a long-range timetable with the evangelist and his team. I have mentioned Luis Palau because he is a personal friend and one whom I have seen in action on many occasions. There are numerous evangelists who are equipped to launch major crusades. In fact, both Luis Palau and Billy Graham have endorsed a number of crusade evangelists who can be tapped for this important ministry.

Third, bathe the entire enterprise in prayer. We must remember that in spite of all our efforts, it is God who brings the increase. Only the Lord can touch people's hearts and bring conviction and life-changing conversion. The greatest crusade evangelist in the world cannot do the spiritual work that must take place for a crusade to be truly successful. Even the greatest of speakers realize that they are but "a voice crying in the wilderness." The "real" evangelists, even from the human point of view, are those believers who invite an unsaved friend, relative, or neighbor to attend the crusade meetings. For this reason effective crusade evangelists insist strongly on follow-up measures to make sure the Christians who brought their friends, neighbors, or relatives can encourage the one who has made a decision for Christ in the stadium meetings to continue with the Lord, to get in His Word, and to become associated with a Bible-believing local church.

The importance of the testimony of each individual associated with the crusade and the vital need for prayer became evident in the San Salvador experience with Luis Palau. In spite of the diligent and effective work of hundreds of volunteers and experienced leaders and an excellent attendance on the opening night of the crusade, when Luis gave the invitation at the close of his superb gospel message, very few responded. We were disappointed to see a relatively small group of people stand at the front in that massive stadium to put their trust in Christ.

Along with all the others who were involved in some way in the crusade, I received an express delivery letter the next morning, asking that I attend a special meeting at our San Salvador Central Church later that day.

The personal invitation and curiosity over the purpose of the meeting caused almost every one of us to make this gathering a priority. The church was filled. Luis stood before the assembled crowd and made a brief but disturbing statement. "We have all witnessed what happened last night," Luis explained in Spanish. "Everything seemed right about the opening evening. Attendance was good and the service went exceptionally well. But the response to the invitation was not what any of us might expect. Something is wrong."

There was an unnerving silence over the crowd. Luis simply waited quietly behind the pulpit. Suddenly a lady stood to her feet and said, "I happen to know that the leader of our choir is not living right before the Lord." After several moments, a man spoke up, "Well, I am aware of several of those in the choir who are living in sin." More hushed moments followed before another gentleman stood and said, "It hurts me to say it, but I feel compelled to reveal that the treasurer of this crusade is not walking with the Lord."

Then Luis spoke up. "Friends, it is clear. We have sinned. We must confess our sins if God is going to bring blessing and reward our efforts with His harvest of souls. Let's gather in groups of two or three and pour out our hearts to God for His gracious cleansing."

The auditorium became a great temple of fervent prayer as confession filled the air. I noted that some made their way across the hall to pray with a person whom they may have offended. You could almost sense the cleansing of God over the assembly of believers asking for His forgiveness.

You can probably guess what happened. The second night of the crusade and every night thereafter the attendance continued to grow and each service was blessed. The notable difference, however, was in the harvest. As soon as Luis finished his message and gave a simple invitation to respond, hundreds rose to their feet all over the stadium and made their way forward, some almost running down the stairs and across the field. God worked to accomplish His purpose for His glory.

Hearts that have been cleansed and a spirit of fervent prayer serve as a foundation for an effective crusade ministry. So if you are considering a city-wide crusade, start the entire endeavor in systematic and consistent prayer, and watch God work.

FAITH PROMISE FOR PEOPLE—EACH ONE WIN ONE

I had been teaching at Dallas Seminary for several years. My wife and I determined that it was time to set aside an entire summer to live and work overseas. We kept the months of June, July, and August two years thereafter free from any commitments so that we might fulfill this plan, although we did not yet know where we might serve.

In the following year we received two invitations. One was to join the CAM team in Spain, the country in which we had served just before I joined the faculty of Dallas Seminary. While we contemplated this opportunity and prayed for God's guidance, friends from El Salvador called and asked if we might get together while they were in the United States to attend a short training conference.

Three of these men then came to our home in Arlington, Texas. Two respected laymen whom we knew well were elders of the Nazaret Church. Luis Bush, an Argentinean whom I had come to know very well when he studied at Dallas Seminary, was the third man in the group. Luis had been led of the Lord to become pastor of this vibrant, growing church.

Francisco Choriego, one of the elders, invited me to serve as interim pastor in the months of June, July, and August in the following year to free Luis Bush to attend some important conferences during those months.

We told them of the prior invitation we had received from Spain. They were not shaken at all. They said, "That's fine. If God wants you in Spain, we want you in Spain. But we would like for you to ask for the Lord's guidance and if He opens the door for you to accept our invitation we would be very grateful for His good favor." We prayed together that night in Spanish. It was a glorious time of fellowship and worship.

After several weeks of continued prayer, we were certain that God wanted us to serve with the believers in El Salvador. We knew it was not an easy assignment, but once it became clear to us this was God's will, we had no choice but to obey.

We had asked if we might bring some Dallas Seminary students to join us. The church leaders encouraged this. Without a great deal of re-cruitment on our part, the Lord led six seminary students to join us in this three-month assignment. For those who had wives and children, the whole family made the trip, of course. Libby and I and our three children and the Dallas Seminary team moved to El Salvador for three months.

When we arrived, El Salvador was engaged in a guerrilla offensive in a bloody civil war. In spite of the imminent dangers and extreme unrest in the country, God worked in a marvelous way. Perhaps because of the dangers, people were very open to the gospel.

Early in our three months in this troubled country, Mark Choate, one of the students who accompanied us, suggested a simple plan for evange-listic outreach. He called it the campaign of "Five Friends." Each believer in the church was challenged to join in the *Campaña de Cinco Amigos*, the "Campaign of Five Friends." To join, a person had to commit to pray systematically throughout the year for five friends who were unbelievers.

"Faith-promise" cards were printed for the campaign. These were faith-promise cards for souls rather than money. The larger portion of the card indicated the commitment to pray for the salvation of five unsaved friends in the coming year and had five blanks in which the participant wrote the names of his or her five friends. The smaller portion of the card simply indicated the commitment, a signature line, and the date of the commitment. The card was perforated so the two parts could be detached.

We launched the campaign in each of the three morning services. I preached on the need for evangelism and multiplication and then left ample time for response to the Five Friends faith-promise appeal. Those who were led of the Lord to respond were asked to fill in the names of five friends, sign and date the commitment card, and bring the signed portion of the card to be placed on the platform as a sign before the Lord and the church of their commitment. Hundreds responded.

I explained, "Even if you cannot think of five friends who do not know the Lord, you can still respond. Covenant with God that before the year is up, you will have five names on the card, five friends for whom you can ask that God might bring them to Himself." We also made it clear that one of the ways in which we might pray was that God would give us the opportunity to share the gospel with at least one of the five in the coming year and that this one would come to Christ.

It was amazing to note how quickly the Lord worked. In the midweek service just a few days after the Five Friends commitments had been made, two of the men gave vibrant testimonies of how God had opened the door. One man said, "The ink was hardly dry on my card when my neighbor dropped by to talk. He was obviously sent to me by God to lead him to Christ."

We have initiated this simple Five Friends faith-promise plan throughout the areas in which CAM missionaries serve. In an evangelism consultation with missionary representatives from each country, plans for this grass-roots campaign were refined, and the campaign has spread throughout Central America, Mexico, and Spain.

If every member of your church could be challenged to participate in this simple form of evangelism that builds on already established friendships, and if God would respond to prayers that at least one might come to Christ within the year, your church could double in size through conversion growth! That is 100 percent growth—not transfer "sheep-stealing" growth, but true "new-lambs" growth in the body of Christ and in your local church.

Try this faith-promise plan personally first. See what God will do. If you feel it is something that could capture the vision of the people of your fellowship, join with some of your leadership team, lay out the plans, and launch one of the most effective means of evangelism I know. By the grace of God each one can win one. This is the road to explosive growth. This is God-ordained multiplication.

THE LEAST EFFECTIVE— DOOR-TO-DOOR CAMPAIGNS

I was walking along Gaston Avenue in Dallas, Texas, toward Baylor University Medical Center to visit an ailing friend when I sighted a couple of Mormon missionaries walking along ahead of me. I came alongside the two young men and greeted them with a friendly, "Hi." They responded with a bit of caution but were genuinely kind to this stranger.

"You are missionaries, aren't you?" My question seemed to help set them at ease. "Yes," they responded, almost in chorus. "I used to be a missionary too," I volunteered.

Now the two were very warm. The older of the two "elders" introduced himself and his companion. "We are serving here in Dallas. Elder Smith is from Provo and I am from Salt Lake City," he added.

"It is good to meet you," I replied. "I too was a missionary, but not with the Mormon Church."

"Oh," the spokesman of the two muttered. He obviously had thought I was one of them. "How did you know we were missionaries?"

"By your uniform," I said with a smile. They both laughed.

We chatted as we walked the brief distance to the Baylor Hospital main entrance. At the doorway we stopped for a moment. I turned to Elder Taylor and said, "I know you keep good statistics. What have you found to be the most effective means of evangelism?"

He seemed pleased that I recognized their efforts. He said, "Could I tell you the least effective first?"

"Yes," I replied, "I'd like to know that."

"Door to door," he said.

"Door to door," I said in a genuinely surprised tone. "Why do you keep doing it?" Mormons are probably most noted for their tireless door-to-door endeavors.

"Our door-to-door ministries are really not so much for the ones behind the door," Elder Taylor explained. "It is done to strengthen and confirm those who knock on the door. If we have a young person do this ministry for two years, we never lose him."

I was amazed at this astute explanation. The Mormon Church draws in some converts from these diligent efforts, but according to this young man door-to-door visitation is the least effective means of evangelism.

"We have found," he continued, "that people generally come into the Mormon Church through a friend, neighbor, or relative. Most come through a relative."

We parted to go our separate ways in the hospital, but that brief encounter has left an indelible impression on me. Of all people in the world from whom to learn that door-to-door campaigns are the least effective means of evangelism, I hardly expected to have a Mormon as my teacher.

Facts are facts. There are certain obstacles to door-to-door evangelism. This is not to say it should not be done. It is only to say that it is not the most effective.

It is not overly difficult to understand the obstacles to a door-to-door endeavor. Most people consider their home a private enclave and increasingly dislike any invasion by an uninvited party. Anyone who has worked as a telemarketing agent knows that even by phone there is a certain resentment toward those who have interrupted the activities of a person who is in his or her own home. It is far more offensive when someone rings the doorbell to try to sell something, even when it is as priceless as eternal salvation offered at no cost to the one who will listen and respond. The one who answers the door does not usually respond with a cheerful spirit. He or she sees this as an intrusion and is generally convinced that the one who is there on the doorstep is some high-powered salesperson peddling an unwanted product.

Furthermore it is rare to find someone at home in this exceedingly busy society. In most homes both parents work and the children are off at a day-care center or school. The best time to find people at home is in the evening, and yet that is when interruptions are most unwelcome.

Jehovah's Witnesses, who are as active in door-to-door efforts as Mormons, often limit their visitation to Sundays. They look for the people who are not attending church! Not a bad strategy.

Having said all of this, I believe door-to-door evangelism need not be considered an impossible approach to reach people for Christ. Several pointers may help. Always go in pairs, deciding ahead of time who will take the lead in the conversation. After ringing the doorbell, step back from the door. A little distance makes the approach seem less threatening or aggressive. Always introduce yourself and your companion immediately and state the purpose of your visit. "Hi, I'm Joe Carlson and this is Charlie Green. We are from First Baptist Church, and we are visiting in the neighborhood to let people know about the ways in which our church wants to serve our community."

A friendly tone and smile are essential. The one at the door needs to capture right away that you are not salespeople. One way to get to chat for awhile is to ask for the opportunity to do so. "May we come in and talk with you for a few minutes? We have some materials we would like to show you." It may sound a bit forward to ask to enter the home, but if stated in a positive tone with anticipation of acceptance, it is amazing how many people will invite you to come in.

The visit should be brief unless the person wants to extend it. It is a time to get acquainted and to introduce the church and, above all, to introduce the Lord to the people with whom you speak. If the TV is on, it is best to ask, "I don't want to interrupt. Is this your favorite program? If it is, maybe we can come back at another time." These comments can serve as a suggestion for the person to turn down or turn off the television set. If he or she does not take the hint, you can ask, "Do you mind turning the TV off for a few minutes?"

It should not take long to discover if the person with whom you are speaking knows the Lord or not. If he or she is a believer, you can express your gratitude to the Lord for the privilege to meet a brother or sister in Christ and to fellowship briefly.

If the person does not know the Lord, this is the opportunity to share how you came to Christ and why He means so much to you and then give your newfound friend the opportunity to find the same new life you have encountered in the Lord. You can lead him or her in prayer. Of course, follow-up is very important for each person who receives Christ.

Be sure to offer a business card and some helpful literature before you leave. I have noted that the Mormons and Jehovah's Witnesses seem to focus on a commitment for further Bible studies. This is a commendable approach. People may not be ready to place their faith in Christ, but many are searching for answers. Future visits to study the Bible are an attractive alternative and might be a more realistic step.

Perhaps the most effective door-to-door campaign I have ever seen was conducted by Robert Schuller when he became pastor of the struggling church that has since grown to become the gigantic and renowned Crystal Cathedral in southern California. He personally visited the neighborhood door to door but in a unique way. "I'm Robert Schuller, new pastor of the church here in your neighborhood. Do you attend our church?"

When the person of the household being visited said no, Schuller quickly said, "Oh, good. I'm trying to determine what people might look for in a church they would like to attend. What would you suggest? What would you like to see in a church that might meet your needs and interests?"

Schuller took copious notes from each person. He then worked diligently to incorporate some of these suggestions in the church. People soon became aware that here was a church that was trying to meet the needs of those in the neighborhood. Many attended out of sheer curiosity.

This is the best approach for door-to-door visitation. It is not a salesman's approach. This is an honest desire to meet people and ask them for helpful suggestions. Like the "I Need Your Opinion" survey approach discussed earlier, this approach in door-to-door visitation appeals to people who like to offer advice.

Part Four

The Lifeline—Leadership for Missions

Chapter Fourteen

A Burden for the World—Pastoral Staff

THE ROLE OF THE SENIOR PASTOR

A MISSIONS-MINDED CHURCH almost always has a missions-minded pastor. The God-ordained leader of the flock generates world vision and an active interest and participation in world outreach. The pastor not only teaches God's clear plan for world missions, but he also demonstrates his commitment to this endeavor by his personal involvement.

Being a senior pastor is not unlike being captain of a ship. There are so many responsibilities it is virtually impossible for the captain to manage every activity on his vessel. He can't control and direct everything. So he depends on a diligent crew and informed passengers. When everything works, he enjoys smooth sailing. But when a crisis arises, he is held accountable. If the ship goes aground, the captain is considered responsible.

The mere mention of missions might seem to be an overload to a busy pastor. He doesn't need more activities as captain of God's ship, especially when he is trying to plug leaks in the hull and has a crew working on a dead boiler in engine room two.

Here are three simple suggestions to help any pastor take the lead in missions.

Lead in prayer for the world. Plan to include an international touch in every prayer. Think globally and pray accordingly. Use the world news as fuel for prayer. When disaster hits somewhere on the globe, include this need in your pastoral prayer. The congregation will be moved by the concern their pastor demonstrates when he asks God to work on behalf of those who are facing a crisis reported in the daily newscasts.

Each local church needs to connect to the whole world. In communications, politics, and business, globalization is increasingly evident. The church by nature is comprised of people from every continent. The international body of Christ is a reality, and every pastoral prayer should reflect this fact. A global perspective in prayer will keep the congregation aware of the needs around the world and foster a greater world vision.

Lead in contact with the world. Churches should give top priority to sending their pastor overseas. Youth mission trips are admirable, but it is far more important for the pastor to be exposed to what God is doing around the world.

An investment in a pastoral visit to come alongside a missionary family that is supported by the church will bring incredible returns. The missionaries visited will be encouraged. The people with whom the missionaries serve will be enriched, especially if the pastor is given opportunity to minister. The pastor will be exposed to the needs and advances in the country he visits. Most of all, the church will be enlightened through firsthand reports of all God is doing. Everyone benefits in this endeavor.

Lead in awareness of the world. A pastor need not be an expert in geography, but it is helpful when he is has some awareness of the diverse world in which we live. A few minutes a day in Patrick Johnstone's wonderful little volume *Operation World* will revolutionize a pastor's view of planet earth.[1] It is encouraging to talk with those who know Kenya from Cambodia and can visualize the location of Ecuador and Equatorial Guinea.

The pastor sets the tone for the entire congregation. If he carries no burden for lost people, it is unlikely that many church members will be concerned. I pray that every pastor would be able to echo the apostle Paul's exclamation, "Brothers, my heart's desire and prayer to God . . . is that they may be saved" (Rom. 10:1).

THE ROLE OF A MISSIONS PASTOR

If world outreach has its rightful place in the church and the size of the congregation permits, a missions pastor is essential. While a senior pastor provides leadership for every aspect of ministry in which the church is engaged, he can't possibly be directly involved in every church activity. Delegation is a key to his survival.

Unfortunately some churches seem to feel that a choir director is of greater importance than an experienced and fully qualified missions pastor. Usually the missions budget alone would indicate the need for someone to supervise this vital element of church ministries.

Missionaries whom the church supports are best seen as members of the church staff on assignment overseas. These dedicated servants in God's work abroad are in need of pastoral care. Sometimes this is the most important role a missions pastor has. His care and concern for the missionary staff can greatly enhance their ministries.

Ideally a missions pastor has served on a foreign assignment. With this experience a missions pastor can better understand the dynamics of missionary adjustments and provide wise counsel and empathetic support.

A missions pastor bears at least five essential responsibilities.

Missions education. Perhaps the main reason more believers are not excited about the role of missions in their church is lack of understanding. Both biblical and practical training are needed at every level of the church curriculum. Starting with young children in Sunday school and going on up to the senior citizens there must be an ongoing presentation of God's global plan and of the many open doors for the gospel around the world.

Missions conference. A special focus on missions at regular intervals in the church calendar is especially helpful in educating the congregation to missions needs and opportunities. An effective missions conference can light a fire for world outreach in a unique way. It should be so well orchestrated that the people of the church look forward to the conference with great anticipation.

The missions pastor needs to initiate preparations and be sure that every detail is well executed in the church missions conference. He should set a high standard of excellence for this important event. Most important, he needs to engage a large part of the congregation in this endeavor. Participation in planning, promoting, and presenting a missions conference will help ensure success. Further practical advice for a quality missions conference can be found on pages 161–64 of this volume. It is important to recognize the major role a missions pastor plays in this key event.

Missions communications. Never before have there been so many ways to keep in touch with missionaries. The missions pastor needs to become a trusted and intimate friend of each missionary with whom he can maintain contact.

E-mail has provided a simple and reliable way for a missions pastor to be in close contact with each missionary under his jurisdiction. Information is available at the flick of a few keys, and the message is current and accurate. Gone are the long days of waiting for a letter to cross the ocean. Occasional use of the telephone is still advisable, but in many ways electronic mail supersedes the phone. Furthermore e-mail saves money that was formerly spent on phone bills and airmail postage.

A missions pastor can easily keep in his computer the e-mail addresses of all the missionaries the church helps support. If his "address book" is designed so that large numbers can be reached under one "blind copy" entry, the missions pastor can forward edited copies of messages by hitting just one key on the computer. This may well be one of the most revolutionary breakthroughs for missions communications today.

Missions pastoral care. The missions pastor needs to maintain close contact with every missionary of the church. If he has a close friendship with all those under his charge, the missionary pastor will undoubtedly be called on from time to time to provide counsel, guidance, and encouragement to each missionary.

William Taylor, a former missionary colleague of mine, speaks to this issue in his book *Too Valuable to Lose.*[2] Extensive research for this classic volume has revealed that pastoral care is essential to keep missionaries and their families intact and productive. Far too many wonderful workers in overseas ministries have been lost simply because they had no pastor to whom they could turn when they needed some help.

What a privilege it is for a missions pastor to provide a well–timed word of encouragement or some thoughtful counsel at a moment of need. A missions pastor tends a flock of deeply committed Christian workers who are scattered around the globe.

Missions finances. The missions pastor is responsible for being sure that each missionary, as well as each related missions ministry, is adequately funded and that appropriate accounting procedures are in place.

It is helpful when the missions pastor has had some business or accounting experience. Since missions budgets can be exceedingly large, this is no place for a novice who has never prepared or even read a financial report.

One of the greatest challenges and most enriching experiences for a missions pastor is to watch God provide well beyond what could be imagined. The missions pastor will experience the delights of God's material provisions in ways that we mortals can barely comprehend. Watching the Lord move His children in a faith-promise rally is especially exciting.

Missions recruitment. The key to missions is people. A missions pastor needs to be alert to qualified members of the congregation whom God may be leading to serve in missions. It is helpful to be proactive in this endeavor. A few choice words can be used by the Lord. "I have noted the unique gifts God has given you. Have you ever thought about using these gifts for the Lord overseas? I'd love to explore with you opportunities around the world where you might be used to help accomplish His work."

Too much of the recruitment responsibility has been assigned to mission agencies. Furthermore I feel the arena for recruitment has been overly restrictive. Most recruiting is presently directed toward Bible college and seminary campuses. This is good, but it is far more important to challenge for missionary service those who are active in the work of the church. As seen in God's Word, the church is the primary sending agency. The church is perhaps the best training facility and offers the best opportunity for careful screening and personal direction.

Missions deployment. Besides recruiting key individuals for missionary service, the missions pastor can help each candidate or appointee depart for the field of service in a timely manner. It is a great challenge to engage members of the congregation in an effective sending role.

The missions pastor becomes a herald for biblical patterns of giving and a champion for those missionary appointees who are anxious to be on their way to their country of service.

Missions motivation. In summary, a missions pastor is the point man for the church's ongoing outreach ministries. He is a link to the world and an emissary for international service. He can help impart a God-given vision to reach people in every continent, nation, people, culture, and language who have not yet come to Christ. Nothing could be more challenging and as rewarding as the unique assignment of missions pastor. The scope of this ministry is immense and the returns are eternal.

CHAPTER FIFTEEN

Reaching Out to the World—Missions Committees and Missionaries

MISSIONS COMMITTEES

THE SENIOR PASTOR can set the tone for missions and a qualified missions pastor can provide needed supervision for this immense ministry. But to realize maximum returns, more personnel are needed.

For churches of all sizes a missions committee is essential. For the church that may not be in a position to employ a full-time missions pastor, the missions committee assumes full responsibility for this vital ministry of the church.

The committee members must be carefully selected. Those who participate in this important assignment must have a deep passion for the cause of Christ around the world and be willing to dedicate needed time to this task.

I would recommend a committee of six to twelve members with a good representation of the church family. Retired missionaries might best represent the senior members of the church, and a young couple who has served overseas on a short-term assignment may be the best voice for families with small children. A vibrant single who is excited about his or her ministry or work-team experience on the mission field can speak for other singles. A teenager who is deeply committed to Christ and has the desire to serve the Lord as a missionary might well be included on the committee. Every member should be carefully selected and appointed by the church board with full approval of the senior pastor and the missions pastor.

It is imperative that missions committee members have the resources, authority, and longevity to fulfill their assignment. The church board needs to include in the annual budget sufficient funds for the anticipated operations of this vital committee. Under clear guidelines the committee should be able to move forward with bold and visionary plans that will impact the world for the glory of God.

To ensure continuity and stability the committee members must have extended terms of service. Ideally each member should be appointed to a term of at least three years and on a rotating basis, so that at least one-third of the committee members are in their third year of service. Renewable appointments will further help achieve this goal.

Whatever it takes, the committee must sense continuity. It is devastating to the cause of missions to have entire missions committees replaced every year. It is even more destructive in those churches where there is no continuing missions pastor. Missions outreach is too important to assign to transitory volunteers who do not sense the awesome responsibility of their assignment. If every church could provide this kind of continuity and stability to the missions committee, the cause of missions would advance in ways we might never imagine.

For information on qualifications and duties of missions-committee members, consult the excellent resources provided by ACMC (Advancing Churches in Missions Commitment). [1]

"How can they hear without someone preaching to them? And how can they preach unless they are sent?" (Rom. 10:14–15). Without senders there are no goers. The church is the sending agency ordained by God. This effort requires a senior pastor providing essential leadership, a missions pastor, if possible, directing the endeavor, a missions committee diligently making and implementing every facet of the church's world outreach program, and a church body fully engaged in God's work worldwide.

MISSIONARIES

After his penetrating question, "And how can they preach unless they are sent?" Paul quoted from Isaiah 52:7: "As it is written, 'How beautiful are the feet of those who bring good news!'" (Rom. 10:15). We thank the

Lord for those whom He directs to leave the security of their homes, family, culture, and community to reach those who might never come to know our Savior if the former are not obedient to His leading.

Of course, God obviously does not direct every believer to serve cross-culturally. All believers must bear this responsibility before the Lord, but not everyone must become a missionary.

When I was a student at Dallas Theological Seminary, my wife, Libby, and I attended Berean Memorial Church in Irving, Texas. I remember well an impressive sign in the church auditorium: "Every heart with Christ a missionary. Every heart without Christ a mission field." The sign was motivating to every believer. It was quite accurate if by "missionary" reference is made to being sent by God as His witness to the lost. As Christ said, "As the Father has sent me, so I am sending you" (John 20:21). The generally accepted meaning of the word *missionary*, however, refers to those who are sent to serve in cross-cultural ministries. It is a more technical meaning for those engaged in a unique assignment.

Maintaining this professional definition of "missionary" helps identify those who are sent out by the church as cross-cultural workers. These missionaries are vitally linked to the church and serve as extended staff in those areas of spiritual need being touched by the church.

Ideally the church will be constantly challenging qualified individuals in the congregation to consider special assignments overseas. The greatest and most effective source for missionaries is the local church. The senior pastor, missions pastor, and missions committee need to be engaged in recruitment and deployment. The truly missions-minded church is one that is recruiting, training, and sending missionary workers in accord with God's guidance and His clear command.

When Christ said, "I will build my church" (Matt. 16:18), He meant more than what is commonly called "church growth." It is fairly certain that Christ was not implying that He would make sure there was increased attendance at every service in your local church. His comment related to Peter's confession, "You are the Christ, the Son of the living God" (16:16). On this vibrant confession Christ said he would build His church.

The church the Lord referred to is the body of true believers all over the world, all those who are redeemed by His blood, not some local church located at a busy intersection of a bustling city in the East or a little chapel nestled on a country road in the Midwest.

To build the church all over the globe calls for each local church to get involved in God's mission. Missionaries have "beautiful feet" (Rom. 10:15) because they are willing to go. The rest of the congregation can respond with beautiful hands. Each believer can clasp his or her hands in prayer and draw generous offerings from his or her billfold or purse to send those who serve as missionaries.

By working closely with reputable mission agencies, each local church can be sure there is quality screening and training, God-honoring accountability, effective culturally sensitive strategy, and continuous communication and partnership in the mission task.

The senior pastor, missions pastor, missions committee, and missionaries form a dynamic team in partnership with a reliable mission agency, which adds expertise and careful supervision. The task is immense, but the Lord has given the resources needed to accomplish His purpose.

PART FIVE

The Supply Line—Strategies for the Sending Church

CHAPTER SIXTEEN

The Game Plan—Policies, Prayer, and Promotion

I VIVIDLY RECALL my childhood days during World War II. Ration coupons were a way of life in those difficult days. Essential staples were in short supply. Purchase of meat, sugar, butter, and bread were strictly controlled. Without a valued "ration coupon" our neighborhood merchant was not allowed to sell these valuable items.

We felt it was our duty to collect newspapers and save used tin cans. Housewives carefully removed both tops and bottoms of canned goods and smashed the cylindrical middle portion of the can so that the metals might be reused.

Since most able-bodied men were on the battlefront in Europe, on some Pacific island, or confined to a combat ship or plane, women by the thousands worked difficult shifts around the clock to keep production going.

World War II was won in large part because of the determination and sacrifice of those who served behind the battle lines. Manufactured goods and essential supplies at the point of battle were produced by faithful, hard-working citizens across the United States and in every Allied nation.

In a similar way world missions is dependent on the spirit of the people who serve as senders. Those on the front lines of mission ministries are just as dependent on those back home as those who served on the front lines in military maneuvers. Much is said about sacrifice and diligence in relation to missionaries. No missionary is accepted unless he or she is fully committed and is willing to leave behind family, friends, and material possessions and move to another land and culture to serve in God's army. Perhaps more should be said about the spirit of sacrifice and diligence needed among senders. Support personnel are desperately needed.

Here are some helpful ideas to develop strategies for an effective sending church. Without an adequate sending base the whole missions enterprise will crumble. People around the world who need the Lord are dependent on sending churches and each person in these congregations.

POLICIES FOR MISSIONS

Someone has wisely said, "Plan your work, then work your plan." Too often missions pastors and missions committees resort to instantaneous, independent decisions on issues as they arise. All too often decisions made on the spur of the moment are wrong decisions. In an enterprise as big and important as world missions, guidelines need to be developed in a prayerful, unhurried manner. A carefully prepared missions policy focuses on pertinent issues and provides workable answers that are not based on personal whims or pressured response.

All churches have policies, written or not. Unfortunately unwritten policies are interpreted differently by each person and decisions are often inconsistent and sporadic. As a result there is little sense of continuity, confidence, or cohesion.

A well-written missions policy provides needed guidance for effective outreach. Time invested to develop this important church document will yield amazing returns for years to come.

The Missions Policy Handbook of ACMC (Advancing Churches in Missions Commitment)[1] addresses almost every issue that might be considered in an effective missions policy: the purpose of missions, missions committee structure, missions committee responsibilities, and financial and support policies. The handbook defines sixty specific issues one by one, gives guidance on how to determine if each issue is applicable to your church, presents options to be considered, and prompts you to write out your church policy on each issue if it is applicable to your church. This *Handbook* also includes several sample missions policies developed by churches of all sizes. A well-designed missions policy distributed to every leader in the church provides an effective game plan that will bring ongoing successful advance and outreach.

PRAYER FOR MISSIONS

I spent almost two years on a destroyer in the Pacific fleet. After that I was glad to receive "shore duty," although I had no idea what my new assignment might be in the place designated in my orders.

"What is the navy doing in Clarksville, Tennessee?" I pondered. "No body of water is big enough for a ship anywhere near Tennessee!" I finally found a warrant officer who was somewhat familiar with the navy base to which I was assigned. "It's some type of classified atomic facility," he explained.

When I arrived at Clarksville Naval Base, I was told I was being assigned to Fort Campbell, the famous army facility of the 101st Airborne located at Hopkinsville, Kentucky. Our naval base was just across the state line to the north and therefore had a Tennessee address. Actually we were hidden behind Fort Campbell.

The warrant officer was right. I was assigned to a top-secret base. For the first three months I was given menial administrative tasks while waiting for top-secret clearance. FBI agents were checking me out. You can imagine the stir this created in my little hometown in Iowa. All my friends in this farming community were wondering, "What has Ronnie Blue done?" The agents quickly explained that their hometown boy was not being sought for some crime. They were just doing a security check for the armed forces.

After I received top-secret clearance, I was assigned to "watches" down in the section we called the "pit." This base was remarkably secure. The entire perimeter was fenced like a federal prison. Marines patrolled a road inside this fence twenty-four hours a day. Inside the outer fence and patrol road were three more fences. Touch the middle fence and you would be electrocuted. All of this protected the administrative area.

The "pit" was the most secure area of the base. It too was fenced with one heavily guarded entrance. Only government-approved vehicles could enter this area. Any passengers transported through these gates had to get out of the vehicle and walk through a checkpoint to be inspected and interrogated. A special identification badge was essential.

When I reported for duty, the officer I relieved would pull from the safe a card to show me a top-secret word.

In the location in which I stood watch there was a red telephone with a direct line to the Pentagon in Washington, D.C. If any emergency were to arise, I could pick up the telephone and have immediate access to top military brass. But I had to know the secret word to assure I was a legitimate caller. This was just one more measure of security.

I never had the opportunity to use that red phone. I used to sit there with my eyes on that phone. I was tempted to pick up the receiver just to see if someone was actually on the other end of the line.

We who know the Lord have a red telephone. We have a direct line to the Creator of the universe, to God Himself. But there is a top-secret word. We must address our prayer "in the name of our Lord Jesus Christ." This should not simply be a phrase we habitually tack on to our prayers. It is tragic that so often we hear these words and interpret them to mean, "I'm about to end my prayer now."

Apart from Jesus Christ we have no access to God the Father. We approach God through Jesus' atoning work on the cross and victory over death. Christ has opened the door to heaven and given to us the wonderful blessing of prayer.

In a day in which the world is linked together by e-mail and satellite connections, nothing can compare with our "red telephone" of prayer. We never get put on hold. We never have to punch our way through a voice-box maze. We never hear a recording. God is always there to hear us. He graciously listens to our requests and understands our needs. He can do above what we can ask or even think to provide answers. He is God.

Prayer is the greatest need in missions today. If every missionary could recruit at least one hundred people who would make full use of their "red telephone" and consistently take to the Lord every related prayer request, the advance in missions would be spectacular.

Church leaders need to lead in prayer. A pattern of prayer should be evident. When a need is expressed, a godly leader should immediately guide those around him or her in prayer. This is especially true for challenges in world missions. Needs in a distant land and another time zone can best be met through God's intervention. Quite often solutions are possible *only* through God's intervention

The sending church can be of invaluable assistance in missions if it is a praying church. The greatest supply line is a prayer line.

PROMOTION OF MISSIONS

Spiritual life starts when a person comes to *know* the Savior. The newborn believer then must *grow* in Christ. He or she will then *show* to others the wonderful message of the gospel.

Missions development must progress in the same way. Each believer must *know* what the Bible says about world outreach and be aware of spiritual needs around the globe. With this knowledge, the believer will *grow* in vision and compassion to help meet those needs. Missions activity is contagious. Each believer who is involved in missions outreach will then *show* others the importance of this key activity.

To be biblical, a church must have a central focus on missions. An educational program is incomplete if there is not continued awareness of God's commission to reach the whole world. Children, youth, and adults of all ages need to be exposed to God's worldwide plan and be increasingly aware of what He is doing on every continent.

Missions is not some extracurricular activity scheduled for special occasions. This needs to be central to everything the church does. Every member needs to see the church as a lighthouse to the world.

Promoting missions in your church and making your congregation aware of the missionary enterprise may be achieved in numerous ways.

Missions maps. An attractive map of the world in a prominent location is a constant reminder of the international scope of the church's ministries. A large map in the church foyer with ribbons extending from field locations to photographs and missionary name identifications or attractive maps representing the Eastern and Western hemispheres at the front and on each side of the auditorium will keep everyone focused on the world. Miniature lights can be used to show the location of each missionary representing the church.

Missions bulletin boards. Announcements of missions activities, pictures and displays of church-supported missions endeavors, and attractive, uncluttered presentations on a well-placed bulletin board can be used to great advantage. It is not advisable to cover the board with missionary letters. Excessive material will only turn people away. Colorful, well-designed layouts that are changed frequently will maximize this means of communication.

Missionary picture gallery. Uniform, framed, color portraits of each missionary or missionary family appropriately identified will help church members become acquainted with those sent out by the church. A member whose hobby is photography can be in charge of this project. The photos should be top quality and should be updated frequently.

Missionary directory. A pictorial directory that includes a photograph of the missionary or missionary family, a list of members of the family, birthdays, wedding anniversary dates, place of service, missions agency under which they serve, a brief description of the type of ministry in which they are engaged, and a current address, telephone number, and e-mail address can be of great help. A loose-leaf format facilitates revisions.

Missionary newsletters. Rather than post missionary letters on a bulletin board, it is far more effective to include excerpts in the church bulletin or church newsletter. Missionaries should be encouraged to send letters directly to those in the church who feel a part of the support team and therefore want to keep informed.

News releases and broadcast media. The local press, as well as radio and television stations, will often accept newsworthy material, especially if it is related to current events. An interview with a missionary in a country facing a crisis will provide a personal touch to the news. Someone in the church employed by the media or who will take the time to develop personal relationships with religious news editors or other key press or broadcasting people should be the church's proactive liaison for this invaluable exposure.

Missions periodicals and books. Pamphlets, brochures, and other literature on missions should be readily available. An attractive literature rack will help keep these materials in order. The church foyer or library is an ideal location. A special rack for youth-related materials can be installed where young people gather. If the church has a library, the missions section should feature current books, particularly missionary adventure and biographies. Just like missionary letters, missions literature is most effective in the home. Every church family should subscribe to at least one periodical related to missions.

Audiovisual resources. Videos, compact disks, films, overhead transparencies, and audiocassettes that emphasize missions should be a part of any church's resource library. Occasional use of visuals in church services will make members aware of missions outreach and encourage more involvement.

Flags, banners, and posters. A display of flags representing every nation in which church-sponsored missionaries are located is both colorful and stimulating. For special events, large banners and attractive posters will increase interest and excitement. Airlines and travel agencies will often provide posters of countries of the world free or at minimal cost.

Missions is so important that it needs to be promoted continually. We can't assume that members will automatically maintain high interest in the missions ministries of the church. So a well-planned schedule throughout the year for missions information and inspiration will keep the congregation attuned to God's work around the world.

Missions conferences. A missions conference in your church can add great exposure to God's work around the world. In addition to informing your congregation about missions, an annual conference can inspire your people to pray more fervently for missionaries, to give more generously to missions, and even to consider the possibility of serving as missionaries, whether on a short-term or long-term basis. A missions conference in which you have missionaries speak who are supported by your church can be a great encouragement to them too, as they have opportunity for personal interaction with your people.

In a society that is filled with activity and prior commitments, it is probably not advisable to schedule a conference with meetings every night for an entire week. Far more effective is a missions emphasis launched on Sunday, with missionaries engaged in every church activity already scheduled through the week, and an appropriate closing rally the following Sunday. If missionaries supported by the church or those seeking support can become a part of every group meeting through the week, including choir practice, prayer meeting, softball games, youth meetings, and home Bible studies, they will have the kind of close personal exposure that is most effective. This scheduling also allows for more flexibility for those who participate in the conference. Some may not be available for the entire week. The two Sundays provide broad exposure, and other events give depth in "high-touch" relationships.

Several steps are important in carrying out a meaningful conference with high spiritual impact.

First, appoint a conference coordinator. Perhaps the best place to start planning for a missions conference is with a carefully selected leader who assumes responsibility for this key event. The leader may be a member of the missions committee, but it is not necessary. He or she needs to be a person of deep commitment to missions, a diligent worker who knows how to recruit and engage many people in fulfilling specific assignments, and one who has a reputation for high achievement and excellence. Most of all, this leader must have an unquenchable inner passion to make the missions conference a great success.

Second, choose the dates for the conference. In consultation with the church staff and missions committee, the conference coordinator needs to set dates for the conference. These dates must be on the church calendar at least one year in advance and should not conflict with other church and community activities. The staff needs to consider this an essential activity in the ministry of the church and take an active part in the conference. Nothing is more disconcerting than to have the senior pastor accept an out-of-town speaking engagement at the time of the conference or, worse yet, to see this as a time to take a vacation.

Third, recruit a conference team. As soon as the dates have been set, the conference coordinator needs to recruit a core team to assist in planning and leading the conference. Each one should be carefully selected and personally recruited. The more experience the coordinator has, the more effective he or she will be in this recruitment endeavor. Each one can be challenged with specific areas of responsibility, if these are already determined. If not, the assignments can be made after plans are fully developed, and others may be recruited for expanding opportunities for service. It is important, however, that those who are leaders for the conference be included in the planning stages.

Fourth, determine the conference program and participants. The selected team of leaders will need to engage in initial extended and hopefully highly productive sessions to outline plans for the conference. They need to determine a conference theme that will meet the perceived needs of the congregation, choose an appropriate main-session speaker, determine likely missionary participants, outline the initial conference program, including appropriate special features, plan publicity and decorations, develop a conference budget within already determined limitations, and care for any other key elements that will help make the conference a success.

Fifth, mobilize the conference. Every leader who has participated in the planning meeting needs to assume direction of a segment of the conference under the guidance of the conference coordinator. Before the above-mentioned meeting is adjourned, each individual should be assigned a specific responsibility and sense the freedom within the approved guidelines to fulfill the assigned task.

Each area of responsibility should be clearly defined. For example, someone needs to be in charge of post-conference evaluation and cleanup. Each leader must then recruit as many people of the church as needed to prepare for and carry out the conference. One great key to an effective conference is participation. Each duty needs to be clearly defined and someone challenged to fulfill this task. The leader charged with hospitality, for example, will need to find a host family for every guest, someone to provide airport pickup and local transportation for those without cars, a detailed meal schedule, and many other details.

Sixth, plan other special conference features. Plans that emerge from the conference leadership meeting may include the following activities: a men's breakfast, home meetings with missionaries, separate sessions for children and youth, an all-church banquet or potluck supper, an outreach ministry to a local missions organization or a tour to a nearby missions headquarters, and special missions seminar sessions. Special features of the major church gatherings should be determined. A parade of flags, missionary introductions and interviews, musical revues, power-point or video presentations, and other unique features should be a part of the plans.

Seventh, prepare for a conference follow-up. One of the conference leaders should assume post-conference responsibilities. These include careful follow-up of those who have made decisions of commitment to possible missionary service and faith-promise financial and prayer commitments. Acknowledging these decisions immediately will be of great encouragement to those whom God has touched. In consultation with the conference coordinator this leader needs to have a special evaluation session right after the conference to outline suggestions for improvement. These suggestions are invaluable to those who will plan future conferences. Constant improvement will ensure long-range advance. Soon after the conference has ended is the ideal time to find a new team to begin plans for the next conference. Many of those mobilized to assist in some of the responsibilities of the conference will be ideal candidates to take greater leadership responsibility in the next conference. This is discipleship in action.

CHAPTER SEVENTEEN

Returns That Are Out of This World—Financing Missions

I AM AMAZED how people seem to get nervous when money is mentioned, especially if there seems to be some indication that the one who brings up this topic is in the ministry. For some reason many visualize a ministry leader or missionary as a dangerous thief who is about to pick their pockets.

The Bible does not mumble about money. According to the Scriptures every believer must recognize the responsibility God has given us. We are not owners. We are only stewards of the resources He has entrusted to us.

"Do not store up for yourselves treasures on earth.... But store up for yourselves treasures in heaven.... For where your treasure is, there your heart will be also" (Matt. 6:19–21). How we use our money reflects our priorities and commitments. Major spending for houses and cars is a clear sign that our priorities are on personal comfort and satisfaction. Generous gifts to God's work prove that we are vitally interested in what He is doing in the lives of people around the world. Those who give demonstrate a commitment to eternal values.

Giving is not an option for God's children. "On the first day of every week, each one of you should set aside a sum of money in keeping with his income" (1 Cor. 16:2). God never asks us to give for His work what He has not already given us. He wants us to give as He has prospered us. Giving is to be systematic, personal, and in proportion to what He has entrusted to us.

"Give and it will be given to you. A good measure, pressed down, shaken together and running over, will be poured into your lap. For with the measure you use, it will be measured to you" (Luke 6:38). This is a wonderful promise. God blesses those who give. In fact, He promises abundance to those who are generous.

The early church is a wonderful example. "Out of the most severe trial, their overflowing joy and their extreme poverty welled up in rich generosity. . . . They gave as much as they were able, and even beyond their ability " (2 Cor. 8:2–4). Even in the midst of extreme difficulties and dire economic need, these Christians believed that giving is a privilege, and so they participated with joy.

The apostle Paul outlined God's design in giving. "Remember this: Whoever sows sparingly will also reap sparingly, and whoever sows generously will also reap generously. Each man should give what he has decided in his heart to give, not reluctantly or under compulsion, for God loves a cheerful giver" (9:6–7). I tell people, "Don't give until it hurts. Give until you're happy! If you aren't happy, give a little bit more. Keep giving until you get happy!" God does not want gifts given with reluctance or under pressure. He loves cheerful givers.

Abundant, joyous giving is the biblical way. And to those who give in this way God makes a marvelous promise, "You will be made rich in every way so that you can be generous on every occasion, and through us your generosity will result in thanksgiving to God" (9:11).

Without apology or hesitation church leaders need to encourage every believer to get involved in giving, especially giving for one of the church's most important ministries—witness to the lost world. World missions should not be limited for lack of funds. The church has a responsibility to call its people to be a giving church. The church that fails in this responsibility fails its people.

BUDGETED MISSIONS GIVING

Perhaps the most traditional way to be sure missions outreach is adequately funded is to include a sufficient amount for missions in the church's annual budget. This must be seen as an essential ministry of the church. The budget needs to include support for missionaries and also funds for the missions pastor and missions committee to fulfill their duties. There should always be room for expansion in the budget. To reduce the budget for missions is to call for a reduction in God's work around the world.

FAITH-PROMISE MISSIONS GIVING

A number of churches encourage "faith-promise" giving. Instead of having a few church leaders in the finance or budget committee indicate what amount will be dedicated to missions, believers in the congregation are given opportunity to indicate the amount they each sense God would have them give. Based on faith in God's provisions, each believer makes a promise before the Lord to give a designated amount in the forthcoming year. In other words the entire congregation helps write the budget in prayer before the Lord.

Some people ask, "Are faith promises biblical?" The answer is yes. For Paul wrote, "So I thought it necessary to urge the brothers to visit you in advance and finish the arrangements for the *generous gift you had promised*. Then it will be ready as a generous gift, not as one grudgingly given" (2 Cor. 9:5, italics added).

Filling out a faith-promise card is a challenging—and personal—assignment. It demands sincere prayer and divine guidance. It must truly be a step of faith. Based only in part on the way God has prospered in the past, a faith promise projects into the unknown future. It should go beyond "sight." Then the actual amounts given in the coming month depend on God's supply. This can be one of the most stretching and rewarding experiences of life. Without any certainty of how God might provide, a believer records an amount that can challenge his or her faith.

Faith promises may be approached in one of two ways. Faith promises can be directed toward the total missions budget, or they may be designated for individual missionaries, missionary families, and mission projects for the coming year. In other words the designations may be generalized or individualized.

Listing each missionary and project on the faith-promise card on which each member responds will create a closer bond between the giver and the one who receives this financial support. Each missionary can thereby know those who are part of their support team and keep close contact with these individuals and families in the church.

If individualized faith-promise cards are used, provision should be made so that each missionary and project is adequately financed either through a designation "where needed most" on the card or by having a reasonable support goal for each missionary or project. As soon as a goal is met, church members who have not yet filled in their faith-promise cards can be encouraged to help provide for those who still need support.

While couples and families may want to consult together in prayer and submit a joint faith-promise card, another approach is for each family member to participate, including young children giving out of their meager earnings or allowance. This is a faith builder that can be of benefit to all.

Almost without fail, when church members are called on to make faith-promise commitments and thereby "write" the missions budget, the resulting amount far exceeds what anyone could have imagined. This proves that when adequately challenged and when given the opportunity to respond prayerfully, the people of the church will be more generous than any budget committee might have anticipated.

Whatever means the church uses to finance missions outreach, this part of the church's ministry must receive proper attention. Just as each believer who is generous in giving will be blessed by God, so the church that is generous in supporting missions will receive His blessing. God in His sovereignty has entrusted His children and His church to provide for His work around the world.

CHAPTER EIGHTEEN

Will You Be the One?—Involvement in Missions

RECRUITING OF MISSIONARIES

NEXT TO PRAYER, the greatest need in missions is for qualified personnel to join the ranks of missionaries who are presently serving the Lord in world outreach.

I rejoice that CAM International, the missions agency with which I served as president, continues to grow. Each year we have many new appointees who more than make up for those who are retiring.

But this is not true of all mission boards. A number of well-established mission agencies are facing a crisis. More missionaries are retiring than are joining the mission. In other words, these missions are declining. There are fewer and fewer missionaries each year. Unless something changes, a death warrant looms over the agency. This is a serious matter.

What is the secret for a growing missionary force? What can be done to be sure new candidates and appointees fill the ranks and provide needed leadership for the future?

Effective recruitment revolves around relationships. Conferences, displays, literature, advertisements, and direct mail are helpful tools to inform and interest prospective candidates, but most missionaries join the global force through personal contacts.

Every leader, especially those already engaged in missions ministries, must engage in recruiting others. Among the friendships already established, a wise leader is on the lookout for men and women who demonstrate the qualities needed to be productive missionaries. A simple comment at the appropriate moment can open the door for a likely missionary candidate. "I have noticed how adaptable and effective you are in your ministry. I think you would make a good missionary. Have you ever explored this possibility?"

If a prospective candidate shows even the smallest spark of interest in missionary service, we should do all we can to help them explore this option. Most mission agencies have a simple preliminary questionnaire that provides basic information on a prospective candidate. This helps the mission agency get to know the person and gives an opportunity to maintain contact. The preliminary questionnaire also provides an initial screening that will eliminate unrealistic pursuits.

Ultimately the Lord is the One who sends out missionaries. Yet it behooves every church leader, school teacher, college professor, and career missionary to engage in missions recruitment for the glory of God and the advance of His work around the world.

Christian parents have tended to be the greatest obstacle to missionary recruitment. Most parents tend to encourage their children to pursue professions and positions that are financially secure and highly respected. They coach their children to avoid a career in ministry, especially missionary service. Often this is an unconscious endeavor, but it often results in young men and women turning from the idea of serving the Lord in missions outreach.

Parents can be challenged to give their children into God's hands for missionary service. Everyone needs to acknowledge this important calling for service and to support those who sense God's direction toward this goal for their lives. A commitment service for parents and members may be helpful in many churches. Young men and women are much more prone to respond to God's leading if they sense this kind of encouragement and support.

The task of every leader in God's work is to produce productive followers of Jesus Christ. As Paul admonished Timothy, "And the things you have heard me say in the presence of many witnesses entrust to reliable men who will also be qualified to teach others" (2 Tim. 2:2).

Missionary recruitment must be a high priority for every one in the ministry. It must be a goal for every believer to identify and encourage those who will serve as God's ambassadors to other peoples and nations.

In recent years I have devoted my attention to qualified people without trying to present to them a specific place for them to use their training and talents on the mission field. I have found that it is far more effective to explore with a person open to the Lord's leading a possible place of service designed by God. In other words, I no longer present a list of "job descriptions" to prospective candidates. I prefer to learn about their interests, gifts, talents, experience, and training. With this approach I always respond with an immediate "yes" when someone asks, "Could God use me in missions?" I may not know exactly where this individual might best serve or the details of what he or she might do, but I am confident, if God is leading, that He will help us find the place and assignment within His perfect plan. We can engage in this pursuit with the assurance that God will answer our prayers and accomplish His will.

This is an unprecedented day of opportunity for vibrant new missionaries to spread out around the globe and touch those of every language and culture with the good news of our Savior. Thousands and thousands of young men and women are needed to reach the billions who need the Lord.

MISSION AGENCIES

Unfortunately some mission agencies have become distant from local churches. They recruit personnel, fund their activities, and direct their ministries with little or no contact with the churches from which their missionaries have come and from which funds have been donated. No wonder an irritated pastor once complained, "If this mission agency is an arm of the church, it is certainly disconnected from the body."

When I was president of CAM International, I worked hard at keeping a close tie with sending churches. We even installed a vice president of mobilization, who is responsible for this link with pastors and churches that partner with us in reaching the Spanish-speaking areas of the world and beyond. One of the major objectives of CAM International is "to enable the outreach of North American churches through strategic partnerships." We view our mission agency as an arm of churches in North America. Also CAM is closely linked with thousands of churches that have been planted and nurtured by our missionaries in Central America, Panama, Mexico, Spain, and the Hispanic USA. These churches in turn are becoming increasingly engaged in missions outreach. Many of these receiving churches are now sending churches.

A number of churches in North America are turning their backs on mission agencies, thinking they can "run" their own missions outreach. This is especially evident among megachurches. Rather than sending missionaries as such, many of these churches organize teams from the members of their congregation and hold workshops and seminars in other countries to "train the nationals" to replicate what they have done in the United States or Canada. They introduce people overseas to their megachurch concepts: contemporary music, new worship styles, the use of drama, and a "seeker-friendly" approach. The budget for this type of "missions outreach" is consumed in airline tickets and hotel bills for the church members and staff who make the trip overseas. The budget may also include a gift of written materials (often in English) that outline the program they are trying to reproduce on foreign soil, a program that was born in the United States.

Rather than "transplanting" their product, megachurch leaders would do well to ask, "How did our church begin? What factors helped this movement mature into the dynamic and influential church it is today? What was done to understand and meet the needs of the community in which the church has prospered?" Then they should help churches overseas find answers to these and similar questions in their own situations.

North American churches need help in the missionary task around the world. No church can be sufficiently acquainted with the many cultures overseas to direct effectively those who serve as resident missionaries around the globe. This work must be outsourced to reputable mission agencies that are equipped to fulfill this task.

As exciting as church teams may be, resident missionaries are needed to build local churches in other cultures and to leave a witness that will endure. Mission agencies are able to give guidance to each new missionary, help them adapt to the new culture and language-learning, provide key contacts with evangelical leaders in the target country, and provide adequate supervision and direction in the anticipated place of ministry.

Usually missions agency leaders are veteran missionaries. So because of their experience they can give the type of guidance every new missionary needs in order to be productive and spiritually effective.

Church leaders and mission leaders need to bond together in this gigantic task of world outreach. Pastors and other church leaders need to recognize their limitations and seek the help of reputable missions agencies. And those who lead in missions agencies need to show rightful dependence on and to express deep gratitude to church leaders and congregations for the essential role they play in missions. This is a divinely ordained partnership to accomplish God's purpose.

Constant communication between the supporting church, missionary, and mission agency is key. Through e-mail, phone calls, and correspondence the partnership can remain vibrant and effective. Consultations are essential in a missionary's placement or change of ministry or field. Church leaders who wisely outsource the work of mission direction to a reputable agency are not abrogating their interest or responsibility for the missionary they have sent out and faithfully support. They want to feel a vital part of the ongoing care and guidance of the one who represents them abroad.

At the same time the missionary must not feel frustrated by multiple directors and micromanagement from every church leader who has a part in his or her support. Church leaders need to demonstrate confidence and trust in their missionaries and the mission agencies.

SHORT–TERM MISSIONS TEAMS

Short-term opportunities abound today. A builder in St. Louis can take two weeks off from his job, hop a plane to Costa Rica, and in hours be mixing cement in the construction of a new evangelical camp property there. A pastor in Seattle can utilize a week to minister through translators at a growing church in Mexico City. A seminary professor may use his sabbatical year to serve on the faculty of a Bible institute in Hungary.

This is a new wave in missions. Never before have so many people been directly involved in missions outreach. The experience can be as brief as one week and as extensive as two full years.

The trend in short-term missions is toward a decreased time commitment. More and more people want to be involved for fewer and fewer days. Many people may disagree, but I feel that anything less than two weeks should be considered a field visit. Ministry or work might be accomplished in this brief span of time, but it is hardly a missions "term." Those who serve beyond two years should be considered career missionaries.

Gone are the days when every person is expected to fit one standard career missionary status. Special-service personnel, associate missionaries, special-assignment missionaries, and short-term missionaries join the ranks of the core force of career missionaries. A complex, diversified world requires more flexibility in mission structure.

The growth of short-term missions is astronomical. There appears to be greater demand for opportunities for short-term exposure than there is supply of adequate destinations. Career missionaries could easily drop the work to which they feel God has led them in their place of service and dedicate all their time to provide liaison for short-term teams. In some cases this is literally what has happened. An increasing number of missions agencies focus exclusively on short-term opportunities.

Short-term missions is a vibrant, growing force that must be channeled for maximum benefit to the cause of Christ around the world. We can thank the Lord for what He is doing through this growing movement.

Motivation. Why are short-term missions so popular? There are many altruistic motivations: the desire to become involved in God's Great Commission; to help those in need; to utilize talents and experience to help others; to invest time, energy, and resources in world missions for God's glory.

Other motivations, not readily voiced, are still real: to visit other parts of the world, to engage in something adventurous, to take advantage of financial assistance for overseas travel, to fulfill a sense of responsibility for greater involvement in missions, to have fun with friends on an exciting trip abroad.

Everything that is done in missions needs to be evaluated by biblically ordained goals. Missions exists to bring people to Christ and help them grow and multiply. Because these goals are within His perfect plan, they bring glory to God.

Often a short-term mission is evaluated on the basis of what is gained by participants rather than what is achieved to increase the number of believers and advance God's work in the country visited. It is natural for pastors and church leaders to focus primarily on those under their care, but these very leaders will have to exchange these "natural" inclinations for a "supernatural" viewpoint. What seems spiritual may actually be suspiciously carnal.

For short-term missions to be a success from God's perspective, one's motives must be in line with His motives. From the outset, plans for a short-term project should be carefully evaluated with honest, forthright answers to the question "Why?" and see if the reasons are thoroughly biblical. Short-term outreach is a wonderful, dynamic movement that can be used of God to change the world. We must do everything in our power to encourage continued advance in accord with His Word and His will.

Selection. Rather than plead for large numbers to participate in short-term missions, leaders should carefully select those who may best contribute to well-established goals for the proposed trip.

To provide maximum benefit it may be best to recruit from the mature leaders of the church. The senior pastor, church elders, and other recognized leaders are probably those who have the most to offer on a short-term ministry and who have the best opportunity to convey vision to the rest of the congregation.

Obviously there are benefits for all ages from participation in a short-term exposure, but the benefits often diminish in direct proportion to the youth of those who participate. College students are generally more equipped to contribute to short-term trips and better able to benefit from them than high-school students, and high-school students are normally preferred over junior high.

Whatever the short-term trip, it is beneficial to develop a screening process and make careful selections of those who desire to participate.

Training. Every person who engages in short-term opportunities should receive thorough orientation. A church- or school-sponsored short-term trip should include adequate training classes that will include a practical introduction to the destination culture, basic language training for common phrases, effective evangelism and discipleship techniques, and other vital matters to be mastered before departure.

To qualify for participation on the short-term team each member should be given a list of books and articles to read as part of the preparation. Some instruction and supervision on communicating the team plans and recruiting prayer and financial support can be included, with specific practical assignments in which this training is implemented.

Increasing the requirements for short-term participants will increase the quality of those who serve and the effectiveness of the team. Work teams need similar orientation and training to be most effective. They require more briefing on the construction project as well as ways in which they can be effective witnesses to those with whom they have contact in the host country

Deployment. To make the most of short-term teams a special commissioning service is of great value. Those who pray and give for each member of a short-term ministry or work team need to feel a close tie with those who are going. From the outset every missions endeavor must be seen as a partnership that involves the entire church or school body.

A special send-off at the airport or other departure site by those who can participate, including family members, friends, and supporters, is an added touch that can be very encouraging.

Involvement. The ultimate purpose of short-term endeavor is to make an impact for Christ in the place of service. Leaders and team members must be committed to this high calling. Every person should fulfill his or her duties with a cheerful spirit and servant attitude. The on-site liaison, missionary, or national, ought to be treated with respect and ready obedience; and contacts with nationals should be cordial and uplifting. This interchange with the nationals can be the most rewarding experience in a short-term exposure.

Communication. It is often helpful to have one member of the short-term team assigned to serve as a special reporter. If there is an e-mail connection, fairly frequent, concise, and dynamic reports can be forwarded to those who would like to keep informed. Someone in the sponsoring church or school needs to be designated as liaison to glean from the reports a few selected items to convey to the church congregation or student body.

Debriefing. Short-term experience never ends with the return trip home. Some of the greatest benefits come after the work or ministry teams have completed their assignment.

Plan a welcoming party to meet the short-term team on their arrival back home. Balloons, flowers, signs, and even a pep band can make this a joyous and meaningful occasion. News media may cover this type of human-interest story if the local television or radio station is notified well ahead of time.

Within a week or two after the team returns, all the members need to meet together for a debriefing session to review the highlights and successes of the trip and to note suggestions for improving future short-term opportunities. Soon after the team returns, schedule a service with personal testimonies and visuals of the team at work in the target country. This can be a great blessing to all who attend this service.

Advancement. An opportune time to identify and recruit future short–term leaders and possible career missionary personnel is shortly after an effective short-term trip. Leaders of each short-term team, with the input of missionaries and nationals at the site in which the team serves, should be constantly evaluating each team member. It is wise to set a goal of three to five most likely candidates to advance in their role from team participant to team leader or career missionary.

The multiplication factor for the cause of continued missions outreach must be one of the primary goals of every short-term endeavor. By multiplying the number of leaders and career workers, the work of God is advanced in accord with the biblical mandate to "make disciples" (Matt. 28:19).

"ADOPTING" MISSIONARIES

I was somewhat disturbed. The missions conference for which I was keynote speaker seemed to be centered almost exclusively on money. A large thermometer designed to mark the progress of financial gifts to the missions budget goal was the most visible item on the church auditorium platform.

Every aspect of the service seemed to be directed toward meeting the missionary offering goal. At one point I wondered if the church leaders were going to lock the doors and keep passing the offering plates until the financial goal was met. The pressure to give was palpable and it continued through the week I was there.

On Tuesday I attended the women's luncheon. I was not the speaker for this event. I sat there munching on a stick of stuffed celery, not too happy with the whole money-centered conference.

Suddenly, I got an inspiration. "Why do we continually talk about 'supporting' missionaries?" I mused. " "Missions is not driven by money," I thought to myself. "Missions is people sending people to reach people."

"How can we shift our thinking from money to people?" I continued to ponder. "I have it! Let's shift the focus from 'supporting' missions to 'adopting' missionaries."

Fresh ideas began to tumble across my mind. I grabbed a napkin and started jotting down my thoughts on this new approach to link church members with missionaries sent out to reach people who need the Lord in other parts of the world.

By the end of the women's luncheon, I had a fivefold adoption plan that I felt could revolutionize missions outreach. This plan gives every Christian a practical way to get involved in world missions. No one need be a bystander. Everyone can participate in a way that brings personal satisfaction and eternal rewards.

The idea begins with selecting a missionary or missionary family for "adoption." Similarities can help in the selection. For example, a young married couple with three small children might best relate to a missionary family with small children. A working single person would be wise to find a single missionary of approximately the same age. An elderly couple with numerous grandchildren should find a missionary couple who is rejoicing in their grandchildren. In other words, each person or family could adopt a missionary with whom they can best identify.

Here are the five steps in this adoption plan.

Daily—pray. Probably all of us are challenged from time to time to pray often for as many missionaries as possible. This is commendable. But in addition to this admirable goal, special focus can be given to one adopted missionary or missionary family. Put their photograph or prayer card in a place where you see it each day, and pray for them as you would for any other family member. In fact, you can use a "P.S." method of prayer. As you pray for God to meet your specific daily needs, just add a "P.S." for the needs of your adopted missionary. They are undoubtedly facing each day the very challenges that you face.

Weekly—give. Yes, missionaries need financial help. Rather than give out of a sense of duty or external pressure from those who plead for your help, you can now give with the joyful sense that through your weekly contribution in worship to God you are keeping your adopted missionary on the field. It gives a new spirit to your giving by personalizing the purpose of your gift. One of the great delights is to see how God takes what may seem to be a modest offering and multiplies it to achieve His purposes around the world. Missions giving is truly a joyous experience.

Monthly—write a letter. I know what you are thinking. You are probably saying to yourself, "Write a missionary? I don't even write my own mother." However, this need not be a painful experience. If you and your adopted missionary have access to e-mail, you can easily keep in touch with brief notes by a simple click of the "reply" button.

Even if you don't have a personal computer, you can easily write a letter by use of "snail-mail" aerograms available from the post office. These clever devices provide ample space to write a brief note, and with two simple folds they are ready to be sealed and sent on their way. They are already stamped, and for the price of a coke they go anywhere in the world. It is a great bargain when you consider what it achieves.

You can hardly imagine the joy it is for missionaries to receive mail from interested friends. Your letter need not be long. Just a quick note will do.

Missionaries who are isolated in distant lands will cherish simple, brief notes from you. This kind of communication is very encouraging to missionaries.

Quarterly—send a care package. Every three months slip a few special items into a large envelope or box and ship them to your adopted missionary. Find out the things that may be unavailable where the missionary lives. For example, when we lived in Spain we couldn't purchase marshmallows or dry yeast. My wife, Libby, liked to bake, but without dry yeast it was not convenient. She would have to obtain some yeast from a nearby baker. And while we could live without marshmallows, occasionally we missed this special touch in a cup of hot chocolate. Some of our friends learned of these unavailable items and took action. They sent us a large mailing envelope with marshmallows and packets of dry yeast. You can imagine our delight to receive these priceless items.

Check customs regulations before shipping your care package. Sometimes the authorities will assess a large fine or customs charges for incoming packages. I have discovered, however, that custom charges can be avoided in most parts of the world by attaching a green sticker on your package indicating that the contents are "samples with no resale value." These green stickers are available at any post office.

Missionary children are thrilled to receive age-graded books. This is a good way to get your children involved. They might even be willing to share with their adopted missionary children some favorite books that no longer have the same attraction they once did. Or they can participate in shopping for appropriate volumes for the missionary children. Your care package each quarter is like a modified Christmas four times a year. It brings you and your family great joy and gives even greater joy to your adopted missionary family.

Annually—send birthday and anniversary cards. Just as you celebrate special days in your family, you will want to recognize birthdays and anniversary dates of your adopted family.

Birthday cards and anniversary cards bring special joy to each recipient. There is something personal about a greeting on these important days of celebration. Be sure to include a little handwritten note. Another item we found unavailable when we lived overseas was birthday and anniversary cards in English. So I suggest you sign the card lightly in pencil rather than in ink, or enclose a little note. On your note write, "You can recycle this card it you want to." Sure enough, you might well get it back for your birthday!

Missions, as I have said, may best be thought of as "people sending people to reach people." The more we are personally involved in the missionary-sending process, the more effective missions will be. Think of how greatly encouraged and motivated our missionaries would be if every one of them was adopted by a Christian family who engaged in this fivefold plan!

MOMENTS OF CRISIS—MISSIONS PASTORAL CARE

It was a horrible automobile accident. In fact, some wondered whether Tom would live. I was deeply moved when Tom's home church in Dallas sent their senior pastor to Europe to provide pastoral care for the injured missionary.

Missionaries are not exempt from crises. In fact, those who serve overseas are generally more subject to severe trials. Furthermore, since missionaries are often the spiritual leaders of emerging congregations of new believers, the missionaries are essentially without a pastor. Mission agency field leaders do their best to fill this important role, but they are generally stretched in their assignment with more personnel than they can adequately oversee on an intimate pastoral level.

One of the great services the sending church can perform is that of pastoral care. The lines of communication should be of such a nature that leaders in the home church are aware when there is need for spiritual counsel and encouragement. Much can be done by e-mail, fax, and phone calls, but at times a personal visit may be needed to give in-depth spiritual assistance and advice.

Missionaries have indicated that lack of adequate pastoral care is one of the major causes of missionary failure.[1] Mission agencies are doing what they can to be sure that sufficient care is provided for every member. Perhaps too much responsibility in this area is being assigned to mission board leaders. Mission agencies do their best to give pastoral care for their field personnel, but the sending church can have a significant ministry in this area.

When missionaries are facing a crisis, they take comfort in the fact that in addition to receiving care from mission administrators and field leaders, they can also look to their pastor back home for the assurance and care of a loving congregation and a caring pastor.

For this reason every missionary should have strong ties with a home church. It is not enough to be supported by a number of local congregations. One of those churches should be claimed as a "home church." If the tie is strong to this home church, in times of crisis the missionary will undoubtedly be the beneficiary of loving pastoral care.

PART SIX

~~~~~~~~~~

The Front Line—Strategies for the Missionary Force

WITHOUT "SENDERS" THERE ARE NO "GOERS." The key to missions outreach is the body of believers who believe in the Great Commission of the Lord Jesus Christ to the point that they are willing to stand behind those whom God has chosen to be His representatives around the world as missionaries. A "missionary" is a "sent one."

The word *mission* comes from the Latin verb *mittō*, "to send." The Greek verb rendered "to send" is *apostellō*, from which we get the word *apostle*. In one sense the missionary is an "apostle," one who is sent out to serve as Christ's ambassador.

The missionary force is the body of God's servants who are serving on the front lines. These colleagues are choice people. Many of them have left everything most people hold dear to fulfill a cross-cultural assignment.

I salute these missionaries and rejoice in the way God is using them. I consider it a privilege to have served in these ranks. This section of the book offers advice and suggestions for those who are contemplating missionary service or already engaged in this special assignment, as well as counsel for those who send them.

CHAPTER NINETEEN

A Settled Conviction—Responding to the "Call"

O FTEN A STUDENT at Dallas Seminary would confide in me after class. "Prof, I would be more than willing to serve as a missionary, but I haven't been called."

I always responded to this comment with a leading question, "What do you mean when you say you haven't been called?"

"Well, you know, I just haven't received God's call for missionary service."

"But what do you mean by 'call'?" I persisted.

"Prof, I'm not sure. But whatever it is, I have not been called," the student insisted.

Sensing that the student might be thinking this way as a means of avoiding missionary service, I would often reply, "I'm not sure you need a 'call.' You may need a 'kick in the pants.'"

This rather forceful confrontation generally served as a helpful admonition to those who simply wanted to dismiss any consideration of missionary service.

GOD'S "CALL" AND MISSIONS

Many people talk about God's calling without actually determining the biblical meaning of this term. The Greek word *kaleō*, "to call," in its various forms appears almost three hundred times in the New Testament. Most of these biblical references focus on a calling to relationships and standards in a Christian's life. God calls all Christians "saints" (Rom. 1:7; 1 Tim. 6:12) and He calls each one to be like Christ (Rom. 8:29–30). And all believers are called to the following:

- peace (1 Cor. 7:15)
- grace (Gal. 1:6)
- liberty (5:13)
- hope (Eph. 4:4)
- glory (1 Thess. 2:12)
- holiness (1 Pet. 1:15)
- light (2:9)
- suffering (2:21)
- blessing (3:9).

However, of the many uses of the word *call* in the New Testament, only two refer directly to missionary activity, and both are found in the Book of Acts.

When the leaders of the church in Antioch met together to worship the Lord, the Holy Spirit said, "Set apart for me Barnabas and Saul for the work to which I have called them" (Acts 13:2). Only five men are listed in this passage: Barnabas, Simeon called Niger, Lucius of Cyrene, Manaen (who had been brought up with Herod the tetrarch), and Saul.

In this international, multiracial meeting of a handful of men God worked to select two who became the first missionaries sent from the church at Antioch. These two, Barnabas and Saul, were called by the Holy Spirit, presumably a unique calling.

The second passage that uses the word *call* in reference to missionary service is in Acts 16. When Barnabas and Paul determined to go their separate ways, Barnabas took his nephew Mark and sailed for Cyprus. Paul chose Silas and headed back across what is known today as Turkey. The Paul-and-Silas team was strengthened by the addition of Timothy, and they moved northeast to spread the good news to this spiritually needy area of the world.

Strangely enough, this missionary team was "kept by the Holy Spirit from preaching the word in the province of Asia," in present-day western Turkey (16:6). Moving all the way to the border of Mysia, they tried to enter Bithynia, a part of Asia Minor to the northwest, "but the Spirit of

Jesus would not allow them to" (16:7). Then they moved on to the coastal city of Troas, and in the night Paul had a vision of a man who said, "Come over to Macedonia and help us" (16:9).

Luke wrote that after Paul had seen the vision, "we got ready at once to leave for Macedonia, concluding that God had called us to preach the gospel to them" (16:10). This "calling" was communicated through a vision in the night. This call was not to missionary service, but was one of direction given to a missionary team that was already on the move.

MISSIONARY "CALL" OR "SETTLED CONVICTION"?

These two biblical uses of the word *call* in relation to missions are unique. One involves a voice, that of the Holy Spirit, and the other a vision. Neither of these passages seems to convey the modern use of the word *call* in reference to missionary service. People who advocate a missionary call do not insist on God's voiced command or some heavenly vision.

Could it be, then, that the modern use of the word *call* refers to God's guidance rather than some mysterious voice or vision? It seems to me that those who speak of God's call are more likely talking about a deep, settled conviction of God's guidance. To say, "I have been called to serve as a missionary," probably means "I have come to the conviction that God wants me to serve as a missionary."

This is not to contend that God does not call or invite His children to give their time, talents, and lives in missionary service. But to be thoroughly biblical, it might be better to reserve the word *call* for relationships and standards to which the Bible refers when the word *call* appears in God's Word.

It is imperative that Christians sense God's direction in a decision as momentous as missionary service. All missionaries need a deep, settled conviction that they are engaged in world outreach through God's clear guidance. Many factors will contribute to this conviction. God can use circumstances, one's spiritual gifts, the counsel of others, personal interests, the persuasion of the Holy Spirit, persistent prayer, the Word of God, and other means to bring a prospective missionary to the place of confidence that he or she is moving in accord with His perfect plan.

So a deep, settled conviction is probably more biblical and therefore more appropriate than the word *call* in relation to missionary service. While God could give an audible *call* or somehow communicate His directions to those who serve in missions, it is more likely that He graciously guides His ambassadors to a place of confidence that He wants them to serve Him in world outreach.

CHAPTER TWENTY

A Perfect Wedding—Choosing a Mission Agency

WHEN ONE OF GOD'S CHILDREN senses the inner conviction that He is directing him or her to missionary service, the question immediately arises, "Now what do I do?"

While it is not mandatory for a missionary to be a part of a mission agency, it is certainly advisable. To serve on the mission field without any direction or accountability usually results in ineffective service and may end in defeat. Many reputable mission agencies are available to give training and direction in the challenging task of world outreach.

Choosing a mission agency with which to serve is not unlike choosing a spouse. The commitment to an agency is not the lifetime commitment required in a biblical marriage, but there are serious consequences if the choice is not done with utmost care. Several factors need to be considered in finding a mission agency that is a workable match.

GEOGRAPHY

With the Lord's guidance to missionary service He often impresses a certain part of the world or people group on a prospective missionary. This may be the first factor to consider when looking for an appropriate mission agency. If God has given a "deep, settled conviction" that He wants you to serve Him in Africa, you will not want to serve with an agency that works exclusively in Latin America.

However, if there is no clear guidance from God to a place of service, this factor need not be considered. Often the place of service becomes clear through consultation with the mission agency. As someone has wisely said, "It is more important to play on the right team than be preoccupied with the stadium in which the game will be played." The team and game plan are far more important than the field. If you find the right team, the owner and coach will make sure your talents are used in a way that will ensure maximum potential for your personal fulfillment and a "winning season."

DOCTRINE

One of the most important considerations for a Bible-believing Christian's choice of a mission agency is doctrine. Without unity in what missionaries believe, the team will exhaust its energy with inner battles rather than reach the lost and build up new believers.

For example, a missionary who does not "speak in tongues" will be very frustrated in a charismatic mission. One who is convinced that the Bible speaks clearly about future events in God's calendar will find difficulty working in an agency that ignores biblical prophecy or takes an entirely different view of prophetic Scripture.

It is wise to determine how inclusive or ecumenical the mission agency might be. A missionary who finds it difficult to relate to others who do not adhere to a clearly defined doctrinal position will struggle in a mission that pays little attention to the doctrinal perspective of those with whom they work.

Every prospective missionary needs to review the mission agency's doctrinal statement. Most doctrinal statements sound good at first reading, but lack of definition in areas that seem important may be "red flags" in the selection process. It might be helpful to start with a list of beliefs you consider essential and compare this list with the mission agency's doctrinal statement. Take special note of those areas the mission does not cover. If not properly addressed, those areas of silence may result in difficulties.

Harmony between the missionary candidate's belief system and the doctrinal position of the mission agency will help make his ministry more effective and enduring. Disunity in this basic area will often spell defeat and pending division. Unless people hold common beliefs, it is difficult, if not impossible, to achieve common goals.

REQUIREMENTS

Reputable mission agencies have clearly defined requirements for those who seek membership. This is an essential factor in considering membership with a mission agency.

For example, agencies generally indicate Bible-training requirements. More and more agencies now recognize Bible training acquired outside academic institutions or make provision for further acquisition of needed Bible training after the candidate becomes a member. Nonetheless this and other basic requirements can help give guidance on whether the agency being considered is the one of God's choosing.

If you are woefully deficient in requirements listed by the mission agency, it might be advisable to consider another agency. At least make this a point of inquiry when considering an agency.

PERSONNEL

One of the best ways to get to know a mission agency is to get to know its people. Get acquainted with missionaries serving with the agency being considered. A short-term opportunity to live with a missionary family and work with them on the field is ideal.

A mission agency is best reflected in the personnel who serve in the agency. Exposure to those in the mission headquarters is helpful, but it will not give a full picture if you limit your acquaintances to those who are mission leaders. Interacting with field missionaries gives a more realistic picture.

In any agency there is a wide spectrum of personalities and talents. An agency must never be judged by limited contact with one or two members. To judge a mission on the basis of one missionary would be as erroneous as judging an entire church by one member. Make it your goal to get acquainted with as many individuals serving with the agency as possible. Time spent getting acquainted with members in all areas of the mission agency is time well spent.

VISION

Take a close look at the mission vision. Is the agency advancing, is it in a maintenance mode, or is it retreating? Do the vision, mission purpose, and goals of the mission agency excite you? Do you share a passion that might contribute to the corporate mission agency goals?

If a mission agency is moving in a direction that is not in some way linked to your passion, you may need to consider some other alignment. For example, a candidate anxious to utilize radio expertise and training needs to focus on an agency in which this is a live option. A pilot will be grounded in a mission agency that does not have a plane or any desire to obtain one.

God uses many talents to achieve His purposes. Reputable mission agencies recognize this and are open to form teams that will advance stated goals and objectives. Ultimately evangelism, discipleship, and church planting will be achieved if every member of the team contributes his or her talents and experience to these central tasks.

The direction in which the mission agency is headed needs to be in line with the direction you feel led to invest your time and energy. It is only wise to board a train that is heading in the direction of your destination—unless, of course, God issues a new ticket written to a new destination.

PLACEMENT

Find out how the agency places each missionary. Ideally the missionary, field director, and mission leaders work together on this important assignment. It can be most frustrating to be ordered to serve in a country and fulfill a ministry without any opportunity to discuss the options. A directive or dictatorial leadership style can be extremely difficult for a missionary.

If you want to be part of this decision, be sure to join a mission in which you are given the opportunity to discuss options together with your leaders and to determine God's plan together.

A change in assignment, except for some temporary unexpected emergency, must involve the same joint consultation. Some agencies are finding it beneficial to involve supporting churches and donors in some way when a change in assignment for a missionary is contemplated. Even though they might not insist on having a voice in the change, they want to be informed and to have opportunity to pray for decisions of this magnitude. Often church leaders and donors are simply advised of changes after the decision has already been made.

Reputable mission agencies work diligently to sustain effective teamwork. Joint prayer and consultation are a part of every major decision. It would not be wise to join an agency in which this spirit is not evident unless you are a person who enjoys working under a strong leader who makes decisions for you.

REPUTATION

Does the mission agency maintain good relationships with supporting churches, donors, and other mission agencies and missionaries? What do others say about this mission agency?

Donors and supporting churches are usually reliable references. They have a good sense of accuracy and accountability through mission agency receipting and correspondence. Reliable mission agencies receipt every gift accurately and promptly, thereby assuring donors that their gifts will be used for the person and project so designated.

It is equally enlightening to hear what personnel with *other* mission agencies, especially missionaries who work in the same areas of the world, say about the agency being considered. If these colleagues give positive commendation on a mission agency of which they are not members, you can be sure it is worthy of consideration. If they indicate reservations or give negative response, pursue the inquiry to discover specific concerns and evaluate them with care.

"Public relations" is not just some science in which secular companies are engaged. Relationships are of utmost importance in God's work.

References outside the fold of the mission agency being considered can often be some of the most reliable sources in evaluation. Positive marks in this area will give added confidence in the pursuit of a quality mission agency.

ADVANCEMENT

In the mission agency being considered, what is the policy on personal development? Do they encourage advanced studies on home assignment? Do they value educational and professional development pursuits?

One of the greatest investments any organization can make is in its people. If the agency does not see the value of personal progress and enhancement in ministry skills, then membership with that agency ought not to be pursued.

If a mission agency shows no flexibility in extended home assignments to complete a program in higher education, it is clear evidence that this is not a very high value. To obtain advanced degrees will often require two or three years instead of the traditional one-year "furlough" now usually called "home assignment." Inquire about this policy, and see how it has been employed in recent years.

Of equal or greater importance is the policy on missionary children's education. If the agency insists that your children be sent to one of its boarding schools, you may want to move with caution. Ideally a mission agency will grant the parents the option they feel most appropriate for each child. Quality "MK" (Missionary Kid) schools are but one viable option. It may be more helpful to home school, enroll the child in a national school, utilize a secular private school, or consider a nearby American or other similar school.

Ultimately the parents are responsible for the welfare of their children and must be given the authority to act accordingly. I would hesitate to join an organization that offered no flexibility in this important area.

FLEXIBILITY

In this area of personal advancement and children's education the real issue is flexibility. Is the mission agency rigid in its approach, or do you sense a more open spirit to pursue paths that may seem different but are readily agreed to be much better?

In an age of immense diversity mission agencies and their leaders must be open to new ideas and be willing to explore a variety of options. Rules should not be viewed as "the laws of the Medes and Persians"; instead, they should be considered guiding principles.

It is always helpful to utilize the question "Why?" when applying rules to any specific situation. The underlying reason behind each rule is of greater importance. There may be other ways to comply with these basic principles than blind compliance to some rule.

Flexible agencies seeking to advance God's work around the world should be the ones of greatest attraction to a prospective candidate. A changing world requires flexibility and adaptability. Wise missionary prospects look for a mission agency with these vital qualities that point to vibrant life and continued progress.

PRAYER

Ultimately all the advice and exploration in the world cannot match the direction God can give to His children. It could be devastating to follow the seven areas of concern and inquiry I have suggested and not consult constantly with the only One who can see the whole picture and knows exactly where you should serve and what you should do in His service.

Constant prayer is essential. Your prayers and those of every friend and relative you can enlist will help guide your choice of a mission agency. Choosing a mission agency is no small task. The mission family with which one serves is of utmost importance. It can make the difference between a rewarding, productive experience in ministry or one filled with frustration and conflict.

Chapter Twenty-One

A Solid Foundation—Enlisting a Support Team

For over a year it seemed that nothing was happening. The big sign announced bold revolutionary plans for a new luxury hotel in the heart of Dallas, Texas, an impressive structure that would tower above the city skyline.

A board fence surrounded the entire city block and the only movement seemed to be a multitude of trucks and workers. Not one sign of a new building was in view. However, workers were driving pilings deep into solid bedrock. This took about a year. The glittering hotel that stands tall today could not have been built without a firm foundation.

Every missionary faces a similar assignment. People and church congregations who provide faithful support are the bedrock of mission ministries. No worker in world missions can launch his or her ministry without this essential foundation. With an increased focus on short-term missions and independent church-directed activities, career missionaries are faced with a greater challenge to engage supporters in their service to the Lord.

This task can become much more effective with a change in perspective. Rather than see the assignment as "fund raising," it should be seen as "friend raising."

A detailed guide to this endeavor has been written by William Dillon in a book entitled *People Raising.*[1] Valuable, workable principles outlined in this popular volume are now available in a vibrant video presentation

197

that will instruct and encourage those who have the responsibility to build a support foundation for ministry.

The following pointers can be helpful in establishing a mission support base.

LIST FRIENDS

Explore bedrock that is already on the property where you intend to build. Spend extended time listing every friend, work colleague, church member, neighbor, and relative you can recall. No doubt you already enjoy relationships with hundreds of people that you have built throughout your life. This circle of friends is the place to start.

Include everyone in this list. Do not exclude distant friends, estranged relatives, or unsaved business colleagues. Every person with whom you have had contact, even for limited periods of time, may become part of the foundation. God is the master Builder. Unsaved friends will often be touched by your example of commitment to God's work. They may join your support team and some of them may become believers as a result of their contact with you.

Prepare an electronic computer file or three-by-five card file on every person in the list. Include as much information as you can on each individual. Include correctly spelled first names of husband and wife for each couple, children's names, names of house pets, addresses, both home and work numbers, e-mail addresses, and other helpful details you can recall or discover. This reference file is an initial and essential foundation. Those with whom friendships have already been established are sometimes sufficient to complete the entire support base to move out in the assignment to which God has called you. This is the place to start.

CONTACT FRIENDS

From your prepared list of friends select ten to twenty whom you feel will be most receptive to your decision to serve the Lord in missions. Try to include at least one from each category of friendships. Start with immediate family members. Add your closest friends at church. Include at least one of your closest business associates or colleagues at work. Then consider a neighbor or two with whom you have had closest contact.

Contact these friends by phone and ask if you might get together with them, one at a time, at a time convenient to them. Suggest a date and time and, if this is not possible, offer another specific alternative. Keep working until you are able to settle on an appropriate date, time, and place. If possible, arrange to meet at a friendly, nonthreatening location like a restaurant for a cup of coffee.

This is a time to hear more about what is happening in your friend's life. Try to learn everything you can. At an opportune moment, explain to this trusted friend how God is working in your life and the ministry to which you are committed. Without apology, explain how missionary support operates and your need to form a support team so that you can fulfill this ministry. Be attentive to any questions your friend may have, and do your best to answer them as honestly and frankly as you can.

Some feel comfortable asking a friend what part he or she might be able to consider in needed support. Others prefer giving their friend a packet of literature and a faith-promise card and asking that they prayerfully consider helping with support. Still others prefer to follow up this initial visit with a phone call and mailed material to encourage their participation in this mission assignment.

While it is biblically incorrect to promote giving under compulsion or pressure, the Bible says nothing against making giving convenient. No candidate should feel ill at ease asking for prayer and financial support. That's because the support given is not for personal benefit. It is for God's work. You are simply asking your friend to take a step of faith similar to the one you have already taken to fulfill the Lord's work. You are giving your talent, time, and life. Your friends are often pleased to have a part in this ministry through faithful prayer and financial assistance.

By starting with those who may be the most responsive, it should become very apparent that this is not an unpleasant or distasteful experience. Getting together with friends should be a delight. Hopefully, out of the initial ten to twenty appointments you make you will see some positive results. This should serve as a great boost to continue further personal contacts with as many friends on your list as possible.

Many missionary candidates seem to depend too heavily on mailed prayer letters. These can be helpful communication tools, but they are especially weak in developing a support team. They are too indirect and impersonal to provide a warm, encouraging encounter with people who know you and appreciate you.

A missionary appointee must take the initiative to make personal contacts as suggested above. This is absolutely essential to the foundation-building process. Set a goal of sitting down with at least five of these individuals each week.

In the unlikely case that one of those listed as the most responsive says bluntly that he or she does not want to meet with you, even though you have offered several optional times and dates, don't insist on a meeting. If this person is a true friend, however, he or she should remain on your list for future contact.

Once the initial list of high potential friends has been contacted personally, and hopefully many have responded with an initial desire to help your ministry in prayer and finances, take another segment of the list and continue until every person on your list has been contacted.

For those who are not in the local area, there are two options. One option is to call each one in the same way you did those in your area. Tell him or her how much you wish that you might get together. Arrange for a time when you might chat by phone at greater length to catch up on news and to share details about your mission outreach. In other words arrange for a meeting by phone much like your encounter with friends locally over a cup of coffee.

A second option is to plan a trip to connect with as many of your friends as possible and to arrange the same type of fellowship you had with friends in your local area. Some see this as impossible, but this is exactly what my wife, Libby, and I did shortly after we had been appointed with CAM International. During the summer after graduation from Dallas Theological Seminary, while we worked at Word of Life camp in New York, Libby and I planned an itinerary that would cross the entire country. We traveled a northern route to California designed to connect with as many friends as possible and returned on a more southern route that finally took us through my home in Iowa to Libby's home in Ohio.

In preparation for our cross-country drive we let our friends know exactly what day or days we would be in their cities and we asked if we could get together. In most cases these friends asked us to spend the night with them. We soon discovered this was an exceedingly effective way to develop a support team. We did not ask these friends to support us. Without any prompting on our part, they asked us, "How much support do you lack?" We told them we honestly did not know. We suggested they contact CAM International to find out where we stood.

At the end of this lengthy excursion from coast to coast, we received news from our mission headquarters that our full support had been promised. Within months we were on our way to the mission field.

It was in this endeavor that we soon learned that the most advantageous approach was to stay overnight with friends. This helped reinforce friendships and bond us together.

Far too many missionary appointees are looking for opportunities to speak in church services. This is helpful, but on our cross-country trip we discovered that formal church services are the least effective means to build a support foundation. Next to spending a night or two with friends, we found a home Bible study very helpful. This setting provides opportunity for effective interaction. In a church setting we discovered the most advantageous was a prayer meeting or a Sunday school class. The least effective is the normally very limited time in a church service for a quick five-minute presentation that tends to be isolated from interpersonal contact.

Building a support foundation requires personal contact. Increasingly God is using what is often called "high-touch" relationships to accomplish His purpose in forming the kind of mission teams needed to bond missionaries with senders. And contacts with friends can sometimes result in their encouraging their church to include the missionary candidate in the church's missions budget.

ENLIST FRIENDS

In contacts with present friends who comprise the initial list, opportunities constantly arise to make further friends. Sometimes a friend will suggest someone you might like to call or will arrange to introduce you and serve as your liaison. These new friends require the same personal touch given to those you originally listed. Either have your friend call this prospective contact or you call them and set up an appointment that includes your mutual friend.

When Libby and I traveled across the United States, we made numerous friends through those with whom we stayed. In many cases we were given an opportunity to share our vision in a home Bible study, Sunday school class, or church service, and through this exposure, made numerous new contacts.

The goal is not simply to increase a mailing list. The objective must be to establish and nourish the new friend. Any mailing should include a personal note that makes it clear that you know their names and something significant about them from your contact with them.

THANK FRIENDS

Two of the most motivating words in the English language are "Thank you." Handwritten thank-you notes are vital in the friend-raising process. After staying with friends in our cross-country trip, we wrote a thank-you note by hand to express our deep thanks for their interest in us and their gracious hospitality. We included our photograph prayer card. This gave them a prayer reminder and the address they needed if they wanted to contact our mission to help in our support.

After each visit with a friend your handwritten thank-you note should be in the mail within a day or two of the visit. These do not take long to write, are relatively inexpensive, and are remarkably effective.

INFORM FRIENDS

I have already alluded to prayer letters. Well-designed, informative prayer letters are a link to your friends. (Further suggestions on prayer letters are given in chapter 24, "A Challenge of Communication—Keeping in Touch.") These letters are essential to the ongoing development of friends who are in any way associated with you in prayer or support.

The most important part of each letter is a personal note alongside your signature. Even if these are sent by bulk mail, you will achieve much by taking the time to add a personal note to each letter. Here are two examples:

"Paul and Mary, What a great time we had with you at the Bible study last March. You are a blessing! Ron and Libby."

"Dear Jeff, Libby and I still chuckle about the way your cat Tabbie woke us up. Ron."

Obviously e-mail is a fresh new way to keep up with friends. More frequent "blind-copy" notes can be sent to your list. Every personal response merits a quick answer. I suggest a brief two- or three-line response, followed by hitting the "send" and "delete" buttons. This important personal touch need not be time-consuming.

In every activity related to missions prayer is the bedrock. God is the master Builder. We depend on Him to provide a support team of His choosing. For this reason, it is wise not only to pray earnestly for those who should be included on your list of friends but also to pray for each person already on this list. It is not a mere prayer-letter mailing list. It must truly be a "prayer list" for mutual encouragement and supplication before the Lord. Support moves both directions, from your friends to you and from you to your friends. This is true partnership.

CHAPTER TWENTY-TWO

A New Way of Life—Adapting to a New Ministry

LEARNING A LANGUAGE

STUDENTS IN MY CLASSES at Dallas Seminary would often say, "Prof, I'd love to serve in another country, but I could never learn the language."

I had a standard response, "Do you remember when you learned English?"

Most people never think about the arduous task of learning a language and often fail to realize that they have already worked through this process as a child.

Every child is coached to speak those first words: "Mama," "Papa," or "bye-bye." In spite of careful coaching, children usually start with their own vocabulary: "no," "oh-oh," or "hot." Parents and grandparents are always overjoyed when a child begins to talk, no matter what the vocabulary.

In time a child begins to put sentences together and in due time is fully conversant. Special tutoring continues through this process. If a word is mispronounced or some grammatical construction is in error, someone is always there to point it out and correct the error. Language learning is not as complicated as some might think.

The major problem for adult learners is that pride can stand in the way. It is fine if a child makes some cute error, but an adult feels foolish when he can't speak another language with ease and accuracy.

The most important aspect of language learning is attitude. Jesus' words, "Except you become as a little child," are invaluable in learning another language. Like a child, a missionary is thrust into a new world. He or she must relax, enjoy life, listen to all the strange sounds, and try to imitate them.

The parallel between early childhood formation and essential orientation for a new missionary is of value. Just as the rest of life depends on the care and instruction given to a small child, so the entire missionary career is enhanced or severely hampered in the first years on the field.

To be effective a missionary must learn to speak the language of the people with whom he will minister. Effective evangelism and discipleship are dependent on effective communication.

While it is true that translators can serve as a bridge in communication, this method is not adequate to make a lasting impact in the community, society, and country of missionary service. Bonding relationships so essential in true discipleship require an ability to talk freely together.

When God wanted to provide salvation for the people of this earth, He sent His Son to live in the midst of humankind. Being God, He identified with humanity. He walked among us and communicated with us. He did this to provide salvation. But He also gave us a wonderful example of how to reach people for Him. He left heaven, went to a place of spiritual need, and lived among those whom He wanted to reach. Missionaries too must be willing to leave their place of security and comfort, family, and place of work, travel to a place of spiritual need, and live among those who need to be reached.

Language learning is a key step in this process. Reputable mission agencies make provision for every new missionary to spend the time needed to become adept in the language of the people with whom he or she will minister.

Carefully selected language schools provide the setting for this important assignment. An example is the language school in Costa Rica used by many mission agencies. Founded by the Presbyterian Church and now owned and administered by an independent board of selected mission and church leaders, this language school has helped thousands of new missionaries develop fluency in Spanish.

Unlike normal academic institutions, a good language school focuses on verbal skills rather than intellectual achievement. Classes are small with native speakers as teachers. In the first week there are no textbooks. Every student is immersed in a simple dialogue that is repeated over and over again. Simple little drawings give some idea of where the conversation is heading, but not one word of Spanish appears in writing.

After this first week of saturation in sound in an intense "listen-and-repeat" mode, students, according to their language ability, begin the arduous process of assimilating a new language. Vocabulary is not learned through English-Spanish word lists. New words are introduced in conversation centered in picture books. Increased vocabulary is also introduced in "pattern practice." Rather than learn individual words, they are presented in pattern sentences that are repeated over and over again, changing only one or two words in the sentence.

These are but a few of the techniques that are indicative of a good language school. The goal must be to speak the language with proper phonetics and intonation. Speakers are not considered fluent because of their great ability to use correct grammar. They are judged primarily on their ability to sound right. The words are pronounced the very way a native speaker voices them (phonetics), and the sentence flows just as they do when people in the country talk (intonation).

A good language school will not always succeed in producing fluent speakers. The missionary has to do his or her part in the process. If language-school students reside in an English home, they are immediately hampered in language learning because of their constant contact with English speakers. Finding housing with national speakers is far better.

Immediate use of the language is of importance as well. A simple rule that has helped me immensely is this: "To master a language you must first murder it." I encourage new missionaries to "murder" the language. Learn to laugh with those who laugh at you. People will feel free to correct your mistakes if they know that you are very anxious to improve and that you welcome correction.

Just as a child learns to speak with many self-appointed tutors, so missionaries will learn with the aid of those willing to give assistance. Some of the most effective language learning takes place in the street, in homes, and in church foyers. I probably learned as much in Cartago, Costa Rica, each weekend during our first year at language school as I did in classes in

San José. Some of my best teachers were the young people with whom we served in the Cartago church.

I would encourage anyone who is planning to spend two years in a country to dedicate one year to language school. You can't fully identify with a people with whom you cannot converse. Language is a key that unlocks the door to relationships with the populace to be reached for the Lord.

CULTURAL ADAPTATION

There is no need for "culture shock." The only reason missionaries experience "circuit overload" in foreign settings is because they have not learned to adapt.

By means of radar a ship can detect the course and speed of other vessels. If another vessel seems to be headed on a collision course with a ship, the C.I.C. (Combat Information Center) will engage in "dead reckoning," a simple procedure projecting the course of one's ship and that of the other ship. They will quickly tell the exact second in which a collision might occur. If there is any danger, they will sound the alarm. The officer in charge on deck will respond immediately by changing course to avoid a collision. He will quickly order, "Right full rudder." In moments the ship will veer off course to avoid the intruding vessel. To fail to heed the warning will guarantee collision. Those in C.I.C. will prove to be correct. Collision will happen right on schedule.

A missionary who is trying to navigate in foreign territory must be alert to possible collisions with the culture surrounding him or her. To fail to change course will insure a collision called "culture shock."

For this reason every new missionary must explore cultural differences with active interest rather than judgmental attitudes. He should constantly be intrigued by those differences and seek to adjust. There is no need to collide with those who do things differently or think in a different way. It can be fun to make changes and come alongside those of another culture. People in other places have different values, different customs, different dress, and different ways of thinking.

When a national seems to crowd closer to you as you converse, rather than feel pressed and step backward, take notice of the difference in "personal space" and delight in the warmth of close contact. Enjoy the warm bear hugs called *abrazos* given when you greet some of your new national friends and learn to reciprocate. Take note of the uncanny ritual of shaking hands with everyone in the group before departing and develop the ability to do the same as a natural part of life.

The more difficult adjustment may be in thoughts and feelings. Outward change of action and dress are not as challenging as inner change. Value adjustments may take more time, but they too can be achieved. When people do not arrive at the appointed hour for some function, don't mutter, "These people are so irresponsible! They don't seem to understand punctuality. No wonder this country is so far behind the United States!" Instead, observe the differences, "Obviously punctuality is not of high value in this culture. This is interesting. I wonder if I should tuck my watch in my pocket so I can more adequately adjust to their way of doing things." It is helpful to replace a high value on time with a high value on relationships. Focus on the person, and don't worry about the time. I keep telling people, "Come to Latin America. We don't use clocks. We use calendars."

It is virtually impossible to review the myriad of cultural differences a missionary will face. Every missionary needs to note the differences with a positive attitude and take the challenge to adjust as much as possible. It can be fun to blend with those of an adopted community and culture. The Lord will honor this with effective and rewarding results. "As the Father sent me," Jesus said, "so send I you" (John 20:21).

Language school offers an initial adjustment. Veteran missionaries can assist in other ongoing adjustments that are needed. Most mission agencies not only provide guidance through language school but also offer on-site training and even assign a resident missionary to be a personal adviser through a new missionary's first term. These veterans can be of invaluable assistance, but even if they are not assigned or readily available, a new missionary can succeed in the important adjustments if he is alert and willing to flex as needed.

ENGAGING IN MULTIPLICATION

The world's population now exceeds six billion people. Demographic authorities predict that in the year 2020 the world will strain under the load of eight billion people. Every day some people die and others are born, so that the net daily population increase is 260,000!

Faced with this mushrooming population it may seem at times that the commonly expressed missions goal to reach the world is an impossible dream. Can this global task actually be achieved?

If mission and church leaders continue to focus on merely *adding* believers to the existing family, the worldwide task is totally impossible. Even if every believer suddenly became a flaming evangelist, it is totally unrealistic to think that adding new believers will reach the world.

Missions must take seriously the strategy Christ outlined in His command to those whom He left behind when He ascended into heaven. "Therefore go and make disciples of all nations" (Matt. 28:19). Making disciples is the only effective—and biblical—way of reaching the world for Christ.

Multiplication, not addition. Multiplication, not addition, is the key to reaching the world for Christ. To test the difference between addition and multiplication, I took a pocket calculator and compared the growth achieved by winning someone to Christ every single week with winning one person a year and getting each new convert to reach one in the following year and each year thereafter.

At first glance we might think that leading one person to the Lord every week would be more successful than discipling one person a year. Addition does look better than multiplication for almost a decade. Then the process of multiplication takes an astronomical jump. Check the figures out yourself.

Year	Winning One a Week	Discipling One a Year
1	52	2
2	104	4
3	156	8
4	208	16
5	260	32
6	312	64
7	364	128
8	416	256
9	468	512

10	520	1,024
11	572	2,048
12	624	4,096

Keep the calculations going, and the result is absolutely astounding. After thirty-two years, the rigorous activity of the supreme evangelist who has led one person to the Lord without fail every week would have a group of 1,664—no mean harvest! But the one who has followed God's plan of multiplication in discipling one person a year for thirty-two years would see a "harvest" of 4,294,976,296. Through addition hundreds can be reached, but through multiplication billions can be reached.

Of course, all "pyramids" such as this break down. Even in Amway they fail. Regardless of the reality that multiplication and compounding do not function with the same precision as a pocket calculator, it is abundantly clear that if God's children will simply follow His strategy, His assignment to reach all nations may be achieved.

Make disciples. The priority of every missionary must be centered in discipleship. No matter what the assignment, each missionary should find a few individuals with whom he or she can share in depth, lead these people to the Lord, and then coach them to reach some people in *their* sphere of friendship and influence. For example, a missionary engineer who is assigned to provide technical support for a radio station abroad shares the gospel with other technical personnel or family friends who do not know the Lord. In God's grace as one or two of these individuals come to saving faith in Christ, the engineer will encourage these new converts to reach out to others. The multiplication has begun.

With a new appreciation for the power of multiplication I no longer view a person with whom I have contact as a single individual. I see each person as a link in a giant chain that can circle the globe. Only God knows how He may use the individual with whom He has granted me some brief contact. A chain or web could multiply from this person that might ultimately reach some distant corner of the world.

Multiplication application. I propose that in mission strategy every missionary be challenged to develop a multiplication strategy. Each missionary should list from five to ten prospective disciples. An annual update of this list will show the progress of those who have come to Christ and are now reaching others for Christ. Appropriate annual changes and revisions of the "discipleship" list are in order. The multiplication process must be fresh and dynamic. This basic God-given strategy could literally revolutionize mission activity and produce significant advance and sustained growth.

Maintenance may be one of the greatest blights to missions today. It is time to shift to multiplication and watch God work in fulfillment of His divine plan.

SETTING VISIONARY GOALS

It's always helpful to know your destination before starting on a trip. In fact, you will never know if you have arrived at your destination if you didn't determine where you intended to go.

It all sounds quite basic and maybe a little silly to suggest that a destination be determined before starting a trip, but far too many people engaged in missions are wandering in a dense forest of uncertainty or chugging across an uncharted wilderness of confusion.

Missions is not some romantic cruise into oblivion. Jesus has clearly ordered what must be done: "Make disciples of all nations" (Matt. 28:19). He has instructed us to "preach the gospel to every creature" (Mark 16:15, NKJV). He is "not willing that any should perish but that all should come to repentance" (2 Pet. 3:9, NKJV).

The ultimate mission objectives are already determined. Every missionary must contribute in some way to evangelism, church planting and multiplication, and spiritual growth in the body of Christ. Within these basic objectives those who serve in world missions need to outline specific goals that will contribute to God's plan and purpose.

Setting goals, a stretching and rewarding experience, is essential for effective mission outreach. Individually and corporately, missionaries need to define specific goals that give meaning, direction, and guidance to all activity. Effective goals will have five essential qualities.

Good goals are simple enough to be understood. Every goal needs to be clearly stated. I have seen goals expressed in lengthy discourses and complicated terms that defy comprehension. Clarity is of utmost importance.

For example, here's a sample of a poorly expressed goal: "To engage national leaders in a predetermined course of study that will enable them to evaluate and assimilate theological concepts and biblical constructs so that they might more effectively communicate these truths and more adequately engage in productive ministerial activities." God presented this in understandable terms by simply stating, "Make disciples."

Good goals are short enough to be remembered. Goals that are lengthy and complicated are not only difficult to understand. They are also seldom learned or all too soon forgotten. Some of the most effective goals may sound very much like slogans.

"Each one win one," is clear, concise, and catchy. Obviously not all goals can be expressed with this degree of brevity nor be as memorable. Yet every effort must be made to devise goals that make a lasting impression and encourage implementation. A goal presented in a captivating way and that sticks with all those who hear it or read it will be much more effective than one that is long and poorly worded.

Good goals are sensible enough to be achieved. Sometimes goals are wild dreams. "To reach every person in Mexico with the gospel of Christ" is clear and concise, but is it achievable? Broad, sweeping objectives may sound good, but they are often unrealistic.

Well-established goals are designed to encourage diligent effort and action directed toward achievement. Goals are destinations toward which people travel. Goals are finish lines in the race of life. Goals motivate participation and measure progress.

To establish a goal that is not realistic is to frustrate the whole process.

Good goals are specific enough to be measured. If a goal can be achieved, it can also be measured. It is frustrating to work toward immeasurable goals. No one is sure if the destination has been reached or the finish line crossed.

Five couples serving in Central America formed our first team to Spain. I was named the field director for this new enterprise. We spent a week in prayer, setting goals, establishing policies, and outlining plans before any of us departed for Spain. It was an unforgettable week.

We sensed the deep need for sustaining prayer. The suggested goal "to enlist prayer support for our team's efforts in Spain" was one of those admirable but immeasurable goals. We refined this goal. One suggested, "to enlist five hundred people to pray every day for our team in Spain." This was more specific but not yet measurable. How would we ever know if these people were praying every day?

Finally someone proposed the answer: "to obtain five hundred signatures for a daily prayer commitment for our team in Spain." We could count the signatures on prayer commitment cards. We might never know if they were fulfilling the commitment, but we knew that if five hundred made the commitment we would have more prayer than if we had not asked anyone to pray faithfully on our behalf.

Good goals are stretching enough to be challenging. Small, insignificant goals will bring small, insignificant results. While a good goal needs to be realistic and thereby measurable, it should also be bold and visionary.

Missions is no small assignment. As has been expressed before, this endeavor is as big as the world and as long as eternity. To design tiny, easily achievable goals is to fail to comprehend the magnitude of the task. As William Carey, pioneer missionary to India, put it, we should "attempt great things for God and expect great things from God."

When our CAM Spain team met to pray and establish policies and goals for our new assignment in a place we knew would be difficult, we agreed on a goal that some said was insane: "to establish five new churches in five years." Churches in Central America were multiplying at unbelievable rates, but in Spain we were aware of many reputable missions whose personnel had labored for ten to fifteen years without a single church planted from their diligent labors. Yet after considerable prayer we staked our claim to God's power in a bold endeavor to see five new churches planted in five years.

This goal was simple enough to understand, short enough to be remembered, sensible enough to be achieved, specific enough to be measured, and stretching enough to be a challenge. By setting this goal, our plans took on new meaning. Our team was comprised of five couples experienced in ministry in Central America and fluent in Spanish. We determined that each couple would take the responsibility of moving into a separate area of Spain and, together with Spanish friends made in the assigned city, look to the Lord for effective evangelistic outreach, discipleship training, and from these efforts to see a new church emerge.

This goal shaped our plans. Earlier we had discussed working together in one locality as a unified team. With our bold goal of five new churches in five years, we knew that we would have to scatter. Had we all congregated in one place, we would most certainly not have reached our goal.

Instead of living in the same city, the five couples moved into five distinct locations, and by God's grace five churches *were* established in five years! Specific methods for these church-planting models varied. Some came into being through high-profile evangelistic efforts. Others emerged in a quiet and unobtrusive way. All five churches, however, emerged through the basic steps of establishing friendships with unsaved people, doing effective personal evangelism, discipling the new believers in the Word of God, and drawing growing believers together in a church fellowship.

Work plans. With both personal goals and corporate goals clearly defined, each missionary and missionary team needs to develop a work plan. This is required in CAM International on an annual basis with periodic review. Each missionary devises his or her work plan and then reviews the plan with the field director or immediate supervisor. A copy of every work plan signed by both missionary and supervisor is submitted to the vice president of field ministries.

The plan presents specific goals and action steps proposed by the missionary to work toward each goal. Both tasks and time of anticipated completion are outlined. It includes goals and plans for ministry, family, and individuals. This simple device has been of invaluable help. It promotes clear thinking and provides structure to every activity. Individual missionaries have been blessed. Families have found new unity and purpose. Our mission has experienced great advance and impressive progress that can be traced to wise use of work plans.

A common tool used in secular organizations and ministries is a job description. I have discovered that while we employ helpful job-description listings of the responsibilities, tasks, and structures of any mission assignment, "work assignments" are much more beneficial. Mission endeavors can hardly be classified as jobs. Work assignments can be more inclusive and innovative. Work assignments incorporate visionary goals, purposeful activities, and new frontiers that are generally overlooked in more routine job descriptions.

Chapter Twenty-Three

A Family Spirit—Getting Along with Mission Colleagues

As you might expect, every commercial airline pilot is highly trained. I have witnessed the intense and effective instruction given to pilots with American Airlines at the flight-training center located just south of the Dallas/Fort Worth International Airport.

A vast computer network with touch-sensitive screens provides the flight trainees with most of the basic technical knowledge each must master. Personal veteran pilots are readily available to give guidance and answer any questions that arise. Classrooms are equipped with every visual aid imaginable, and highly qualified instructors give expert guidance to those engaged in this learning experience. Massive flight simulators provide lifelike experience and present every possible emergency to the pilot-in-training. The simulator is so realistic some trainees have all but fainted.

I was surprised to discover that training in this highly sophisticated and intensely technical program includes a section on interpersonal relationships.

"What does training for interpersonal relationships have to do with piloting?" I asked one of the instructors.

His answer was classic, "A pilot may be the most technically proficient in the industry, but if he cannot get along with his co-pilot, very serious problems emerge."

Interpersonal relationships may be one of the most overlooked areas in world missions. Church and mission leaders can learn from American Airlines. Missions personnel need training in how to avoid and resolve potential problems that can occur between co-workers. In an enterprise as focused on human relationships as missions this must constantly be emphasized with missionaries.

TEAMWORK

Mission outreach is a team effort. Individuals who demand their own way or protect their own personal rights can disrupt or even destroy ministries. In writing Ecclesiastes King Solomon was led by God to outline four advantages of team effort.

First, teamwork provides greater production. "Two are better than one because they have a good return for their work" (Eccles. 4:9). Teams accomplish more than individuals working in isolation. With more workers, more work is done.

A second benefit is more progress. "If one falls down, his friend can help him up. But pity the man who falls and has no one to help him up!" (4:10). It is difficult to keep going when you have no one alongside you, especially in those moments when you fall. Missionaries are especially vulnerable. Complications from limited resources or primitive living conditions coupled with the challenge of radical cultural and language adjustments can "trip" a missionary. Pity the missionary who is totally isolated. A team colleague can reach out and lift up the one who has fallen.

A third benefit is provision. "Also, if two lie down together, they will keep warm. But how can one keep warm alone?" (4:11). People can survive intensely cold weather by huddling together. And in missionary work, workers can help and encourage each other as they minister together.

The fourth benefit is greater protection. "Though one may be overpowered, two can defend themselves" (4:12). Wars are never won with isolated individuals engaging in battle wherever they please. The armed forces are just that—forces of armed individuals working together in accord with joint strategy in an organized, disciplined army. Our entire national defense depends on carefully designed team effort.

Solomon concluded his discourse by noting, "A cord of three strands is not quickly broken" (4:12). In a passage that talks about "two," it is interesting that it concludes with a mention of "three." I picture God included in the intertwined twosome. Two flimsy strings are wrapped around a strong cable that cannot be severed. If two wrap themselves around the Lord, the team becomes formidable in strength and supernatural in effectiveness.

Teamwork is indispensable for mission endeavors. Those who want to be a "Lone Ranger" should not even look for a "Tonto." No one in missions wants some masked man who rides off into the sunset of self-centered ambition.

TRUST RELATIONSHIPS

A group of people will not readily work together unless there is a strong bond of trust, the foundation for every healthy relationship.

Trust is reliance on someone's character, ability, strength, and truth. This reliance is a mutual concern. An individual may entrust information to a friend to benefit from his or her wisdom, sympathy, or advice. If, however, the friend then shares this information inappropriately, trust is eroded or may be destroyed. Trust is a two-way street.

Interpersonal relationships are built on trust. Trust is not simply affection or admiration. It goes beyond feeling or knowledge. Trust finds fulfillment in the soul and is grounded in the will.

For example, liking someone and trusting someone are different. Your interest in an entertainer or salesman does not necessarily mean you have trust in that individual. Trust goes deeper. Trust is more foundational in our relationship with others.

Furthermore you can trust someone you barely know. Every time you take a commercial flight you entrust your life to a pilot you may neither see nor meet. You probably do not know if those on the flight deck are properly licensed. Yet you board the plane with confidence. This is not blind trust. It is logical to fly with trust in the plane and crew. Another example of one you trust even though you may not know a person very well is your doctor.

In missions, trust is an essential ingredient for the field team and is of great importance in relationships with mission leadership. Suspicion and doubt will reduce personal and corporate effectiveness in missions outreach.

Building trust is usually a slow process. Unfortunately what takes time to build can be quickly broken. And once trust is broken, it is even more slowly rebuilt, if ever. Some prominent evangelists, for example, have been caught in immorality or criminal financial maneuvers. While many disappointed supporters were quick to forgive these men, trust did not immediately follow. Forgiveness can be instant, but trust usually requires years to restore.

Some basic principles will help missionaries in trust relationships. Ken Williams of Wycliffe Bible Translators outlines a number of "Trust Builders" and "Trust Busters."[1] Each missionary can work on these "Trust Builders:"

- consistent and dependable Christian life
- expressions of sincere, visible love
- genuine humility
- sincere honesty and transparency
- a servant's heart
- fulfillment of commitments and promises
- concerned interest in the affairs of others
- utmost care in guarding confidential information
- active and empathetic listening
- consistency, consistency, consistency!

"Trust Busters" to be avoided are these:

- cliques and biases
- failure to follow through on promises or commitments
- inconsistent beliefs and actions
- concealed sin or immorality
- communication of confidential information without permission
- personal agendas at the expense of others
- fraud or dishonesty in finances
- a judgmental attitude
- inaccessibility or a secretive demeanor
- divisiveness or pitting one person against another
- No sense of forgiveness or tolerance.

Every missionary can be either a "Trust Builder" or a "Trust Buster." The success of an entire ministry can grow or become stagnant, depending on the strength of a foundation of mutual trust.

Integrity is a key ingredient. Without integrity there can be little or no trust, and without trust there can be little or no teamwork. This is no minor item in mission agendas. It is foundational and essential.

CONFLICT RESOLUTION

When trust breaks down, conflict may soon follow. One of the greatest problems in ministry around the world is interpersonal conflict among those who should be working together.

Conflict is as old as history. The origin of sin was essentially a matter of conflict. Satan betrayed Eve and soon Adam joined her in believing his lie. Suddenly the Garden of Eden was a place of conflict. The first couple was separated from God. The Lord immediately introduced resolution. He sought the estranged couple and provided a way to restore fellowship, even though sin had taken its deadly toll.

The Bible is filled with broken relationships. Both the nation of Israel and the early church give evidence of repeated misunderstanding and division. Two of the most outstanding missionaries of all time encountered severe conflict. The apostle Paul and his mentor Barnabas could not agree on a destination for their second missionary journey or on the composition of the missionary team. They finally split up and went their separate ways.

Actually conflict may be part of God's plan. He is not the Author of conflict, but sometimes He allows it to happen for His glory and for the advance of His work. We may not fully understand what is happening, but it is our responsibility to respond correctly to conflict.

Interpersonal conflict must be resolved as soon as possible. At the outset of most conflictive situations those affected are still talking to each other, some remnant of trust is still there, and the ministry has not been unduly damaged. Resolution is urgent or all these advantages will erode or be destroyed.

From God's perspective, conflict can serve for spiritual growth in His children. He can remove the dross and impurities and produce pure gold. The furnace of conflict can serve as a foundation for greater compassion and strengthened confidence. Conflict can be an adversary or an advantage. Unresolved conflict is an adversary, but resolved conflict can be an amazing asset.

The Word of God outlines key principles to avoid conflict or facilitate resolution. "Love is patient, love is kind. It does not envy, it does not boast, it is not proud. It is not rude, it is not self-seeking, it is not easily angered, it keeps no record of wrongs. Love does not delight in evil but rejoices with the truth. It always protects, always trusts, always hopes, always perseveres" (1 Cor. 13:4–7).

"Carry each other's burdens, and in this way you will fulfill the law of Christ" (Gal. 6:2). "Be completely humble and gentle; be patient, bearing with one another in love. Make every effort to keep the unity of the Spirit through the bond of peace" (Eph. 4:2–3). "Do nothing out of selfish ambition or vain conceit, but in humility consider others better than yourselves. Each of you should look not only to your own interests, but to the interests of others" (Phil. 2:3–4).

If every Christian applied the principles in these verses, there might be little or no interpersonal conflict. However, conflicts do occur. When a conflict emerges, immediate action is needed to apply God's principles of resolution. It is common to avoid confrontation, hoping that the problem will disappear. Confrontation is difficult, but it is absolutely essential. Conflictive problems do not go away by themselves.

At the first sign of friction, misunderstanding, or strained relationships, we must go to the person immediately and make every effort to restore a good relationship. It makes no difference who may be at fault; resolution is important. Christ said that when another person is grieved or offended by something I may have said or done, it is my responsibility to go to that person (Matt. 5:23–24).

It is amazing how quickly trust can be restored when we take the initiative to resolve any hint of conflict. Correct attitudes in meeting with an offended friend are of utmost importance. It is always appropriate to start with a sincere apology. This allows your colleague to welcome resolution rather than be defensive. The point of meeting together is not to win an argument but to win a friend; the purpose is not to assign guilt but to restore a relationship.

Veteran missionary Tom Hale presents a dozen helpful guidelines for effective conflict resolution.[2]

- Show courtesy and listen intently.
- Don't argue; seek to explain.
- Be vulnerable; don't try to defend yourself.
- Don't put words in the other person's mouth or try to be a mind reader.
- Stick to specifics; avoid generalities.
- Be generous; don't calculate or keep score; go the extra mile.
- Be willing to concede; acknowledge that there may be other viewpoints.
- Put yourself in the other person's shoes.
- Work on one issue at a time.
- Recognize external circumstances over which neither party has control.
- Allow for the possibility that your adversary will change.
- Remember what you have in common, including, above all, the Lord Himself.

Most people who follow the guidelines listed above will find a wholesome and encouraging restoration. With sincere openness, sensitivity, and loving empathy, one who seeks reconciliation will often bond even more closely to the estranged individual. Friendships can be greatly strengthened.

If conflict is not satisfactorily resolved and you honestly feel you have done all you can, you need not be discouraged or defeated. God may desire to humble you and mold you through this difficult process. If you are fully reconciled to the Lord and have honestly done all you can to resolve the conflict, you can move forward with full confidence. Just as Christ has forgiven you, you need to forgive, even when you are the victim of false slander. Move forward with joy. Focus on God's blessing. The Lord will ultimately resolve all conflict in accord with His grace and goodness. We can trust Him.

SERVANT LEADERSHIP

The most effective missionary teams are led by those who demonstrate a servant's heart. Christ clearly explained servant leadership to His disciples. "You know that the rulers of the Gentiles lord it over them, and their high officials exercise authority over them. Not so with you. Instead, whoever wants to become great among you must be your servant, and whoever wants to be first must be your slave—just as the Son of Man did not come to be served, but to serve, and to give his life as a ransom for many" (Matt. 20:25–28).

Authoritarian leaders become increasingly possessive about their position. They drive hard to take control and hold on. Leaders who demonstrate this spirit may seem successful, but over time the missions enterprise will suffer. Domineering leaders find it hard to accept suggestions because they see feedback as a threat to their authority. Growth and progress are essentially thwarted by one who "lords it over" others.

By contrast, those with a servant spirit do not aspire to leadership roles. They are willing to assume this responsibility only if they are convinced that this will advance the work of the Lord and bring glory to Him. They feel called to help, not driven to control. They see themselves as stewards, not owners. They are not at all threatened when someone comes along who proves to be more adept in leadership. They readily partner with that person or even step aside to an assignment in which they can more effectively serve. They love suggestions and ideas that will help them serve better and advance the cause of Christ.

Servant leadership is not so much a matter of style or methods. It is born in the heart and is evidenced in character. Christ was by nature a servant leader and has given the greatest example of all. He "did not come to be served, but to serve, and to give his life as a ransom for many" (20:28). Although He had ultimate authority over the entire universe, He did not lord it over others. He came to serve and to be the sacrifice for our sins and to give eternal life to those who believe in Him. No one can match this Leader of leaders and Servant of servants.

Instead of asking, "How many people are serving under you?" we must ask, "How many are you serving?" I like to call it a reversed pyramid. "Number one" in God's leadership plan is not the one "at the top"; it is the one "at the bottom," who sustains the needs of all those being served. It is the person who mobilizes and encourages other individuals in the pyramid to fulfill God's purposes for His glory.

World missions needs servant leaders. Making disciples calls for servant leaders. Those who are driven to maintain control and hold on to their positions will generally fail in the disciple-making process. Servant leaders are much more adept in this important discipleship assignment.

The formula for missions advance is not complicated. A team of individuals who highly respect and fully trust each other, who engage in prompt resolution when any hint of conflict appears, and who are encouraged and mobilized by a servant leader will be richly blessed by God in ministry.

CHAPTER TWENTY-FOUR

A Challenge of Communication—Keeping in Touch

MUCH OF THE WORLD has fully transitioned from the industrial age to the information age. More than ever, people focus on communication. The transatlantic cables that provided a breakthrough in telephone contact between distant continents are now deep-sea relics covered with seaweed at the bottom of the ocean. Satellites now bounce messages around the globe in a split second. The world is truly a global village.

The communications network that circles the globe is a great advantage to world missions. Missionaries scattered around the world enjoy new and unique means for carrying the message of the gospel and the truths of God's Word to distant lands. In addition, missionaries also benefit from new means of access to those who stand with them in prayer and support.

Maintaining contact with supporters is an important assignment for every missionary. If the "senders" have little or no information, it is unlikely that they will want to continue to provide financial assistance. Also without information it is impossible for supporters to pray for specific needs.

Missionaries must keep in touch with those who stand with them in prayer and support. This assignment must be taken seriously. Yet it need not be overly burdensome. Without expending excessive time at this task, close contact can be maintained by various means.

E-MAIL MESSAGES

Electronic mail may be one of the greatest breakthroughs for missionary communication. Almost as ubiquitous as the telephone, computers are now found in the homes of almost every supporter. Most are connected with some electronic mail server and are thus available for printed messages that drop into their "in baskets" with great frequency and at little or no cost.

In a world of immediate news from the remotest corner of the globe, electronic mail is undoubtedly the most effective communication method for missionaries today. It is important to use this means wisely. Short messages of a current event are the most effective. It is not wise to send a lengthy letter or to copy on e-mail what is being sent by "snail mail."

I have found that for the normal prayer or support friend the best rule is to limit e-mail messages to what will fit on the screen without scrolling. Obviously family members will usually welcome as much as you are willing to write. But the average person will welcome concise notes of current activities and will be especially grateful for one or two priority prayer requests.

Another great advantage of e-mail is the ease with which a reply can be sent on its way. With a simple point and click, the screen is ready for a quick reply. This has been one of the greatest blessings in my use of the computer. I have learned to read, reply, and delete immediately. I try to keep my "inbox" emptied. Another feature, of course, is electronic filing for those items that we want to save. There are three easy options: Read and delete; or read, reply, and delete; or read, file, reply, and delete. The key that should get the most use is "delete." This may sounds drastic, but I am convinced that this is the most efficient and effective way to use e-mail.

Each missionary can group his or her e-mail addresses so that one "send" click covers the entire list. Furthermore "blind copy" listings are imperative. This way each person receives the note as though he or she were the only recipient. The lengthy list of other addressees does not appear on the copy received.

The general principle in all communication is to make every message as personal as possible. With e-mail this can be done with relative ease.

TELEPHONE CALLS

Although I was not born until after the Great Depression, I have been impacted by this tragic era of severe economic hardship in our nation. My parents talked about it, and by their example they taught me a strong measure of frugality. International telephone calls and, for that matter, even long-distance calls were made only in a case of dire emergency.

However, today telephone calls are considerably less expensive. Even international calls are not excessively costly. While I still fight the Depression-era syndrome not to dial an international call for mission business, younger members of our missionary team do not hesitate to make such calls.

For donors a brief call to say thanks and share an important prayer request can be most effective. This is certainly advisable when a missionary is on home assignment and can take advantage of relatively inexpensive evening and weekend telephone rates.

One of the disadvantages of telephoning is the increasing difficulty of reaching people with a phone call. It seems that in most of my calls I spend more time talking to recorders than I do to the friends I am trying to reach. Call backs are equally as difficult. It is often a game of tag. Yet the telephone is a marvelous instrument for close, personal contact.

Some missionaries and mission groups are beginning to utilize "telemarketing," but I must confess I have a strong aversion to this device. I would strongly encourage missionaries to avoid even a hint of financial solicitation on the phone. The call should be centered in a friendly greeting, heartfelt interest in what is happening in this friend's life and family, sincere thanks for his or her prayers and support, and possibly a specific prayer request. In a call like this listening is sometimes more important than talking. Personal interest will tie a stronger bond even over a fiber–optic telephone line.

PERSONAL NOTE

Attractive notepaper is another wonderful aid to a busy missionary. It takes only a minute or two to write a brief note by hand and send it on its way. In an age of high-tech mechanical production, a handwritten note is especially welcomed.

If your penmanship is undesirable, you can always make the extra effort to print. Obviously the note must be legible, but even when it requires studious effort to decipher, the recipient is most grateful for something that is truly personal and brief.

Thank-you notes are especially important. As I mentioned earlier, every time I stay with a family or have dinner with a friend, I dash off a simple note of thanks and try to get it in the mail within a day or two. This gesture is important for two reasons. First, when the task is done immediately it does not continue to haunt me as something yet to be done. Second, the one who receives the note is always moved by a prompt thank-you note.

Sometimes little notes written on unusual materials will attract greater attention. George Verwer, founder and director of Operation Mobilization, frequently sends me brief notes written on airline baggage tags, restaurant napkins, and other unique materials. He obviously pens these little notes on the run. They have always moved me deeply. They usually say something like, "Ron, I was thinking of you today. How are things going? George" or "Ron, I prayed for you today. Keep up the good work! George."

All this reinforces the basic principle of effective communication. The more personal the communication, the more effective it is. Every person appreciates individual attention and concern. Handwritten notes are one of the most effective means of communicating this kind of personal attention.

PRAYER LETTERS

The standard means of communication for most missionaries is a prayer letter. Even in our age of e-mail and phone connections, prayer letters are still effective, if done properly.

These printed letters sent to large numbers of friends can accomplish much. But the production of these bulk mailings can be expensive in time, energy, and financial cost.

As a missionary appointee, I found a few secrets to make what I called "junk-mail" productions both efficient and effective. My wife, Libby, and I tried to streamline the process and to seek to get maximum response from every letter we sent.

God put us in touch with a lady who directed the print shop of a major bank in Dallas. She graciously agreed to print all our prayer letters for us during her coffee break. The bank charged us for only the cost of the paper.

The church in which Libby and I served during our Dallas Seminary days agreed to send our prayer letters on their bulk-mailing permit. The cost of postage therefore was minimal, less than two cents each! This kind of bargain is no longer available, but bulk-mailing postage is still economical. It is costly to send these letters first class. Furthermore the church agreed to use their address machine to ready the bulk mailing of our letters.

With the help of our friend at the bank and our home church, we simply prepared photo-ready copy of our prayer letter and sent it to our friend for printing. From that point on all the work was done for us.

Knowing the amount of "junk mail" each person in the United States receives, I realized we had to make our letter stand out or it would move directly to the wastebasket. From the outset, we avoided the use of envelopes for the hundreds of prayer letters we sent almost every two months. The recipient did not even need to open an envelope.

With a variety of folds we utilize a brochure format with clever art line drawings that I collected from magazines and other publications. For example, when we first departed, our prayer letter featured a bold drawing of a Dodge van that represented our vehicle, which we named "Joshua." Inside the folder, a map outlined our long trek through Mexico and Central America with anticipated dates along the way. The little letter was hand printed as though "Joshua," our Dodge van, were writing. I was amazed to hear from many friends who posted this prayer letter on a wall or refrigerator or kept it on a table or desk for ready reference. They prayed for us during our entire trip.

The first prayer letter we prepared from Costa Rica when we embarked on language study was inspired by one of the drawings I had in my clipping file. It was from an advertisement of a little man looking down at a big, bold asterisk in the middle of his tummy. This figure obviously attracted attention to our simple brochure prayer letter. I entitled it, "What's going on down there?" Inside we told of our experiences "down there" in Costa Rica.

With clip art you don't have to be an accomplished artist. An eye for layout helps, of course, but this type of letter can attract attention and will therefore be read. Computers make this task much easier. The format of every letter is almost as essential as the content. The competition in mail today is much greater than it was when Libby and I first sent out our prayer letters. Anything you can do to attract the attention of each friend who finds your letter tucked in a pile of junk mail stuffed in the mailbox will help. While you would like to believe each recipient is eagerly awaiting your carefully written letter, the truth of the matter is that most people will be prone to discard it. This need not discourage us. It should simply stimulate us to find a way to be sure the recipient will take notice of what we send, read it, and pray.

I am convinced that missionaries should not spend inordinate time on prayer letters. We were grateful that we could send letters to hundreds of friends without a trip to the printer, endless folding, envelope stuffing, addressing, stamp sticking, or any of the other time-consuming tasks that could easily become a chore. Address changes came back to the church from which the bulk mailing was sent. These were forwarded to us. It was only then that we might decide to drop a person from our mailing list. Usually, however, we simply corrected the address and sent it back to the church for an updated list.

Whatever it takes, I would encourage every missionary to send prayer letters faithfully at least once a quarter. Like e-mail correspondence, phone calls, and personal notes, the content should be fairly brief and focus on one central theme. A summary list of three to five prayer requests is especially helpful to the reader. Lengthy dissertations are generally not very effective.

One of the disadvantages in the somewhat detached process we used to mail our prayer letters was the inability to add personal notes to the printed letters. When a note is handwritten on the letter, the recipient will inevitably read this first.

We were able to offset the disadvantage of not being able to write personal notes on our printed prayer letters by writing short, separate personal notes mailed to each donor every month utilizing the printout that came with our remittance check. This list gave the name and address of each donor. They seemed very grateful for this personal, handwritten thank–you note. Because of this personal touch I think our limited number of donors were more anxious to receive and read our prayer letters.

HOME VISITS

Obviously nothing can match personal, face-to-face contacts. Today, the most effective personal encounter is not on home assignment or frequent visits to the donor's home. A visit by the donor in the *missionary's* home on the field makes a far greater impact. Travel has become more afford-able. More and more donors are flying to distant destinations and visiting missionaries there.

Of course if too many people come to visit, the missionaries may have difficulty keeping their focus on ministry priorities. Yet hospitality is a core prerequisite for missionary service. Those who come to visit are usu-ally willing to accept the most modest accommodations and are anxious to assist in any way they can.

I found that visitors were most blessed when I simply took them along in the ministry commitments I already had. I did not change my sched-ule. I simply included them in the schedule as much as possible. I remember when a Braniff Airlines pilot and his wife came to visit us in Segovia, Spain. I offered them a choice of sightseeing with a tour guide I knew or joining me in visiting some of the new believers I was scheduled to see. They chose the home visits. They later wrote me that this was the highlight of their time in Spain.

I still remember, for example, the day we dropped in to visit a Spanish pharmaceutical salesman and his wife who had recently come to Christ. I served as a language bridge, translating both directions, from Spanish to En-glish and from English to Spanish. It was a wonderful time. I feel that missionaries erroneously think that when visitors come they need to drop their ministry activities and entertain their guests. On the contrary, the visi-tors need to witness what God is doing. If they are donors, they need to see that the Lord is providing a spiritual return for their economic investment.

While visits by donors to the field are ideal, it is also advantageous for the missionary to make personal contact with as many donors as possible when he is in his sending country. This is the ideal communication mode. Person-to-person contact supersedes any other means. A good hug and animated conversation are priceless.

Chapter Twenty-Five

A Home Assignment—Retooling in the Land of Departure

WHEN TRAVEL WAS CONFINED to steamship voyages that took many weeks to cross the ocean and living conditions were a hazard to health, a one-year leave called "furlough" was granted every four or five years.

Travel and living conditions have changed radically. Today most missionaries are a day or two of travel away from their sending country and live in cities with "modern amenities" like electricity and phone service.

It may take longer for some missionaries to get to the airport from their home than it does to fly to their sending country, but jet service is available in almost every country of the world. And missionaries who live in mud-brick homes or grass huts "in the bush" often have optional housing in the nearest city to provide relief from the strain of primitive living.

Not surprisingly the term *furlough* has been replaced with the more appropriate wording *home assignment*. This is a period of time granted for ministry or study in the sending country or land of departure. Mission agencies generally grant home-assignment options of a few months to a year or more to be away from the field of service. It is common practice to grant from three months for two years of active service abroad to a full year for four or five years abroad.

This link to time of foreign service has contributed to an erroneous conclusion that home assignment is a privilege or reward that is due each missionary. It is seen by some as a merited break from active service like a deserved sabbatical leave of absence. However, home assignments are not vacations. They are times to achieve some important goals that will contribute in some way to God's work.

DONOR RELATIONS

When missionaries think of home assignments, they usually envision visiting supporting churches and donors. This, of course, is an important objective. Even the most effective communication from abroad can't match the opportunity to get together with those who are part of the sending team.

This goal can best be achieved by more frequent visits for brief periods of time. This may not even require a home assignment.

When we lived in Spain, I took advantage of some low airfares for trips to the United States. With a "Visit the USA" ticket for unlimited travel throughout the country for a limited number of days, I was able to bounce around the country to visit churches and donors. It was much more effective than a lengthy home assignment.

People were anxious to get together, knowing that I would be in town for only a day or two. Also I was able to report what had happened last week and ask prayer for events planned for the coming week rather than relate stale news of a year ago.

I found the donors appreciated my commitment to keep the overseas ministry going. Donors rightfully question missionaries who seem to spend excessive time away from their place of cross-cultural ministry. While they appreciate personal contact, donors are most interested in making an investment in missions outreach, not in self-satisfying fellowship with the missionary they have sent for ministry in another culture or place. In fact, they would much rather visit the missionary in action overseas than have that missionary at their doorstep for extended periods of time.

While financial support is of utmost importance, no missionary should make fund-raising the most important part of his or her home assignment. The goal is to reach the world, not raise needed funds.

ADVANCED STUDY

One of the most important objectives for home assignment is further training. Missionaries need to be equipped for more effective ministries. Just like those of any other profession, people who serve in cross-cultural ministries will benefit from advanced studies.

Most Bible schools, Christian colleges, and seminaries welcome missionaries for further training. Some advanced-degree programs are designed specifically for those engaged in cross-cultural ministries.

For those who may seek graduate studies that involve more than one year, most mission agencies are willing to extend a home assignment. Mission leaders are alert to the advantage of this added training. Increasing numbers of missionaries now hold master's and doctor's degrees, a great asset in mission outreach. Mission-based educational institutions continue to upgrade the programs they offer. Most mission schools now seek professors who hold the same graduate degrees commonly expected by similar institutions in the sending country. The most common graduate degree desired for teachers is the Ph.D. degree.

Those who do not expect to teach in a formal institution overseas may want to pursue a Doctor of Ministry degree. A doctorate designed especially for those already engaged in ministry, the D.Min. program usually allows for greater flexibility in classroom work and gives credit for projects that relate directly to the ministry in which the candidate is already involved. Much of the work is done in the country of missionary service, thus allowing for continued study, which enhances rather than disrupts the ministry. Whatever the level or duration of home assignment study, this is a worthwhile objective for every missionary.

MISSIONARY RECRUITMENT

One of the most touching lessons Christ conveyed to His disciples was His plea to consider the plentiful harvest and the serious lack of workers. His conclusion was powerful. "Ask the Lord of the harvest, therefore, to send out workers into his harvest field" (Matt. 9:38).

All Christians need to be in constant prayer for God's supply of workers to reap the massive harvest around the world. So many areas of the globe are "ripe for harvest," but there are simply not enough workers to do the reaping.

Missionaries on home assignment must be attuned to this important aspect of God's plan. They must constantly be on the lookout for likely candidates who might be touched by the Lord to join our missionary ranks.

It is totally erroneous to expect a director of recruitment to fulfill this gigantic task. Those involved in mission-agency recruitment are obviously active in challenging possible missionary candidates, but their major assignment is to follow up on the contacts missionaries and other leaders have made with likely prospects.

I think every missionary should prayerfully set a goal of a significant number of possible missionary candidates for the period of time designated for home assignment. It is a special challenge to find those who might be led of God to serve alongside in the country or area of service to which the missionary will return after home assignment. There is no better recruiter than the person who is actively serving in the ministry or location to which God may be directing another of His children.

ETHNIC MINISTRIES

In most cities people from other parts of the world are moving right next door. Rather than seeing this as a threat, we should accept it as a God—given challenge.

One of the fastest growing mission fields is Hispanic USA. Spanish—speaking people are flooding into the country. Our mission agency, once known as the Central American Mission, originally ministered exclusively in the countries south of our border. Now these people are crossing that border in large numbers. CAM was founded in Dallas and continues to headquarter there. One of our CAM board members, who also serves on the Dallas City Council, recently informed me that demographers anticipate that in the 2000 census Dallas will be 52 percent Hispanic. Other cities in Texas are open doors of opportunity for Spanish ministry. For example, San Antonio is 98 percent Hispanic! Those to whom we have long sent missionaries are now moving in next door.

Missionaries on home assignment will find wonderful opportunities to utilize their adopted language, cross-cultural training, and overseas experience in mission outreach to the people they have come to love. Time away from the foreign country of missionary assignment need not be time away from an active ministry to people of that country.

Home assignments should rightfully include active outreach to people of one's country of foreign service. Even more important, home-assignment missionaries can help mobilize some of their sending churches to open their eyes to this mission field that is right next door. Missionaries on home assignment can assume the role of active consultants to give guidance in this important new dimension of church outreach.

HEALTH NEEDS

Although health care abroad is constantly improving, North America is still the benchmark of quality medical personnel and facilities. For this reason many missionaries take advantage of a home assignment to take care of special health needs and have thorough medical examinations.

Sometimes a home assignment will be used to provide needed health care or arrange for the medical needs of family members. Aging parents are often the concern of missionaries who return on home assignment. Some missionaries have found a new solution to parental care. Rather than leave their field of service to care for parents, they have taken their parents back to their field of service. The health care may be quite good and the cost is much less. I have been blessed to see how content these parents are on the mission field. They seem fulfilled to be a part of what God is doing through their children and grandchildren in their newly adopted land.

Health is of primary importance. If a person is not in good health, the ministry in which he or she is engaged will suffer. So it is appropriate that needed time for this important aspect of life be allotted during one's home assignment.

REST AND RELAXATION

Though home assignments are not designated as family vacations, it is important that some time be set aside for renewal and family fun. For some reason many people see missionaries as people who grind their way through life in some impossible world of spiritual burdens. This is simply not true. Some of the happiest, most fulfilled and balanced people I know are missionaries. Both in the challenge of cross-cultural ministry and in spare moments dedicated to personal or family recreation missionaries are generally very satisfied people.

I have not found many donors who would be disturbed with a missionary family taking a few days of their home assignment to relax at the beach or enjoy a family outing at a ballpark.

A week at one of the many excellent Bible conferences is an ideal way for a missionary family to meet new friends, experience spiritual renewal through the ministry of the Word of God, and to be refreshed in a relaxed setting. Missionaries can profit greatly from a week in which they are not under the pressure of ministry demands.

CHAPTER TWENTY-SIX

A Walk with God—Maintaining Intimacy with the Lord

FOR YEARS I was inconsistent in my time alone with the Lord. I had come to know Christ early in life. As I progressed from junior high school to high school, I was well informed on the importance of what we called "quiet time." I simply did not know how to accomplish this apparently vital part of each day.

Even though I loved the Lord and was very active in church life, I was not consistent in a daily time with God. At best, in the hectic schedule of school and church activities, I found occasional moments early in the morning or late at night for a quick read of some passage in the Bible and a rather hurried prayer.

Things were no better in college. At the University of Nebraska I got involved in a myriad of extracurricular activities. I loved the whirlwind of responsibilities and did my best to do all that might be expected of me in each assignment and still maintain a high grade-point average. The calendar was soon crowded with demands that preempted a consistent daily time of devotions or "quiet time."

After college I spent three years as a supply officer in the United States Navy. This was an all-time low in my spiritual life. My assignment on the destroyer was very demanding. In my early days aboard the ship I tried to evangelize some of my fellow officers, but they were not interested. After a few weeks I simply stopped witnessing. Then I determined that I just did not have time to read my Bible. Eventually I stopped praying. I was in a precipitous fall.

I finally came to my senses. Like the prodigal son I realized I was far from the Lord and was suffering because of it. I took one step up. I prayed, "Lord, please send to this ship some officer who knows You." God answered my prayer when Bill Marshall, a recent graduate of the Naval Academy, came aboard. He was a wonderful, vibrant Christian from North Carolina. Bill and I studied the Word and prayed together on a regular basis. We obtained permission to have church services on the mess decks and soon many guys on our ship were coming to Christ.

Our captain called us up to his stateroom. Bill and I thought we were in deep trouble. We faced our captain with fear and trembling. He was known to be very tough. As soon as we stepped into his office he looked at us with a cold stare and blurted, "I notice what's going on on my ship! And I like it!" We could hardly believe what he was saying. He continued, "I'll tell you what I would like you to do. I want you to lead the ship in prayer over the loudspeaker system every morning, and you'd just as well end the day that way too." I didn't know of another ship in the fleet where this was happening.

You would think that I would have learned my lesson. I left the Navy and took graduate studies at Ohio State University. After my training in contact-lens fitting I was offered a position in the University Eye Clinic. I still was inconsistent in my time alone with the Lord. If you are a professional, you will perhaps understand my reasoning. The demands of work seemed to make regular devotions difficult if not impossible.

Active in an InterVarsity chapter and at Calvary Bible Church in Columbus, Ohio, I did my best to serve the Lord, but my time alone with Him was sporadic at best. Yet God was working. I sensed a deep conviction to enter the ministry, so I resigned my position at the eye clinic and enrolled in Dallas Theological Seminary.

It is not easy for me to confess that during my four years as a student at Dallas Seminary, I was still inconsistent in my time alone with the Lord. I was, of course, spending hours in the Word for class assignments, but devotions were not part of my daily experience.

It was not until God led my wife and me into world missions that I finally found an answer to this lifelong struggle. As new missionaries with the Central American Mission we landed in Costa Rica for language school.

It did not take long for me to realize that without the Lord's help this whole assignment was impossible.

I started a plan that has been revolutionary in my life. Instead of thinking "devotions" or "quiet time," I think "appointment." I have an appointment with God every day. It is amazing how we are able to carve out time for meals three times a day and yet be so hard-pressed to find some time alone with the Lord.

For years I tried to understand why it is so difficult to find time alone with God. I have finally concluded why. If Satan can prevent us, he has defeated us. Satan is not nearly as concerned with our hyperactivity in ministry as he is when we spend quality time alone with God.

My appointment system has worked. I'm a morning person, so I choose a time early in the day. If you are a "night owl," the morning is obviously not the best time for you. Choose a good time in the day and make an appointment with God each day. There may be times when you will need to reschedule, but don't cancel.

To be sure that I don't fail in this important event each day, I learn what time I have to be "on deck" in the morning and then get up one hour before that. By rising one hour before my obligations begin, I have ample time for a shower and all the other things I must do to get my body going. This leaves equal time for my soul. For example, if I am to be at breakfast at 7 A.M., I rise at 6 A.M. If we need to leave for the airport at 5 A.M., I get up at 4 A.M. It is amazing how a daily shower gets me going and how the Word of God and time in prayer energizes me no matter how much or how little sleep I have had the night before.

If you struggle to maintain a regular time alone with the Lord, I would suggest you try this appointment plan. I had a business friend in Texas tell me how effective this was. He said, "I told my secretary, 'I have a very important appointment at 9:30 this morning.' She jotted a note on her desk calendar. At 9:30 she stepped into my office and said, 'I need to remind you about the appointment.' 'Oh yes,' I exclaimed, 'Please close the door.' The secretary glanced around a little baffled and closed the office door as she stepped out." He was obviously moved when he concluded, "I had a wonderful time with God!" This businessman had discovered how easy it was to spend some time each day with the Lord. Make an appointment with God. Just schedule it!

PERSONAL PRAYER LIST

It would be erroneous to think of an appointment with God as the final solution to all spiritual needs. Devotions, quiet time, or an appointment are only a means. It is not some little short-cut prescription for spiritual vitality. It is, however, an excellent start. I have become convinced that the length of time or what is done in that time is not as important as a sense of the urgency for time with God.

In my morning encounters I read God's Word in a devotional way. I want Him to talk with me and feed my soul with what He says. I read exclusively for application and edification. Then I go to Him in prayer. I talk with Him about all those things that are on my heart. I want Him to work in my life and through my life for His glory.

In Spain I started something that has been of great help in my prayer life each day. I folded a piece of paper twice to make a little accordion with eight columns. I labeled the first column "Every Day" and on the remaining seven columns wrote a day of the week on each column.

This became my personal prayer list to help me with continuing prayer requests. On the "Every Day" column I listed my top five prayer requests:
- Renewed submission
- Cleansing of sin
- More wisdom
- Spiritual growth
- Finish well

These are my initial prayer requests every morning. I want to be available to the Lord each day as a "living sacrifice" totally committed to Him so that He can do anything He desires. I want my life clean from sin by means of His spiritual "shower" that matches the shower I have each morning to help get my body going. I pray for wisdom, in answer to His promise, "If any man lacks wisdom, let him ask of God who gives to all men liberally" (James 1:5). I ask God to help me grow each day; I don't want to be stagnant or static. And then I pray that I will finish well. I don't want to "wash out" in my walk with the Lord. I have seen far too many of God's choice servants fall into moral or spiritual failure and be removed from the ministry. I earnestly pray each day that I will cross the finish line faithful to Him in every way. In fact, I often pray, "Lord I would rather be dead than be an embarrassment to you. Please keep me close to your side. Help me to stand in your power and in your grace."

In my "Every Day" column I then list my wife, children, relatives, mission colleagues, and others I have chosen to pray for each day. On the remaining seven columns I list those I pray for once a week. This has been a great help for me to follow up on what were previously vain promises to pray consistently for friends and colleagues. Now I have their names listed to remind me to uphold them in prayer as promised, even though it is weekly.

This prayer list has also served to keep me attuned to the fruit of the Spirit (Gal. 5:22–23), which is the true measure of spirituality. I pray each day for one of the evidences of the fruit of the Spirit:

- Sunday—love
- Monday—joy
- Tuesday—peace
- Wednesday—patience
- Thursday—kindness and goodness
- Friday—faith
- Saturday—gentleness and self-control

Throughout the day I keep checking to see if I am truly controlled by the Spirit. I evaluate my life to see if the qualities for which I have prayed are evident. This has been a wonderfully beneficial exercise each day.

In a recent conference in Honduras we were talking about the fruit of the Spirit, and I suddenly had an inspiration for a simple little personal examination. I tested myself by listing the nine items in the "fruit of the Spirit" in order from the most evident to the least evident in my life. I found this a good test of my strengths and weaknesses. Here is the revealing list I made in evaluating my life:

- joy
- love
- peace
- kindness
- goodness
- faith

- self–control
- gentleness
- patience

My friends agreed with me. I am a happy person who loves to be with others. But my weakness is that I lack gentleness. I tend to be forceful and aggressive. I am overly task-oriented, always pushing to get things done. And I do not have a lot of patience. In fact, the little prayer, "Lord, give me patience, and give it to me right now!" seems to fit me all too well.

You might like to take this little test. List these nine items in your life from the most evident to the least evident. It is a good measure of your personal spiritual vitality.

MEDITATION ON GOD'S WORD

The Bible is not an ordinary book. It is the voice of God speaking to us. Bible study is exceedingly important. One of the great difficulties, however, is limiting our study of the Scriptures to exegesis and diligent interpretation. Bible study is never fully complete until God's truth is transferred into life practice.

As a missionary I soon discovered that I could tell you the outline of a Bible book and give you the authorized, doctrinally correct interpretation of each passage, but these facts were lodged in my head. They needed to be turned into life-transforming truths that filtered into my heart and out through my hands, touching those who needed to "read" the Bible in me. This is really what missionary work is all about. People need to see the Lord and His Word in the one who has been sent into a cross-cultural setting.

Each missionary needs to learn the art of biblical meditation and application. In my appointment with God, I am especially moved by the simplicity of the Bible and its message to me. I read with a burning passion to apply lessons God has for me in His Word and thereby watch Him change my life more and more into His image.

Even intense, detailed Bible study should start with meditative reading. When I was asked to write on the Book of James for *The Bible Knowledge Commentary*, a thorough exposition of every book of the Bible with in-depth, verse-by-verse analysis,[1] I started by reading the Book of

James about forty times. I read it and reread it to feel the sweep of the book and let it become a part of my being. It was through this meditative reading that I began to realize this book is one of the most practical books in the Bible. It touches who we are, what we do, how we speak, how we feel, and what we have. I found some commentaries regarded James as a disconnected collection of sayings and ideas with no central theme. On the contrary, I found this book exceedingly well ordered and intensely practical. What I wrote to fulfill my assignment reflects the discoveries I made through repeated reading as well as in-depth study.

Meditation on the Word of God is an essential part of the Christian life. As basic as sustenance is to the body are the Scriptures to the soul. In my daily Bible reading I have found it helpful to read through Bible books, alternating between the Old Testament and the New Testament. I read and meditate on a portion of Scripture that is sufficient to give me the spiritual food I need for the day. Sometimes I read a few verses, sometimes I consume entire chapters.

When our children were small, I found it helpful to take an early morning walk and read the Bible as I walked. I read outloud. If a jogger happened to come along, I would be silent until he passed and then go back to my passage with vigorous reading.

My approach is not necessarily the best approach. I admire those who read through the entire Bible each year through a very systematic schedule. If this works best for you, I would encourage you to do the same.

The point is obvious: We need the Word of God. Every missionary needs to be saturated with biblical truth that has filtered into life patterns. Read the Word. Meditate on the Word. Study the Word. Most of all, apply the Word of God to every aspect of life. The Word works!

DAILY CIRCUMSTANCES

An intimate systematic daily walk with the Lord in prayer and meditation in the Bible is essential for spiritual development and growth. With these foundations each believer is better equipped to handle the circumstances and trials that are bound to come.

God carefully orchestrates trials, persecution, difficulties, afflictions, physical ailments, and a multitude of other undesirable circumstances to get our attention and mold us into His image. James wrote, "Consider it pure joy, my brothers, whenever you face trials of many kinds, because you know that the testing of your faith develops perseverance. Perseverance must finish its work so that you may be mature and complete, not lacking anything" (James 1:2–4).

Trials are often the very best teachers to capture a believer's attention and to produce incredible spiritual growth. Considered by God as a test, the trial presents a challenge for the believer to pass the test or fail it. Depending on the believer's response, the trial can build up or tear down. The test is either beneficial or destructive. The key is how we respond.

Perseverance in times of trial will ultimately produce increased maturity. By growing strong in trials a person can eventually achieve complete spiritual stature, lacking nothing.

MISSIONARY APPLICATION

What does all this have to do with missionary experience? Answer: Spiritual vitality is at the core of all missionary experience. Each person sent to reach the lost, disciple believers, and build up the church must, more than anything else, maintain a vibrant testimony of God's work in his or her life. Missions starts with the integrity and vitality of each believer.

Spiritual vitality is essential to effective missionary ministry. It starts with a daily walk with Christ with consistent time alone with God in prayer and biblical meditation. It is dangerous to get so involved in God's ministries that no time is left for God. He merits our devotion and a close personal relationship. Every day is a new adventure in God's wonderful plan to fulfill His purposes and bring glory to His name. An intimate walk with the Father is the foundation for an effective ministry in missions that will make an impact for eternity. This is the heart of missionary life.

PART SEVEN
~~~~~~~

The Heavenly Line—To the Praise and Glory of God

I WAS HONESTLY A BIT DISAPPOINTED when I woke up alive. The doctor hovered over me after my automobile accident and asked me, "Where are you?" I looked around and said, "Am I at Baylor Hospital?" The doctor's response was revealing. He simply exclaimed, "Good!" He looked relieved as he turned and left the room.

While leaving our CAM Center office complex on a warm July day, I turned onto Interstate Highway 30 access road only to encounter fast-moving traffic. The Interstate was closed at this entrance for construction on the overpass. All vehicles were detoured down the access road. In my attempt to merge left into the oncoming flow of cars and trucks, I did not even notice that a dump truck ahead was stopped. It had been abandoned in the middle of the right lane. There were no triangles, no blinking lights, no warning whatsoever.

When I finally realized the danger before me, it was too late. I slammed into the truck and pushed it thirty feet. This is what the police officer called to the scene of this accident told me. He added, "You were only six inches from being decapitated." There was no bumper on the dump truck. The hood of my Honda slipped under the truck bed. The windshield crashed into a million pieces. The frame pressed inward and left a deep gash in my forehead. If the truck bed had been just a few inches longer I would have been a fatality. The Honda was totaled, but by God's grace I suffered only some rather severe lacerations and a broken sternum. My face was not at all pretty, and I suffered intense pain, especially if I had to cough or sneeze.

Interestingly I have a total blackout of the event from the time I turned onto the access highway until the following morning when the doctor hovered over me to see if my brain was still working. Strangely enough, I was fully conscious through the whole ordeal. The policeman later told me, "It didn't take you long to discover that I am a born-again Christian. You even talked in Spanish with some Hispanics who were there on the scene."

I thank the Lord that my body healed rather quickly. I am grateful for His protection, and I repeatedly thank Him for the mental blackout. Otherwise I might be a much more cautious, if not a paranoid, driver. God is very gracious.

Yet just think about it. I could have been in heaven! Not that I don't enjoy life. Yet I long to be with the Lord. I realize it would have been very hard on my wife, my children, and other members of my family. But aside from this legitimate concern, I would honestly prefer to move on to God's glory.

I am convinced that this is a very acceptable desire for every true Christian. Life on earth is great, but ponder for a moment what it will be like in heaven. The ultimate goal of every Christian is eternity with our Lord. And what will we do? We will glorify God forever. This will be fantastic. We will join a massive international choir. In what will sound "like the roar of a great multitude in heaven shouting" we will sing together, "Hallelujah! Salvation and glory and power belong to our God, for true and just are his judgments. . . . Amen, Hallelujah! . . . Praise our God, all you his servants, you who fear him, both small and great! . . . Hallelujah! For our Lord God Almighty reigns. Let us rejoice and be glad and give him glory!" (Rev. 19:1–7).

Dressed in linen garments— bright, clean, fresh, and radiant—we will feast together at the marriage supper of the Lamb. What a glorious celebration this will be. Furthermore this festive event will never cease. History ends. Eternity begins and goes on, and on, and on, and on.

We should live each day in light of this joyous expectation. However, God never intended that we lounge around dreaming about heaven. The main thing is to keep the main thing the main thing. The Lord has told us that we exist to reach out to those who have not yet come to know Him. We are His witnesses sent into the world to preach the gospel and to make disciples. Evangelism and world missions are His plan. By following His assignment to the best of our ability, we add new voices to the eternal choir. We increase the number of those with whom we will enjoy ever-lasting fellowship and happy communion.

Most of us will enter heaven at the moment of God's choosing through death. It might be instantaneous through an unexpected automobile accident. It may be a slow difficult journey through an extended terminal illness. Either way the result is not something tragic. We will step into the presence of the Lord! The ones we leave behind need not sorrow as those who have no hope. Our destiny is sure. Our hope is secure.

Some of us might be part of the Rapture crowd. In the twinkling of an eye we could be caught up with the Lord. This would be the ultimate blessing. And this culminating day of victory may occur much sooner than we think.

Whether by death or the Rapture, for those of us who trust in Christ it will be the most glorious day in our lives. That's right. Our last day on earth will be the best day because it is the first day of everlasting life in God's presence. In this graduation to heaven I long to meet many of those touched by God's grace through my witness. We will join in the celestial choir. Our voices will blend in incredible harmony. What a delight it will be to sing together forever for His glory.

This is the climax. This is the consummation. This is the commencement. This is the celebration of celebrations. This is the main thing.

ENDNOTES

CHAPTER 1
KEEPING THE MAIN THING THE MAIN THING

1. John Mohr and Randall Dennis, *The Mission* (Chicago: Feed and Seed Music, 1989). Used by permission.
2. John Piper, *Let the Nations Be Glad* (Grand Rapids: Baker, 1993), 11.

CHAPTER 9
ARE THEY REALLY LOST?—ROMANS

1. Arthur P. Johnson, "Focus Comment," *Trinity World Forum* 1 (fall 1975): 3.
2. E. O. James, *Christianity and Other Religions* (Philadelphia: Lippincott, 1968), 173.
3. R. Pannikan, *The Unknown Christ of Hinduism* (London: Daron, Longman, & Todd, 1968), 51, 137.
4. Clark Pinnock, "Why Is Jesus the Only Way?" *Eternity* (December 1976): 32.
5. Another view of 1 Peter 3:19–20 is that Christ in His resurrected state announced victory over sin and death to those in hell who had disobeyed God in Noah's day.

6. S. D. F. Salmond, *The Christian Doctrine of Immortality* (Edinburgh: Clark, 1895), 672.

7. Pinnock, "Why Is Jesus the Only Way?" 32.

8. R. C. H. Lenski, *The Interpretation of St. Paul's Epistle to the Romans* (Minneapolis: Augsburg, 1961), 92.

9. Richard W. DeHaan, *The Word on Trial* (Grand Rapids: Zondervan, 1970), 14.

10. Gleason L. Archer, *The Epistle to the Romans: A Study Manual* (Grand Rapids: Baker, 1959), 11.

11. Malcolm H. Watts, "The Case of the Heathen," *Bible League Quarterly* (July–September 1978): 149.

12. Robert C. McQuilkin, *The Message of Romans* (Grand Rapids: Zondervan, 1947), 29.

13. J. Herbert Kane, *Understanding Christian Missions* (Grand Rapids: Baker, 1974), 102.

CHAPTER 14
A BURDEN FOR THE WORLD—PASTORAL STAFF

1. Patrick Johnstone, *Operation World* (Grand Rapids: Zondervan, 1993).

2. William D. Taylor, ed., *Too Valuable to Lose* (Pasadena, Calif.: William Carey Library, 1997), 38, 287–302.

CHAPTER 15
REACHING OUT TO THE WORLD—
MISSIONS COMMITTEES AND MISSIONARIES

1. ACMC (Advancing Churches in Missions Commitment), 4201 North Peachtree Road, Suite 200, Atlanta, GA 30341. Telephone: 1-800-747-7346. E-mail: atlanta@acmc.org.

CHAPTER 16
THE GAME PLAN—
POLICIES, PRAYER, AND PROMOTION

1. *Church Missions Policy Handbook,* 3d. ed. (Atlanta: ACMC, 1995).

CHAPTER 21
A SOLID FOUNDATION—ENLISTING A SUPPORT TEAM

1. William P. Dillon, *People Raising* (Chicago: Moody, 1993).

CHAPTER 23
A FAMILY SPIRIT—GETTING ALONG WITH
MISSION COLLEAGUES

1. Ken Williams, *Building Trust* (Colorado Springs: International Training Partners, 1998).
2. Thomas Hale, *On Being a Missionary* (Pasadena, Calif.: William Carey Library, 1995), 196–97.

CHAPTER 26
A WALK WITH GOD—MAINTAINING INTIMACY
WITH THE LORD

1. John F. Walvoord and Roy B. Zuck, eds., *The Bible Knowledge Commentary, New Testament* (Wheaton, Ill.: Victor, 1983).

BIBLIOGRAPHY

Beals, Paul. *A People for His Name.* Pasadena, Calif.: William Carey Library, 1985.

Borthwick, Paul. *How to Be a World-Class Christian.* Wheaton, Ill.: Victor Books, 1991.

Brierley, Peter, and Heather Wraight. *Atlas of World Christianity: 2000 Years.* Nashville: Thomas Nelson Co., 1998.

Bryant, David. *In the Gap: What It Means to Be a World Christian.* Downers Grove, Ill.: InterVarsity Press, 1979.

Church Missions Policy Handbook. 3d ed. Peachtree City, Ga.: ACMC (Advancing Churches in Missions Commitment), 1995.

Coleman, Robert E. *The Master Plan of Evangelism.* Old Tappan, N. J.: Fleming H. Revell Co., 1963.

Dillon, William P. *People Raising.* Chicago: Moody Press, 1993.

Duewel, Wesley L. *Touch the World through Prayer.* Grand Rapids: Zondervan Publishing House, 1986.

Hale, Thomas. *On Being a Missionary.* Pasadena, Calif.: William Carey Library, 1995.

Hesselgrave, David. *Communicating Christ Cross-Culturally: An Introduction to Missionary Communication*. Grand Rapids: Zondervan Publishing House, 1991.

Johnstone, Patrick. *Operation World: A Day-to-Day Guide to Praying for the World*. Grand Rapids: Zondervan Publishing House, 1993.

Lingenfelter, Sherwood G., and Marvin K. Mayers. *Ministering Cross-Culturally*. Grand Rapids: Baker Book House, 1986.

McCloskey, Mark. *Tell It Often: Tell It Well*. San Bernadino, Calif.: Here's Life Publishers, 1985.

McDowell, Josh. *Evidence That Demands a Verdict*. San Bernadino, Calif.: Here's Life Publishers, 1979.

McGavran, Donald. *Momentous Decisions in Missions Today*. Grand Rapids: Baker Book House, 1984.

Morison, Frank. *Who Moved the Stone?* Grand Rapids: Zondervan Publishing House, 1979.

Moyer, R. Larry. *How-to Book on Evangelism*. Grand Rapids: Kregel Publications, 1998.

_____. *Free and Clear*. Grand Rapids: Kregel Publications, 1997.

Palmer, Donald. *Managing Conflict Creatively*. Pasadena, Calif.: William Carey Library, 1991.

Peters, George W. *A Biblical Theology of Missions*. Chicago: Moody Press, 1972.

Piper, John. *Let The Nations Be Glad: The Supremacy of God in Missions*. Grand Rapids: Baker Book House, 1993.

Pirolo, Neal. *Serving as Senders*. San Diego: Emmaus Road, International, 1991.

Richardson, Don. *Eternity in Their Hearts*. Ventura, Calif.: Regal Books, 1981.

Ridenour, Fritz. *So What's the Difference?* Ventura, Calif.: Regal Books, 1967.

Sjogren, Bob. *Unveiled at Last: Discover God's Hidden Message from Genesis to Revelation.* Seattle: YWAM Publishing, 1992.

Stafford, Tim. *The Friendship Gap.* Downers Grove, Ill.: InterVarsity Press, 1984.

Stearns, Bill, and Amy Stearns. *Catch the Vision 2000.* Minneapolis: Bethany House Publishers, 1991.

Stott, John R. W. *Christian Mission in the Modern World.* Downers Grove, Ill.: InterVarsity Press, 1975.

Taylor, William D. *Too Valuable to Lose.* Pasadena, Calif.: William Carey Library, 1997.

Telford, Tom. *Missions in the Twenty-first Century.* Wheaton, Ill.: Harold Shaw Publishers, 1998.

Tucker, Ruth. *From Jerusalem to Irian Jaya.* Grand Rapids: Zondervan Publishing House, 1983.

Verwer, George. *No Turning Back.* Wheaton, Ill.: Tyndale House Publishers, 1987.

Ward, Ted. *Living Overseas.* New York: Free Press, 1984.

Wilson, J. Christy. *Today's Tentmakers.* Wheaton, Ill.: Tyndale House Publishers, 1979.

Winter, Ralph D., and Steven C. Hawthorne, eds. *Perspectives on the World Christian Movement.* 3d ed. Pasadena, Calif.: William Carey Library, 1999.

Yohannan, K. P. The *Coming Revolution in World Missions.* Carol Stream, Ill.: Creation House, 1989.

Zuck, Roy B., ed. *Vital Missions Issues.* Grand Rapids: Kregel Publications, 1998.

Scripture Index

Subject Index

The
Swindoll Leadership Library

ANGELS, SATAN AND DEMONS
Dr. Robert Lightner

The supernatural world gets a lot of attention these days in books, movies, and television series, but what does the Bible say about these other-worldly beings? Dr. Robert Lightner answers these questions with an in-depth look at the world of the "invisible" as expressed in Scripture.

BIBLICAL COUNSELING FOR TODAY
Dr. Jeffrey Watson

Written by veteran counselor Dr. Jeffrey Watson, this handbook explores counseling from a biblical perspective—how to use Scripture to help others work through issues, choose healthy goals, and work toward those goals for a healthier, more spiritually grounded life. In *Biblical Counseling for Today,* both professional and lay counselors will find insightful, relevant answers to strengthen their ministries.

THE CHURCH
Dr. Ed Hayes

In this indispensable guide, Dr. Ed Hayes explores the labyrinths of the church, delving into her history, doctrines, rituals, and resources to find out what it means to be the Body of Christ on earth. Both passionate and precise, this essential volume offers solid insights on worship, persecution, missions, and morality: a bold call to unity and renewal.

COLOR OUTSIDE THE LINES
Dr. Howard G. Hendricks

Just as the apostle Paul prodded early Christians "not to be conformed" to the world, Dr. Howard Hendricks vividly—and unexpectedly—extends that biblical theme and charges us to learn the art of living creatively, reflecting the image of the Creator rather than the culture.

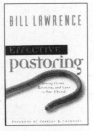

EFFECTIVE PASTORING
Dr. Bill Lawrence

In *Effective Pastoring*, Dr. Bill Lawrence examines what it means to be a pastor in the 21st century. Lawrence discusses often overlooked issues, writing transparently about the struggles of the pastor, the purpose and practice of servant leadership, and the roles and relationships crucial to pastoring. In doing so, he offers a revealing look beneath the "how to" to the "how to be" for pastors.

EMPOWERED LEADERS
Dr. Hans Finzel

What is leadership really about? The rewards, excitement, and exhilaration? Or the responsibilities, frustrations, and exhausting nights? Dr. Hans Finzel takes readers on a journey into the lives of the Bible's great leaders, unearthing powerful principles for effective leadership in any situation.

END TIMES
Dr. John F. Walvoord

Long regarded as one of the top prophecy experts, Dr. John F. Walvoord now explores world events in light of biblical prophecy. By examining all of the prophetic passages in the Bible, Walvoord clearly explains the mystery behind confusing verses and conflicting viewpoints. This is the definitive work on prophecy for Bible students.

THE FORGOTTEN BLESSING
Dr. Henry Holloman

For many Christians, the gift of God's grace is central to their faith. But another gift—sanctification—is often overlooked. *The Forgotten Blessing* clarifies this essential doctrine, showing us what it means to be set apart, and how the process of sanctification can forever change our relationship with God.

GOD
Dr. J. Carl Laney

With tenacity and clarity, Dr. J. Carl Laney makes it plain: it's not enough to know *about* God. We can know *God* better. This book presents a practical path to life-changing encounters with the goodness, greatness, and glory of our Creator.

THE HOLY SPIRIT
Dr. Robert Gromacki

In *The Holy Spirit,* Dr. Robert Gromacki examines the personality, deity, symbols, and gifts of the Holy Spirit, while recapping the ministry of the Spirit throughout the Old Testament, the Gospel Era, the life of Christ, the Book of Acts, and the lives of believers.

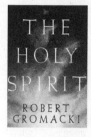

HUMANITY AND SIN
Dr. Robert A. Pyne

Sin may seem like an outdated concept these days, but its consequences remain as destructive as ever. Dr. Robert A. Pyne takes a close look at humankind through the pages of Scripture and the lens of modern culture. As never before, readers will understand sin's overarching effect on creation and our world today.

IMMANUEL
Dr. John A. Witmer

Dr. John A. Witmer presents the almighty Son of God as a living, breathing, incarnate man. He shows us a full picture of the Christ in four distinct phases: the Son of God before He became man, the divine suffering man on Earth, the glorified and ascended Christ, and the reigning King today.

A LIFE OF PRAYER
Dr. Paul Cedar

Dr. Paul Cedar explores prayer through three primary concepts, showing us how to consider, cultivate, and continue a lifestyle of prayer. This volume helps readers recognize the unlimited potential and the awesome purpose of prayer.

MINISTERING TO TODAY'S ADULTS
Dr. Kenn Gangel

After 40 years of research and experience, Dr. Kenn Gangel knows what it takes to reach adults. In an easy-to-grasp, easy-to-apply style, Gangel offers proven systematic strategies for building dynamic adult ministries.

MORAL DILEMMAS
J. Kerby Anderson

Should biblically informed Christians be for or against capital punishment? How should we as Christians view abortion, euthanasia, genetic engineering, divorce, and technology? In this comprehensive, cutting-edge book, J. Kerby Anderson challenges us to thoughtfully analyze the dividing issues facing our age, while equipping believers to maneuver through the ethical and moral land mines of our times.

THE NEW TESTAMENT EXPLORER
Mark Bailey and Tom Constable

The New Testament Explorer provides a concise, on-target map for traveling through the New Testament. Mark Bailey and Tom Constable guide the reader paragraph by paragraph through the New Testament, providing an up-close-and-to-the-point examination of the leaders behind the page and the theological implications of the truths revealed. A great tool for teachers and pastors alike, this exploration tool comes equipped with outlines for further study, narrative discussion, and applicable truths for teaching and for living.

The Old Testament Explorer
Dr. Charles Dyer and Dr. Gene Merrill

Imagine the deep blackness before the dawn of creation. Wander with the Jews through the wilderness in search of the Promised Land. Stand outside the gates as Daniel is led to the den of lions. With *The Old Testament Explorer,* Charles Dyer and Gene Merrill guide you step-by-step through the depths of each Old Testament book and provide a variety of tools for understanding God's message. In contemporary and understandable language, you'll learn valuable information about the stories, people, and life-truths in each Old Testament book.

Spirit-Filled Teaching
Dr. Roy B. Zuck

Whether you teach a small Sunday school class or a standing-room-only crowd at a major university, the process of teaching can be demanding and draining. This lively book brings a new understanding of the Holy Spirit's essential role in teaching.

Tale of the Tardy Oxcart and 1501 Other Stories
Dr. Charles R. Swindoll

In this rich volume, you'll have access to resourcing Dr. Charles Swindoll's favorite anecdotes on prayer or quotations for grief. In *The Tale of the Tardy Oxcart,* thousands of illustrations are arranged by subjects alphabetically for quick-and-easy access. A perfect resource for all pastors and speakers.

The Theological Wordbook
Campbell, Johnston, Walvoord, Witmer

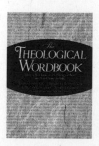

Compiled by four of today's best theological minds, *The Theological Wordbook* is a valuable, accessible reference guide to the most important theological terms. Definitions, scriptural references, engaging explanations—all in one easy-to-find, applicable resource—for both the lay person and serious Bible student.

WOMEN AND THE CHURCH
Dr. Lucy Mabery-Foster

Women and the Church provides an overview of the historical, biblical, and cultural perspectives on the unique roles and gifts women bring to the church, while exploring what it takes to minister to women today. Important insight for any leader seeking to understand how to more effectively minister to women and build women's ministries in the local church.